Droplets of Life

Into Each Life Some Rain Must Fall

Maxine E. Smith

ISBN 979-8-88943-024-7 (paperback)
ISBN 979-8-88943-025-4 (digital)

Copyright © 2023 by Maxine E. Smith

All rights reserved. No part of this publication may be reproduced, distributed, or transmitted in any form or by any means, including photocopying, recording, or other electronic or mechanical methods without the prior written permission of the publisher. For permission requests, solicit the publisher via the address below.

Christian Faith Publishing
832 Park Avenue
Meadville, PA 16335
www.christianfaithpublishing.com

Printed in the United States of America

Present to: _Cordell_____

On this day of: _____

Occasion: _____

Presented by: _Maxine E. Smith_____

Droplets of Life
Maxine E. Smith

With all my Love

To my friends
who share my love
for the literary arts.

Contents

Notes from the Author ix
Chapter 1:   Praise Is Our Weapon..1
Chapter 2:   You Are Precious in My Sight 8
Chapter 3:   Angry...13
Chapter 4:   Sowing Good Seeds...17
Chapter 5:   Opportunity Fading 25
Chapter 6:   God's Unconditional Love....................................30
Chapter 7:   Jesus Is Able to Still the Storm..............................36
Chapter 8:   God's Mercy Imputed..44
Chapter 9:   Cherish Life 49
Chapter 10: The War Room 53
Chapter 11: Spiritual Jealousy...63
Chapter 12: Intimacy with God..66
Chapter 13: You Are Infused in My Being 75
Chapter 14: Fan the Flames of Love..80
Chapter 15: Soul Highly Valued 84
Chapter 16: In Touch with Spirit Self.......................................91
Chapter 17: Forgiveness...96
Chapter 18: He Called Me Servant 130

Chapter 19: Divine Plan 138
Chapter 20: Death Is a Comma, Not a Period 146
Chapter 21: My Journey in a Coma 152
Chapter 22: Encyclopedia of My Mind 160
Chapter 23: He Sings Over Us 166
Chapter 24: Love Makes a Healthy Soul 170
Chapter 25: Indwelling of the Holy Spirit 174
Chapter 26: Launching Spirit Light 178
Chapter 27: He Was There All the Time 210
Chapter 28: Sin Was Nailed to the Cross 217
Chapter 29: Fear 220
Chapter 30: Listen 223
Chapter 31: Jesus Appeared Five Times to Me 226
Chapter 32: Elohim the Creator Knows Our Address 230
Chapter 33: Healing Is the Children's Bread 232
Chapter 34: The Holy Spirit Was in the Cloud 235
Chapter 35: Predestined to Be Redeemed 238
Chapter 36: Above All, Get Understanding 242
Chapter 37: Confront Your Truth 243
Chapter 38: Racism in an Unsympathetic World 245
Chapter 39: Even in the Darkest Night, There Is Light 250

Notes from the Author

There is a delightful joy drawing strength, giving utterance to the feeling I treasure most.

My hope is to capture the imagination of the reader and share the mosaic valley of life with them.

I trust you too will be delighted as you read through the Smith Papers.

1

Praise Is Our Weapon

Praising God should be our weapon of choice. When exhaustion sets in and wearisome feelings are invadings our peace, we become mentally fatigued from beating back the enemy's many faces of camouflage in his attempts to disguise himself as he tries to keep us from obtaining our heavenly abode. Pray faithfully, believing God is dealing with the obstacles that are coming into our lives. Faithful prayer is a must. Jesus prayed faithfully, continuously to his Father, believing the Father heard his prayers and would answer them.

Tests and trials are part of living in this world's system. Overcoming strength shows spiritual development, bringing divine empowerment that is so need in faithful worshiping. Praise brings the endurance that helps us to resist the forces of evil. God asked us to lift him in praise. Come into agreement with God, lift him up in praise, glorifying his holy name. Praise is joyful music in the ears of Almighty God and brings peace to our souls. Praise is an offering of appreciation for what God is doing in our lives.

May our mouths continuously be filled with joyful sounds unto the Lord; praise will defeat the wicked one. The enemy's aim is to receive our souls unto himself. For centuries Satan has been ruining lives, stealing the souls of mankind by filling them with fear and doubt, causing some to question the very strength, the essence of God's Word.

Almighty God gave us divine worship to glorify him. It will push back the works of the devil. Raising our praise to God gives him loving glorification and is a weapon against the enemy's stronghold. Praising will set us free—use praise often; there is no other weapon as strong. At all times, let our hearts and mouths be filled with praise. Praise is the weapon that gives exposure and defeats both seen and unseen ungodliness. Praise a defense mechanism against every evil work that comes against us—use it. Instead of saying, "Woe is me. I've never caught a break. Never a streak of luck ever come my way," with all our might, use the weapon of praise. God will strengthen us to keep the faith. Praise through all difficulties until victory overtakes.

> Make a joyful noise unto the Lord all ye lands: sing to the honor of his name making our praises glorious. Say unto God, how terrible art thou in thy work to all thy enemy. Because of the greatness of thy power, shall thine enemies submit themselves unto thee. All the earth shall worship Thee, and shall sing unto thee; they Shall sing to thy name. (Psalm 66:1–4)

Hate is a virus eating into the soul of man, taking the joy out of life. Hate tares at our ability to love one another. Hate steals the "J" out of joy and puts our eternal soul at risk of damnation. There is no hate in God's kingdom; hate flourishes in hell. Hate sucks the blood out of free will, keeping us enslaved, yoked to its bondage. It is impossible for hate to fellowship with love. Hate blooms in hell; it grows and lives in an incubator that Satan created. Don't let him create chambers of hate in our hearts.

We are to give God the rule over our lives. God will restore, give back what the enemy has stolen.

> The thief cometh not, but for to steal, and to kill, and to destroy: I am come that they might have life, and that they might have it more abundantly. (John 10:10)

Love is infectious; it is an antivirus, an agent opposing the roots of hatred. Love is a covering, a protection against the opponent's extreme intimidation when he is trying to steal our souls' salvation. Hate is a hostile spiritual force coming straight from treasure chest Satan's after the souls of men, offering them gifts of discouragement, mental suffering, physical pain, misery, disease, and poverty. These terrifying gifts coming from hell's treasure chest labeled "the crowned jewels of darkness."

God has given us power from on high to resist the attacks of the devil. Faith is the substance we must exercise if we want peace of mind. Praising is a powerful combative medicine. Come unto the Father through Jesus Christ. When asking for our needs to be met, ask in the name of Jesus. Asking the Father for favor, it is crucial to use Jesus's name. Jesus told us to ask the Father for our needs in his name, and the Father will give it to you.

Our antagonist adversary will contend for man's faith by trying to bring doubt to those who trust in the power of praise. Keep praising; don't stop. God lives in the praises of his people.

There is a mighty conflict going on between good and evil. This conflict is being fought in the heavens and on the earth. Evil wants the rule over heaven and earth. The devil, our tempter, already has the rule over hell. Angels of God and the angels of Satan are warring; they have been at war for centuries. Satan wants to own heaven. He, with his army, has been trying to get back into heaven by force ever since the Lord God Almighty kicked him out of heaven. He is jealous of God's rule. He wants to be the ruler on high, to sit in the throne room of God and to sit on the throne of God.

God said, "Never will Satan sit on my throne." With all Satan's display of cleverness and spiritual insight, God Almighty will always be the ruler of heaven. The spirit of light and the spirit of darkness cannot dwell together—that has been proven. Just look at the condition of the world today. These kingdoms are vying for an exceptional prize—the soul of man. There was a day Satan came to heaven to accuse Job of having the spirit of fear and that the spirit of fear belonged to him. He was walking up and down in the earth with his eyes on Job. The accuser roams around the earth, looking for whom he may destroy. Satan is an outcast. He is under the feet of Almighty God. He is numbered among the walking dead spirits. He is a damned spirit being. Satan is at war with God's army. He has one-third the warriors God has. He is fighting a losing battle, but he keeps pushing, trying to get back into heaven. Our heavenly Father's armed forces outnumbered Satan's armed forces two to one. Satan is the foe of God and man. He is fighting God for the rule of man's soul as well as fighting to satisfy his appetite to occupy and rule heaven. Do not embrace Satan's cunningness; he is the liar deceiving the world, the crafty one, full of trickery, and death is the game he plays; because death is the only game he knows, he crushes the life out of everything he can influence to come to him—death to all that plays his game.

After the great white throne judgment, Satan will be confined to his dungeon of hatred. He will be hated, and he is the hater of all whom he exercises authority over. In the darkness of his disgusting hellish chambers, there is an unending stench the damned will endure forever.

> And there was war in heaven: Michael God's chief warring angel, and his angels fought against the dragon: and the dragon fought and his angels, and prevailed not; neither was their peace found any more in heaven. (Revelation 12:7–9)[1]

> Let us offer the sacrifice of praise to God continually, giving the fruits of our lips in thanksgiving to his name. (Hebrews 13:15)

Enter God's throne room, join the heavenly host where praising and glorifying God never ceases.

---

[1] Doctrinal Footnotes—Tribulation. Michael the archangel is the leader of God's holy angels. At the middle of the Tribulation period, God will empower Michael and his forces to cast Satan and his forces out of access to heaven so that Satan must, thereafter, confine his activities to the earthly sphere.

Let's immerse ourselves in praise unto the Lord. The sound of praise sends love message; the sounds travel through the heavens, into the throne room of God, bringing Him pleasure. Praising a gift from the hearts of his beloved children.

Praise and prayer never die. They are a fundamental entity. They are spiritual activities, divine energy flowing with everlasting life. Unending worship fills the kingdom of God. What a paradise for the righteous soul. Are our souls deficient when it comes to concentration? Can we no longer concentrate on the things of God? Has the mind of man been hemorrhaging—losing its power to divinely concentrate? Is man's mind infatuated with the world's system and has no more time for the things of God? Enduring life without faith is a stumbling block to our peace of mind and a threat to the eternal soul. There are those who have an air of unconcern in how they use their earth time; may we not be one of them. Have we been blindsided by greed to the point we are unable to process our measure of faith? We have a need for God's guidance now as well as in our future. Ask him to open our eyes, to see and understand where we are on life's journey. We may be going through an experience that has left us disoriented, no longer able to focus. We are confused, unable to pray as we should. God will send help from the heavenly storehouse—where we have stored treasures through faith for the rainy days that will come into our lives. God will send ministering spirits to attend the needs of the faithful, so hold on. The richness of our faith is found, in the treasures of obedience. Our obedience beholds the face of God. Many are depositing in heaven's commissary for such a time when they are feeling unforgiven, lost, and forgotten.

In life, we may come to a point when we say, "I just don't have the energy to go on nor the desire to go any further. This situation is over my head. I give up." Never give up.

Amid all adversity, the spirit of God's immense love is with us, working for our good. God will send dreams and visions that will provide insight and will empower our inner man to be an overcomer. His love for us will never die. Adversity comes to all of God's creation. We are not an island unto ourselves; we too are being touched by God. When adversity arrives, don't cry, "There is no way out of this trouble." Praise will open closed doors. Try praising through the unimaginable entanglements of life. The Lord God is with us. The battle against tragedies of the seen and unseen worlds is not ours to fight alone. We are to use the weapon of praise. We are to cast all our care upon him, for he cares for us.

Our Father God has enormous love unmeasurable; the power of his love creates life. Look around. See he is still lavishing his love throughout the world it is his pleasure to do so, yet the world is suffering from a lack of humanity's compassion and love. Showing love for one another and really deeply caring for others, let their well-being be our concern—let it radiate from us. We draw the spirit of love from one another when we show kindness.

> But I say unto you, love your enemies, bless them that curse you, do good to them that hate you, and pray for them which despitefully use you, and persecute you.

There are things unseen that are in motion. There is no limit to the unseen world. We cannot comprehend the secret power of the unseen; divine creation is everywhere, present, living, and growing waiting Jesus's return. There is an infinite abundance of creative substance surrounding us—waiting for its evidence to be called into realization wanting its manifestation to come to light. The powers of the unseen world can be activated through faith brought into visibility through our thoughts and earnest prayer. Through faith We find the key to God's heart. God said, "Let there be light," and the nonexistent light came into being. God did not doubt his words. We sometimes doubt there will be a recognizable answer to the prayers we offer to God. Learn to experience life through faith in God's Word. Spiritual substance lay waiting to be spoken into action by faith. During the storms of life, put faith in the forefront of all our concerns. It will be a cutting edge to God's heart. We are to ask God to meet our needs in Jesus's name, believing he will answer until we recognize the evidence. Believe our prayers are in God's presence. See the actuality, the evidence of our faith at work.

Reverence God's name; don't take his name in vain. We are to place our prayers in the hands of the Almighty then walk away; don't look back. Kneel before the Almighty in faith, press into his presence with love and faithfulness, believing our prayers have been given divine wings, flying from our situation to the throne room of God, and our request has been received and the answer is on its way back to the sender.

2

You Are Precious in My Sight

You are my child. Never doubt my love for thee. You are deeply favored. I have endowed you with spiritual gifts.

Are you prepared to receive the gifts I offer? Know that you are precious in my sight. I long to give the doors of blessings unto you. I offer the keys to you. Are you ready to accept them? Inside my storehouse, you will find many doors. They read "the gift of faith," "the gift of love," "the gift of patience," also "the gift of obedience." You will learn to die to self through these gifts. Let God's will rule over your life, bringing you into his divine presence. I love you, my child. You confessed your love for me through obeying my will. When your love is truly mine, you will come to me in faith through obedience to my Word.

Pray, confessing your need for deliverance from all doubt. Pray God's spirit of faith will abide in you forever. If you believe in my word, the spirit of faith will work through you—to bring me glory. Remember when I work through you, my child—all the glory belongs to me. Never try to steal my glory. I do the work, not you. I bring the miracles, not you.

I am the great I AM, the Alpha and Omega, the beginning and the end, the first and the last. I am whom I say I am. There is no other God besides Me.

Your steadfast love will remove the mountains that are standing in your past because of your strong belief in me. Your past has been cast into the sea. Through faithful prayer, your uncertainty has been removed, Your patience and endurance brought you into a oneness with my Spirit.

Ask me for the desires of your heart. Don't beg. Praise me. I never asked you to beg. I ask only that you praise me. Come before me with your lips spilling over with praise.

> Behold, I have graven thee upon the palms of my hands; thy walls are continually before me.

The word *graven* in Isaiah 49:16 is saying—I have sculptured you, carved you, impressed you deeply, fix you permanently upon the palms of my hands. The usage of the word *wall* shows the wall is serving to enclose you, protect you, and is forming an inner area just for you. God has permanently fixed you in his inner area—he has walled you into his presence. You are continually before him. You are carved in the palms of his hands. Fret not—you are forever before his face. He knows who you are. He knows where you live.

> Fear not, little flock; for it is your Father's good pleasure to give you the Kingdom. (Luke 12:32)

> But I will forewarn you whom ye (shall) fear: Fear him, which after he hath killed (the body) hath power to cast (your soul) into hell; yea, I say unto you (he is the one you should fear) Fear Him. (Luke 12:5)

God is the only One with power over life and the power over souls, so little children, fear not what man can do to you. (Luke 21:19: I tell you man cannot kill your spirit nor your soul.) The way we live our earth life, the decisions we make today, will determined where our souls will spend their unending lives. Don't waste this precious life; it's of high value in God's sight. Keep love in your heart; it's dangerous to have a heart empty of love and kindness—God lives in both the spirit of love and kindness.

In this world, we are given a physical appearance, a presence that is embodying the breath of God. We are a spiritual being sent to earth for God's purpose and pleasure. We live in this world, but our assignments are coming from heaven.

It is written, "In your patience possess ye your souls." God has long patience for the precious fruit of the earth. Patience is a gift. God's children are the precious fruit of the earth; he is waiting patiently to receive his children.

Our estranged soul has been redeemed, bought back, purchased, set free from its offense against God; we were released from the consequences of our sin debt through the blood of Jesus.

God sent us to earth with a divine assignment. Our assignment is the purpose for our being placed on earth at this time. We are to find our purpose and get into it while we are still experiencing life on this side of the green grass. Through prayer, seek God. Ask his help identifying our purpose; it's later than we think.

Comparing human devices in measuring earth time against the endlessness of eternal time, we have been given very little survival time to find our purpose here on earth. We are to find our purpose and get into it, live in it until we go back to God for the next assignment. The limitation put on earth's time system is against man's procrastination. Life on earth is a soul experience with mortal limitations. Call on God for supernatural help, caring out our God-given earth assignment. We need his help as we journey through this system, trying to make it to our eternal reward for our next assignment.

If we are living without faith in God's sacred Word, our full joy in this life is diminishing; every breath is a race against time. Faith is a substance; it's unseen, but it gives evidence of itself, can we see our words as they leave our mouth? No. Faith involves trusting in something that exist in elements unseen to the natural senses. Our words are not corporeal. They are not flesh that last only a little while. They are abstract, spiritual. They will never die. Words are intangible, powerful, forever living substance. The pain of living life causes some to lose faith. Our faith is always on trial. The spirit of God's Word is living substance that is brooding; it is a hovering force covering and protecting his creation.

Faith is the future, leading to greater life. Faith brings into view the presence of God working through his believers, who are affecting the world with the teachings of Jesus. Stand in faith on God's Word until the evidence of his promises come into view. Learn to recognize God as his spirit works through our lives. God built the worlds on unseen substance; he spoke all that is into being. There is wonder working power in faith. When God sends his word out, he knows it will not come back to him void. Not a tinge of doubt can live in the kingdom of God. The Holy Spirit will guide and strengthen our faith as needed. Listen to him. Let him be our guide. God has showed and continues to show the power of his spoken word. By his word, he formed all that is seen. He holds the world's existence in his hands.

God created that which is, not from that which was not but from that which was unseen. God spoke what was in his mind into existence. We see and enjoy God's spoken word. Can we perceive his unspeakable intangible power? The power of God's presence is everywhere, at work before unseeing eyes. We are God's creation—faith brings a oneness with our Creator. Speak in faith that which we want to see come into our lives. We are to exercise faith with expectation. Observe God bringing the desires of our hearts into reality because we believe he will do what we ask in faith. It's a glorious sight when we stand back, witnessing God's power at work on behalf of our trust in him.

Never make this ridiculous statement: God has not answered any of my prayers. God's way of doing business is not necessarily man's way. God is always on the job, answering prayer after prayer. Some of our prayers are best not answered. Sometimes we are not ready to handle the answers. Realize living this life is a gradual learning process for a greater life (a higher prize) to come. We don't always know what to pray for, asking for what we think we want or need. We think things should be done to please our concept. Our capacity of handling what's going on in our lives, or our understanding, is not always the jackpot we were hoping for. Learn patience and obedience; learn to obey while trusting in the Lord's timing. Life experience gives us growing pains; that is part of this game we call life.

Call to God through joyful praising, giving him thanks in every situation. Believing our needs are being met as we wait in faith, continue to stand believing God, believing the answer to our prayers has been received in heaven's throne room and that the angels in heaven are rejoicing as they send back the answered prayers of the faithful.

Yield thyself when praying to the Father God Almighty, succumbing our innermost being to him in loving expectation—anticipate that the desires of our hearts are being answered as we speak.

We are to put our hand in the hand of the man who stilled the water. Believe God. Prayerfully wait while he works things out in his time. He is taking care of all the storms that are trying to intrude into our innermost peace. If we feel our faith is not strong enough to withstand the task that has been set before us, we are to ask God to strengthen our faith that we may stand amid the testing of life for the glory of the Lord. God is always available. His spirit is the very breath we breathe. We cannot run away from God. He is the keeper of our souls; he will keep our souls in perfect peace whose mind is stayed upon the Lord. Nothing—not even the air we breathe—can get closer to us than our Creator. Let God expose our greater self to the world, for we are one of a kind; we are a masterpiece. Our greater life is awaiting us in the kingdom of God. We are in God, and God is in us. Jesus said that we bear no fault; he has been inflicted with our sin, has taken our punishment, suffered our pain. Rejoice—rejoice in the Lord, all ye people of the earth. Rejoice in the Lord always.

3

Angry

When we become angry, we can feel the spirit of anger building. Anger penetrates the body like a bullet in flight. Anger causes the nervous system to become irritable, mental fatigue sets in, we feel a tightness as it strengthens, sending strong protective messages to the brain, so we start defending ourselves, our voice heightened with the excitement anger brings as it inflames. Anger can consume our natural ability to self-control. Anger destroys peace of mind as it progresses. It increases in power, and we decrease in self-control, becoming less than who we really are. Our self-control has been impaired, fading our ability to restrain the harshness of anger.

> Be ye angry, and sin not: let not the sun go
> down upon your wrath. (Ephesians 4:26)

Anger is to be briefly held and replaced by righteous indignation so that the devil will not be given an opportunity to keep causing trouble in our lives. Holding on to anger can become sinful. Keeping the door to anger open is an invitation to evil spirits. They are happy to come in the open doors of our minds. Let us edify one another by lifting each other up. Grieve not the Holy Spirit with stubbornness by holding onto anger. We can find splendor and peace in this life if we stop courting the spirit of anger. Letting anger entertain our minds is a poison to the soul. God will show us that we have blessings already in our hands; we don't have to be angry people.

May our resentment and wrath be overtaken by kindness and forgiveness, remembering God has forgiven us more times than we can count.

We are to monitor our thoughts, thinking before speaking them out. Words can come back to haunt you. Speak slowly and deliberately. Question the thoughts that come into our head—are they from God? With a spiritual ear, we are to listen to our unspoken words, conceive their fruit before sending them into the universe like a pregnancy growing in the mind of man. Words have everlasting life. They can build a person up or break them down. Kindness will make the world a better place in which to live. Be at peace with God, be at peace with your fellowman, and we are to be at peace with ourselves. Can we come to know what total peace is like?

Energy is alive and doing very well. Both godly and ungodly energy is orbiting the earth, surrounding, persuading our thinking. We say things and wonder, "Why did we say that?" We are never alone. The universe is speaking to everyone in many ways. Be still and listen beyond the sounds of earth.

Although the breath, the energy that provided life to my husband's being no longer occupies his body that it once motivated, his spirit recognizes I am lonely without him. I have seen his presence, his energy in our home. He wants me to know that he is still near and cares about my well-being. On one occasion, his voice came from the foot of my bed, calling my name three times—it was 6:00 a.m., time for me to wake up and do my morning studying.

One day, not long after my husband's death, I was saying goodbye to my visitors. While they were leaving, I stood in the open doorway. I notice a white bird walking through the grass. It was not one of those black crows I was always seeing. This white bird had black on the tips of its wings, and at the end of its tail feathers, when they came together, they seem to form a cross. I had never seen a bird around here that looked like that. *Where did it come from?* I thought. For some time, I tried to find a picture of the bird. One day, looking through a magazine, I came across a picture of my strange feathered friend; it was a seagull. That day it seemed the bird had not paid me a bit of attention. He kept walking, pecking at the grass. A light rain began to fall. The bird hunched his shoulders, turned his head to one side, and looked at me. Our eyes connected; his deep black eyes with intensity spoke volumes as he watched me. I knew my husband's energy had entered the body of this seagull, and he traveled back home to let me know that he was still concerned about me and would always try to be there for me. I sold my house; I didn't want to be alone. My husband's spirit responded to my new location by coming to visit and turning my radio on so I would know he was near. There is more to life than what we comprehend. There are some things we don't know, we cannot explain while in our human state of being. We will never be in a state of nonexistence because we are spirit beings fueled by the breath of God, unharnessed energy that is providing life. Our energy was assigned to a physical body controlled only by the master of creation. Although my husband is not physically with me, spiritually he is near. The thought of untouchable life is never far away. He is functioning on a higher level of existence. Someday I too will be set free. My energy will also make its exit. Wherever my husband is, he is concerned about my well-being. It is nice knowing there could be a loved one watching over us no matter what level of existence they are functioning in; they are concerned about us. God in eternity watches over all existence. Even though I cannot touch my husband, I know he is near, and maybe he's interceding to God on my behalf. I would like to think there are souls on the other side of this life praying for their loved ones.

> And the Lord God formed man of the dust of the ground, and he breathed into Adam's nostrils the breath of life; and man became a living soul. (Genesis 2:7)

We are spirit and soul, housed in a physical body, taken from the dust of this earth. We were created to live on this planet in human form. We are what we eat, and our flesh will return back to that from which it came, the earth. Our spirits will go back to the God that breathed us into existence. God temporarily supplied this body of dust with his breath that gave us life. He breathed his breath into a body formed from the dust of the earth, and it became a living being. God's breath was only a loan to this temporary being that became a human being. We pay interest on this loan that is giving us life. We lay up treasures in heaven through obedience.

Human beings are bonded by spiritual laws, the law of flesh, and the law of gravity. The breath of life is given by God for his pleasure. God holds and sustains all life for his pleasure; for his pleasure did he create all things. God is supreme, the highest-ranking being, and the only creative authority. There is no existence nor can authority exist except that which is put into existence by the Creator of all things. God is the only active power that is totality; There is no wholeness except it be given by God. Without God, there is nothing, God is all and all. God is the breath of life; without God's breath, no life would exist. God is always forming life. God is above all—seen and unseen—nothing comes into existence without his creativity at work. Those that he desires will live in his kingdom. They shall be the obedient ones that found their purpose and got into it.

The nature of God defy finite man's explanation. Man's imagination is limited to human insight. Man was never given the intelligence to define the majesty of God.

4

Sowing Good Seeds

Critical words used excessively can work like garden fertilizer placed in the human mind. Words attack mentally, physically. They produce inferiority complexes, causing unhappiness to grow in us like weeds in the open field. They bring inexpressible anguish. The fruits of anxiety caused by cruel words inflict pain that can linger in the heart of man's deepest emotions, spreading through his consciousness like a violent sneeze flying, releasing its infectious droplets through the air, contaminating as it goes, maybe causing sickness to anyone in its reach from the corruption now occupying the air.

With our minds once contaminated by excessive unpleasantness and sometimes unmerciful criticism, some people take delight in dishing out their faultfinding opinions. Unwholesome words are viruses; they have spiritual life that can't be seen but deeply felt, causing mental distress accompanied by temperaments that can bring dangerous reactions. Words in a workplace may work at a low key, like insidious worms spiraling underground, making the workplace environmentally a difficult and unhappy place in which to be. Sometimes the dangerous fallout from words are difficult to detect. Nevertheless, their invisible offensives hurt and are on the move. Words will produce a presence of uneasiness that can cause mental stress for years long after the words have been spoken but still lingering, haunting man's heart. Words can destroy our stability, causing one to second guess every decision they make. Hurting feelings can bring self-confidence to its lowest level. We don't want to become someone's prey. We must learn to stand up for what we believe.

Hurt will occupy all the space allowed it. Hurt steals our peace; unknowingly we give hurt permission to stay in our radar far too long. Mental harm transmits ever so slowly, one day at a time, one word at a time. Hatefulness can be a silent thief. Don't receive bitter words; they were meant to strip us of our personality, stripping us to the bone. They want to bury alive the person we really are. When harsh words are emitting, causing waves of unrest and pain to surface, understand we do not have to receive someone's furious jealousy, their anger, and their insecurity. By not accepting other people's negativity, we do not experience their powerful intentions of giving us self-doubt. Negative spirits will declare war on our peace, trying to take by force the security we now enjoy.

God's Word provides everlasting life. Draw from his word, and live above the negativities that come with life. Walk away from the lies, the tricks produced by the master of sin—he is a supreme spirit of all that is hurtful, and the evil that is coming out of people shows his power at work. The powers of darkness are working overtime to own the souls of men. Do not swap the devil for the witch; either decision would be playing with the corrupted. The evil one comes to us with tempting words, appealing to the flesh's appetite, enticing our flesh to inflict verbal pain on others as we walk through life. There are mean spiritually blind people in this world, blind to their own selfishness, jealousy, and meanness. The devil keeps his fingers in the eyes of many. Jealousy will make us miserable, destroying our peace of mind. It is always looking for vengeance, a way to hurt another. Jealousy makes us wanting, suspicious, feeling someone has something we should have in our treasure chest.

Satan is the chief leader of the dark apostate angels. God had them all kicked out of heaven thousands of years ago. God condemned Satan and his apostate rebellious gang of angels; he kicked them out of his kingdom but not out of his sight. Satan is the ruler of darkness and damnation, whose kingdom is offering fire and brimstone as an eternal reward to all those who obey him and accept his invitation to his ancient palace of darkness filled with evil, He is the officer in this eternal palace, of intense pain, driving our spirit life into unending insanity. He is that dreaded monster of all that is grief. He is extremely schooled in wickedness, the art of evil sadistic torture, the inventor of horror. He takes great pleasure in inflicting punishment. Don't play games with the defeated foe of God. Satan has met his fate. He will not escape the gruesome thorns of the hellish scenes of death and destruction that can never die. Know that he is an accursed and damned spirit being. Don't follow after the evil one's ways; they lead straight to a damnation that will never die.

Jesus paid our sin debt. We have been redeemed, set free from sin. Our salvation was costly. Sinful men placed Jesus on the debtors' cross, driving nails through his hands and feet. They fastened our Lord to the tree of sin until his earth assignment departed. Jesus was the perfect sacrifice for humanity. He did exactly what his Father sent him to earth to do. He came to earth to free the sinner from his payment of eternal death. When we accept Jesus and his teachings, he becomes our personal Savior and the Lord of our lives. We have become the righteousness of God—what an exchange—Jesus's blood washed away our sin; what a privilege. A divine substitute has been offered up in our stead, a God-given miracle. The mending of relationships between God and man took place through the shed blood of God's Lamb. We have been redeemed, made brand new spiritually through the shed blood of Jesus. Freed from the damnation of sin. We have been set free in the sight of God to travel the road of everlasting freedom to the kingdom of our God.

Be diligent, proclaim the Word of God wherever and whenever opportunity presents itself. Get in agreement with God. Decree His Word until Jesus's returns. We are not to struggle, fretting against the different seasons that will come into our lives. By faith, turn the seasons of life over to the Father in Jesus's name then wait on the Father's timing, for the changing seasons must come. Show faith by letting Jesus work through us that people will see the Father's love coming from our innerspring of living water. Fear death only when we do not know the divine Son of the living God. Jesus is our living Savior, anointed of God before he was ever sent from heaven to earth to glorify his Father through the shedding of blood for our sins. Jesus ushered in the dispensation of grace; this was an exemption from the old laws we could not keep; the new law is an announcement of salvation to the repented soul washed in the shed blood of Jesus. The Holy Spirit came to earth to dwell in and guide man, helping man to evangelize the world through the Word of God. Filled with the Holy Spirit through the prayers of our Lord; Jesus said to his disciples. "I will pray to the Father, and he will send you another comforter, the Spirit of Truth."

Some will go out to the mission field to minister, hoping to convert by introducing non-Christians to Christianity, and some will stay and attend the needs of the homeland as their mission field.

Churches today are a representation of the world's system. Many preachers are motivational speakers mimicking the theatrical structured for gain. There are preachers whose sermons sound more like politicians running for office, telling the people how to cast their votes. The democratic party is supposed to stand for the poor man, bring social equality. President Roosevelt said if elected, there will be a chicken in every pot, no American will go hungry, the New Deal will put money in the pockets of the needy. Republicans favor big business, the rich. There are men standing in the altars of the church, mingling their finite truth with the Almighty truth. Men preach with limited theory of how to represent God's will.

Many churches are unable to produce an atmosphere like the prophets of old—men who walked and talked with God, who prayed until the Shekinah glory filled the tabernacle. Some preachers today are busy taking care of their interests, making sure their families become rich, building private enterprises; their joy is watching their securities increase, having more and more investors, strengthening their portfolios; they really don't have time to walk and talk with God. They have become businessmen, busy building an empire creating a name for themselves, their legacy. The world will recognize them by their greatness, their famous name. Many preachers are greedy, measuring their empire as if they are all being challenged in a contest, seeing what preacher is showing the most material wealth.

Greed is weaved in the very fabric of our religious system. We have billionaire preaches living in homes costing millions up on millions of dollars. There is no shame in their game. We the people are the church, not the gorgeous building structure. I don't care how fabulous the structure may be; outward show is not the answer to Christian life. Some church leaders see their people only as dollar signs instead of seeing them as hungry sheep in need of a good feeding from God's Word. Can we hear the Lord saying, "My people are starving—they perish for the lack of divine feeding"? When the people are starving for more of God's Word, the church then is starved and dying from a lack of divine nutrition. Only God can breathe life into dead substance, causing a revival, the state of being brought back to life. Some preachers cannot ascertain God's will. They are so busy hearing only their own voice, feeding on their quest of self-satisfaction through their wealth. It's evident the spirit of God does not abide in the dead substance such as our structural world system, where the Antichrist will arise. Look around at the damage of prejudice, disregarding the rights of others because of their skin color and the texture of their hair. Because of their ethnicity, some are shunned by due process of the law. God abides in the living soul of man, and it was his pleasure to create man in his preference.

Some have made God's Word of no affect until there is no divine manifestation of God's power in the church. Many churches today are lacking divine intervention because of their country club atmosphere. We are putting ourselves in God's way with overblown egos. Man's communications in the church today, in one way or another, the message is all about prosperity—preachers wanting to see their congregations grow larger and larger because of the need to prosper in material wealth. We have more multimillionaire preachers, some billionaire preachers standing before the altar, asking their people for more money, to take care of their private aircraft and their country estates hidden across the globe.

Strolling along life's highway, many preachers are walking hand and hand with God while winking at the devil as they stroll on their way. These winking preachers are straddling the fence, in serious disrespect to God's will, trying to keep their feet in both the Christian world and the world's system.

The affairs of the flesh are manifesting themselves in the churches without accountability. Sexual sin is running rampant—from the altar through the congregation—showing no shame. Sex has become man's pacifier; they feed off it. People who think having sex is without repentance, no excuse needed, nor regrets for their sexual appetite. Today there is no apology needed for our sexual behavior. Sex is not respected as it once was and has no boundary. The threat of rape may come into play; some will force you to let them have their way. Animals are governed, bound by mating seasons; man is bound only by his conscience. We feel that divine sexual law is old school; it does not apply in our lifestyle today. There is no blame or shame in the sex game—so let us sing *que sera sera*—what will be will be. God gave animals a mating season for breeding that the survival of their species be maintained, but God gave man divine law to observe. Sex was to be performed in marriage—after the ceremony of matrimony has taken place.

Whoever does not conform to God's Word are fooling themselves into eternal sorrow. Obedience to God's Word is open to man's choice. Our free will comes into play every day of our lives. Choose this day which master will you be servant to. Sex is running rampant through our society; so is sickness and disease from our sexual behavior. Nowadays, no one dares to speak against premarital sex; is taboo to do so, it's being judgmental, it is no longer against our accepted normal behavior. We have sex because we can, and we have taken the divine spiritual value out of our sexual expression. God intended sex to be a holy ritual, relating to biblical custom, showing we have a lifetime commitment to our partner, the pledging of oneself to another person for life. It seems a demonic spirit has put a sexual ring in the nose of many, leading them into sexual gluttony, a sexual blindness has taken over the world. Satan uses sex in excess; it is his weapon of choice against righteousness. Satan is obsessed with ruining man's relationship with God. We have no knowledge of how many innocent victims that have been assaulted, injured, and even murdered to cover up someone's sexual appetite. The filthy deeds of getting sexual gratification—it's off the chart. Having sex with multiple partners has brought much heartache and unwanted children into the world.

When we obey Satan, he chuckles, laughing at us all the way to his kingdom of dungeons, where the blazing flames of hell dance, awaiting the appearance of heavenly transgressors. We have put our fleshly desires above God's laws relating to our sexual behavior—we bow to what seems right to us in the moment of desire. Jesus said, "If you love me, obey me." Earth has many environmental pressures. God still send us to earth to obey a higher calling; our flesh will be tested daily. We are not to let Satan cheat us, deprive us, defraud us, outwit us out of our eternal godly reward.

If we maintain the same sexual swift magnitude we now have, we will pay a price—a cost we may not want to pay. There is a consequence for every action, and the cost may be more than we can afford to pay. We have had our Calvary hill's representation. Christ was required to suffer and die on the cross for us one time only—are we trying to crucify him again? Many souls are broken, spiritually bankrupt, emptied by sin's pleasures. Do we know what shape our everlasting soul is in? Some have impoverished their soul, laid their soul wide open to sin, bare and naked to the bone; the soul of many have become Satan's playground. I heard men regarding their body as a sex machine. Having sex has become a lifestyle in our society—it's just a thing that happens. Sex means nothing to many. A man may ask, "Would you like to come up to my place for a minute? I would like to talk with you over a cup of coffee." This is him asking you for a date. The act of having sex is just a friendly form of recreation for many. Many women want to please the man, so they play along. Men like to try woman as if they are trying on shoes, to get the size, the fit is it tight enough. Sex is like having a little laughter here and there; it's making merriment. Some use sex to shed boredom; when there is nothing else to do, why not have a little fun? Having sex with Jane Doe or John Doe is just another thing on their bucket list.

Seemingly no longer is sex respected as a sacred act that only takes place in a marital union. The marriage bed is a holy place in God's sight; it's a blessing, a virtuous gift from God. The ideal of having sexual activity only in marriage has become a joke to most. No more do we commit our bodies to one person, saying, "I will be devoted to this person only," and the two pledge themselves to one another—"until death do we part." We are to live by the marriage pledge we taken in the sight of God. The attitude today—sex is something we do whenever we feel like doing it and with whomever we can do it with. Sex is no longer the secret mystery of the virtuous wedding bed. Sex is the toast of the town, and the toast goes round and round, singing, "Come one, come all to my place tonight. Let's have a ball. Don't bring your wife nor your husband. I your host will provide the needs of your choosing."

5

Opportunity Fading

The Neanderthals—the cavemen of years long gone by—are they extinct? The ancient barbarians of Europe—these survivors were accustomed to life in a barren coal, bitter, and unmerciful land. Their hunting tools were not sufficient to take care of their needs, making it difficult to capture enough prey to satisfy their bellies. At times they had to practice cannibalism to survive. The headhunters survived day by day. Hunting food was a constant chore in maintaining life.

Observing man today gives the impression only technically has God brought man a mighty long ways since the age of the Neanderthals. There still are some barbaric attitudes, much like the historic barbarians of the past. Today our civilized headhunters are expanding through time in self-seeking gratification. Think of the Hitlers still to come. As I write, Russia has attacked Ukraine. It seems Putin, the president of Russia, is willing to sacrifice human life for self-glorification. Human life is short; it is just a blink in eternity. We have not learned to live together, to value one another as equals. Our earth is diminishing as companies look for the cheapest way of doing business. We breathe polluted air. Environmental conditions are out of control. How do we harness an out-of-control world?

God is our spiritual engine; his breath gives life. We breathe the breath of God's love as it flows through us. God's will is the power keeping life as it roams across this planet. From day one, life was given a fading opportunity of purpose to be carried out on planet Earth during our life span. The flesh is not independent of its spiritual engine; it cannot survive without the soul—God's engine of love. On the other hand, the engine, our souls, do not depend on flesh to maintain existence. Flesh is only the physiology, a dimension of man, and cannot maintain life once God calls his breath out to be judged. The soul is who we are, our personality, and is composed of our minds, our emotions, and our will. God created us with free will; our attitudes, our position on life will be judged. Did we glorify God, or did we find our pleasures in the world's devices? Each life will be judged. The soul of man will be judged.

The results of spending quality time in God's Word is nourishment to the soul. It goes back to the source. Adam received the breath of God. It was the engine that gave him life. Feasting abundantly on the Word of God is beneficial for our eternal abode. Now is the time to prepare for the infinite duration of life to come, where we will have everlasting fellowship with God in our heavenly abode. Spending time with God now leads to an immeasurable afterlife of fellowshipping with God. The enactment is the fulfillment, glorifying the heavenly Father all the way through our predetermined destiny.

Meditating on God's presence should be our greatest focus in this life. The actions we take and decisions we make today are shaping our eternal spiritual future. Think about who we really are—we are everlasting spirit beings. The breath of God is our engine, making our existence in life possible. One thing for certain—we are eternal beings. We will live somewhere in eternity with eternal life; let that life be under the directions and care of Almighty God. The time is at hand. We are choosing our eternal habitation day by day. Decide this day which kingdom will be our everlasting home. We pass from life to life. We were born with an appointed amount of earth time. We must become experts at getting the most out of every allotted moment.

The amount of earth life that has been appointed to each of us has been entrusted to our care. Life is precious; it's a gift. How will we treat it? It has great value in God's sight. He is the giver of the breath we breathe; respect this gift. Our freedom to serve him came at a very high price. The blood of his Son, Jesus, allows us to be his servant. We are highly cherished. Giving thanks to God every day is a blessing to the soul. We are to ascertain our purpose on earth with love and kindness for one another. May our attitudes be pleasing to Almighty God. He knows what we are thinking. He knows who we really are. He knows us better than we know ourselves.

While living on earth, we ought to live like we are one big family. The whole world makes up the human family. There is but one God. He is the Father of all. We are just one piece of life's puzzle, helping to make up the whole of humanity. When all the pieces of the human puzzle come together, it will make a beautiful mosaic statement showing humanity as it should be. We are to live for God, giving him glory with all vigor and enthusiasm like there is no tomorrow, for tomorrow is not promised. Only our eternal life is promised. The number of our earth days we do not know. Our lifestyle tells the story of our souls' condition. At the end of this present life's cycle, we may say, "I sought. I fought for more time. I even bargained for a little more time to endure on this earth a little longer. I prayed but was denied. I could not obtain any more earth time—it was not for sale. My earth assignment had run out of time. I could not add a moment more to my allotted time. Like those who think they went before their time, I too wanted more time before I slipped into the depth of life unknown, but eternity had called, and I must go."

Consider the joy that Jesus has set before us. His divine eternal light force—is it glowing through us for his glory? A divine holy light shines through God's children, greeting everyone with love. Our true essence never dies. We are who we are—by the grace of God. The Father is one with his children. The children are the seed of their father. They truly love and obey him because they know him as Father. God is the essence of all life. We live out our human existence in the elements of earth's timetable. God has positioned us on this planet for such a time as this. This is our time. Receive what a day may bring. Know that each day is a new day and will never have to be lived again. We are to give each day our very best. We are living in a state of the spiritual and the physical, packaged up in flesh. We will have remembrance of life in the visible and the invisible mind—was it possessed with hate? The fruits of our minds will show its earthly participation on the day of judgment, when we stand before the Lord God. Life will go on, forever animating its intelligence in eternity. The remembrance of earth life goes in part with us in our spiritual existence, and God will cause every knee to bow and every tongue to confess that Jesus Christ is Lord. We will keep our identity after we leave this earth. In heaven we will recognize those we previously knew. We are a derivative derived from God's immense love. We never die. We will see and understand the unseen, for we have become one with our Lord. We are a part of the previously unknown. God has brought us to himself; his children has returned home. We were created through his immense love. He made us in his image and likeness. He wanted us to be one with him in his kingdom. Out of dust was man's body taken. Our human phase is a temporary home, limited to our purpose. Our everlasting appearance started in God's mind. Our lives have no end. We will be with our Creator forever—now ain't that good news? We were created in his image and likeness; we look like him. We were brought back to him through his will for our redemption by the shed blood of Jesus Christ.

God, the creator of all things, is the only true God; there is no other God beside him. Elohim is God all by himself; he needs no validation—he is validation. God breathe breath into the nostrils of a lump of clay that he formed and shaped into his image and likeness; after the clay received life from the breath of God, it was able to communicate and walk with God. When the divine breath entered into the lump of clay, it gave life to the first human being to live in the garden prepared for him east of Eden. God's breath gives life—energy that will never die. God breathes into us, and life goes on the move, reproducing new life as it travels through generations.

Our spirit selves are functioning through divine love. God wanted us to live in the flesh for a purpose. We were to keep our flesh alive by eating plants growing in the dust of the earth. Plants are herbs producing health and nourishment, helping us to sustain physical life. We coexist with the herbs, for we too were taken from the dust of the earth.

The afterlife will be a conscious existence, and if heaven is our home, we will eat from the tree of life. As God allows the human experience to be remembered, there will be people we knew on earth experiencing heaven with us. We will recognize our mother and father, brothers and sisters. Our individual souls are special. Everyone is significant in the sight of God. His Son is our personal Savior and the bridegroom of the New Jerusalem. We are a derivative derived out of God's immense creative love. We were created for his pleasure.

Our Father is the only true God; his obedient children, in every sense of the word, are one with him through the shed blood of Jesus.

The origin of time cannot swallow us. God knew who we were even before the foundation of the earth was laid; we were with him then, we are with him now, and forever shall we be in his everlasting inevitable love. Nothing in God can die.

Having a finite mind, we are limited in our grasping the deep secrets of life; the energy that gives life is not for us to understand. God is all-knowing. We are to make Jesus Christ the love of our lives, and our truth in God came through Jesus Christ. Jesus paid the price for our redemption. We are to walk in his ways that we may live forever with him. Salvation is standing at the door of our hearts; can we hear the knocking? We are to open the door of our hearts, our minds, saying, "Come in, Jesus. I've been waiting for your visit. Wash me, my Lord, in your precious shed blood. Let me know you and the power of your resurrection."

How old is your soul? How old is the breath of God? Prior to the physical form, the breath of God was on the move through boundless vast darkness where there is no time. And he had us on his mind. God is an eternal light force—in him there is no darkness. No end to his endlessness, his Almighty powers are buried in his sacred energy, he is revered and worthy of all praise. There will be souls grievously affected all through eternity because of their disobedience to God, suffering through eternity because they ignored or did not believe he is. God's Word is his will. Those who didn't come to know him while on their earth journey will have to give an answer for their unbelief during the judgment period. My dear friends, don't let one of these suffering souls suffering throughout eternity be yours.

6

God's Unconditional Love

Once saved, always saved—that is the question concerning God's unconditional love. Unconditional love—how do we conceive this statement? What does the word *unconditional* mean to you? What is God offering the sinner? How does unconditional love work? Does it mean we can do whatever we please, deliberately being disobedient to God's will, and still be saved? If we die without repentance, are we still saved because we've been washed in Jesus's shed blood and our sins are hidden in his blood? Some Christians believe just that. If that is the case, it makes us no longer held accountable for our deliberate sin. Being born again means our sins are covered forever, regardless of our attitude. After being sealed in the shed blood of Jesus Christ, we can run amok, no accountability given for our behavior. We think the shed blood of God's Son shall not be trampled in hell, so we go on our marry way thinking, sin does not have the power to crush the blood washed child of God. Sin does not have the power to crush the blood of Jesus under Satan's rule.

Some Christians believe when we constantly sin, it is constantly hidden from God's sight in the blood—so we have the privilege to satisfy our sinful appetites without having the guilt or the shame, having no more fear of retribution. Desiring unlawful pleasures and committing grave sin in the face of God is not a problem anymore to the "*saved*." The solution to our sinning—we are forgiven souls. God will never again judge a blood-washed soul. Our sin account has been and will always be paid in full by the precious shed blood of Jesus. From now on, every time God looks at us, he sees only the blood of his Son; he cannot see our sin because it is spiritually covered in the divine blood of Jesus. That gives us a passport into heaven regardless of the unacceptable circumstances of the life we are living. The gift of salvation is covering our sins—pass, present, and future. A forgiven soul need not be saved again and again; it's covered with the blood of Jesus and cannot go to hell—so many of us think that is the case. Our sins are continually being expunged in the blood. Sin's power will never be counted greater than the power of the blood. God knows our thoughts before they reach us. God will not be mocked.

Sin separates us from God. The wages of sin is death. Can any soul have a relation with God Almighty while living in an impaired state, weakened by mockery concerning God's gift of salvation through continuous sin? There are consequences that must be paid for our actions. God will always be pleased with his Son's finish work. Jesus went to the cross, suffered, and died for the sins of those who truly trust in his finished work. He accepted our sin debt and paid the consequence of our sin. We were obligated to pay that debt but were unable to meet the ransom, nor were we able to release ourselves from the captivity of sin. Only Jesus could free us from sin, for it was the will of God that the breath he put in our human body come back to him. Jesus only was given the power to redeem us. Jesus alone paid our sin debt with his blood. He was the only one that could. We are spirit beings. Without the covering of Jesus's shed blood, we are spiritually dead, and there is no way a dead man can come to his own rescue. God, out of his immense love for the human race, sent an advocate to stand directly before his face to intercede on our behalf.

Our life performance on this earth will be tried by holy fire. When our works come before the living God, will they stand the test of time or will they be consumed by the discerning holy fire? Will our works perish in the second judgment before the white throne judgment? Disobedience is wasted time. Living on this earth in ungodliness is a choice. Our lives have been recorded. How will it read? What will our reward be under the concept of unconditional love? O sinning children, when the time comes and our rewards are handed out, will our unfulfilled purpose be found unmet? How much will our lives' work weigh on the measuring scales of righteousness? Obey—there is no other way to gain heaven. Sinner man, were you ever saved? We are incomplete beings. We need Jesus. If we love Jesus, obey him. Don't let our limited finite existence hang on the vines of foolishness and mockery. Playing with God's gift of salvation is not the way, continually sinning after we say we have been saved. Not asking Jesus into our lives is a no-no, but trying to make mockery out of God's finished work is the greater no-no; it is an insult to the mercy of God.

Are we really under the blood? Are we spiritually blind? We are fooling ourselves, thinking every time we commit adultery or any other sin, all we have to do is to ask for forgiveness, knowing the practice of sin has become our way of life. We want to keep on sinning because it's appealing. All we have to do is to keep asking for forgiveness. Are we sorry for our behavior? Are we mouthing something, thinking, *I confessed. God is faithful to forgive me. I said I'm sorry for my sins. That ought to cover my actions. I will go to heaven.* My dear, we need to look up the definition of *repentance*.

Is willful sin covered? Who makes mockery of God's grace and say, "The victory is mine. My sin is buried in Christ. It can't be seen. We don't have to consider sin anymore"? Jesus is the victor. He is the conqueror. He has defeated our enemy—death. If we love him, we would obey him. Regretting our sinful revile nature, come to God with a repenting heart full of sorrow for our evil deeds. If we are sincere, we will prostrate our souls, humble ourselves before the living God, and ask his forgiveness with repentant hearts. We will face the consequences of our misbehavior in the hereafter; payment is standing at our door.

The so-called saved sinner may be forbidden to see God with clarity and not even have the awareness that they are not seeing God as clearly as other inhabitants of heaven. Maybe our translucent state of being will be hidden from the disobedient few; they will be happy. They do not realize their fate, not knowing their state of being, still spiritually blind. We earthly beings are to keep developing, building a relationship with God through obedience. God is holy and faithful to his word. Respect his will. Day by day, we must learn to die to self. Don't be an egotist. Obedience shows our love for God and our growth in his will. In this world and through eternity, God will always be the fundamental regenerating source of our conscious existence.

We love our children, and if we are good parents, when our children are disobedient, we chastise them. There are many ways to give punishment, bringing to the child's attention their behavior. Teach them there will be consequences for their actions. They are to be held accountable for their conduct—rewards for their good conduct but disciplined when they misbehave.

The child's punishment may be that the parents denied them the privilege of participating in their favorite activities. They are to know there will be a form of retribution for their actions. They must learn what is expected of them as they deal with their fellow playmates. Also, they are to understand rules are a good thing; they are there to keep us safe.

There are spiritual laws that spirits must observe and obey. They are there to protect our souls from living among the eternal damned. God loves us, but we will be held accountable for our conduct. No action taken in our lives goes unseen. Sooner or later, divine light will shine on all our deeds—retribution, the dispensing of rewards for being obedient, and the dispensing of awards for our disobedience.

After our physical death, it's too late to say, "Forgive me, Father, for I have sinned against thee." Many will say, "Jesus, I am truly sorry for my sins. Will you wash away my sins with your precious shed blood one more time?" It is better to go through the punishment of hard knocks on earth while you are still on this side of earth's green sod. Don't wait until you are placed six feet underneath the sod.

God's unconditional love is not carte blanche, condoning corruption on account of once saved always saved. Discipline, self-control, is required of God's children. Satan's artful coaxing may be strong enough to fleece us for a time, but God will not be mocked. Respect the Word of God. Obedience is holiness. God wants us to be holy. Obedience is the path to holiness through Jesus Christ. Jesus said, "I am holy. Be ye holy. Holiness is what I want from man."

Wide is the road that leads to death and destruction. Jesus said, "If you love me, obey me." When the road of life gets rough and bumpy, fasten your seat belt little tighter. Life's surface is difficult—that was in the mind of God. He meant life to be purpose driven. Earth life—it is a journey worth taking for a greater calling (assignment). After our earth's journey has been completed, we will receive our reward, signifying the end of our predetermined destination to planet Earth.

Setting the stages of life, the scenes of right and wrong, through these two choices, we will live our lives. God knows who we are and what we are about to do. Before we do it, listen. Let that small still voice within guide us to God's heart.

God is holy. He said, "Holiness is what I want from my children." How do we become holy? Through obedience. Obeying our heavenly Father shows our love for him. God wants his children to be loving, kind, showing love to their neighbors, giving the world a little TLC. Each day Jesus shows us tender love and care. We are to pattern ourselves after him; be God's example to the world.

The tracks through life's trodden trails are made from many winding pathways. We are to choose prayerfully the path we will follow. The deceiving configurations of unkindness lives amongst us, they are the us, the moving sequence of life beckoning, showing their appealing entrance Emotional destruction. We are to thrive in this life, keeping our eyes on the prize. God has promised us good; wait on him. He is faithful; let him lead the way down the trodden pathways of life's ever-moving sequence. There are worlds in competition. Spiritual conflict is in action opposing God over the soul of man. There are unseen worlds living amongst us. Know that God will win the opposing wars of both man and spirit.

> If I ascend up into heaven, thou art there:
> if I make my bed in hell, behold, thou art there.
> (Psalm 139:8)

God's presence is omnipresence—everywhere at the same time.

> Thou believe there is one God; thou doest well: the devils also believe, and tremble. (James 2:19)

The demons believe there is a God, and they tremble at the thought. Are we smart enough to tremble at the thought of knowing there is life awaiting us, knowing our sin has hidden us from the face of God? What will we do, knowing God does not look on sin? Sin is the stumbling block to greater life.

> And I saw no temple therein: for the Lord God Almighty and Lamb are the temple of it. And the city had no need of the sun, neither of the moon, to shine in it: for the glory of God did lighten it, and the Lamb is the light there of. And the gates of it shall not be shut at all by day: for there shall be no night there.[2]

---

[2] There is no temple in the city since both God and the Son will be present in their fullest manifestation. Its light will be provided by the Shekinah glory of God and of Christ. The glory of God in the New Jerusalem will light the earth. Whether this is the new earth of the millennial earth is not clear. (Footnotes taken from Revelation 21:22, 23, and 25)

7

Jesus Is Able to Still the Storm

Fear is man's oldest enemy. Satan came into the garden of Eden with purpose—steal Eve's innocence and drive a wedge between God and man. Disobedience to God will drive the separation Satan wants between man and his creator. In the midst of the garden stood a tree, bearing seemingly delicious fruit. God told Adam they were forbidden to eat from the tree. The deceiver one bright sunny day was just loafing, hanging out in the garden. He was lying among the branches of the tree, biding hie time, watching the activities below the branches of the forbidden tree.

When the atmosphere seemed right, he delivered his blow. He struck, hissing softly the persuasion of disobedience to the guiltless, gullible Eve. Like a newborn baby, Eve knew no sin. Adam too was covered in innocence. They were a guiltless pair alone in the garden created for them by the hands of God. That day Adam standing near Eve, watching the scene of persuasion. The influence being played out by the serpent, the betrayer, was in action convincing the gullible Eve. By the magic of his persuasion, Eve conceded, not knowing the depths, the deep-seated danger laid hidden, concealed in the treacherous serpent, who spoke tenderly, making an impression on the impressionable, wondering Eve. Under the power of Satan's magical charm, she yielded.

The fruit growing on the forbidden tree begun to look pleasant and desirable for the tasting. She took from the tree a fruit. Taking a little mouthful, she did ascertain the flavor of it was good to the taste, offering also to Adam the tasty fruit, and he did partake. The tree-bearing the fruit of forbidden knowledge opened their eyes to a part of life they had never known. Their disobedience to God's instructions gave birth to fear, an emotion they had never known. The beginning of fear took its root that day in the heart of Adam and his wife, Eve.

The curse of fear has been passed down to the generations. Fear will never let go of man. Look around—man is very fearful. We live in a fearful world. Under our own power, there is no escape from the spirit of fear. Fear is embedded in disobedience to God. When we know we are doing something wrong, fear creeps in, increasing our cunningness to deceive one another by covering up our wrongdoing. Fear is not of God; it is a spiritual gift straight out of hell. Fear has torment in it. The luster of the enemy's silvery voice brought a moment of wonderment to the psyche of motherless Eve. Eve's curiosity was aroused. An excitement came upon her. She relinquished her obedience and exercised her free will, trying something new in a moment of desire. The enticement in the garden east of Eden Flows on. Innocence had vanished. Sin was accomplished. Disobedience and fear were born in that moment of time in the garden east of Eden.

At the close of day, in the cool of evening, they heard the voice of God calling to Adam. The sound of God's voice triggered the spirit of fear, and it surfaced in the heart of Adam. Adam looked for a place to hide. He found no hiding place, from the seeing eyes of God.

Adam told God, "I heard your voice, and I was afraid because I was naked. I wanted to hide myself from you." Adam had God-given protection, shielding him from sin's accountability; he would know no sin. Sin would not be imputed unto him as long as he obeyed the voice of God. In the beginning, Adam had one master, one voice to obey. After the episode of persuasion at the tree of knowledge, Adam was able to hear and be influenced by more than one voice. Now there were two spirits vying for his soul. Through the maze of voices that are coming unto man, the impulse to disobey has bombarded man's ability to decide to obey God's voice. The power of fear is still the number one emotion, invading man's psyche. To pick and choose freely, to know what it is he really wants to do, he is being spiritually persuaded. Overthinking stands before us.

That moment at the tree, in the garden east of Eden, we are still living in that moment of disobedience. Fear will knock at the door of our minds and try to enter without permission. Fear, when it shows up, will try to take over our lives. Without prayer, we live in despair. The sinister effect of fear is worrisome, tormenting, and its depths reach everlasting pain, destroying the peace we once knew before fear came to take up its residence in us. The anguish of fear will be eternal when our souls enter hell's accommodations. In hell we will live with endless fear, an undying pain of regret. Living a longtime courtship with fear will influence our ability to ever escape its grip. Fear will make us do and say things we ordinarily would not do or say. Lingering fear makes one seriously distraught—both physical and mental. Those locked-in fear will live in an unhealthy state of existence. Extreme fear can work against us for years, robbing us of our strength to thrive in life. Fear is a profound emotion that can keep us wondering, *Why can't I do the obvious?*

We don't have to yield to the spirit of fear and live under its influence; we have a friend that sticks closer than a brother—Jesus is his name. Trust in him. We are to give him all our fear. He has overcome the tormentor and wants to deliver us from the grips of fear. Jesus is able to still the storms of life. He walks above the storms. He walks upon the waters. "Fear not." Fear wants to draw near, causing us to say, "I do not know the man," when we know the man is our closest friend.

Peter was asked, "Are you one of this man's disciples?" He answered in fear, "I am not."

In John 18:25, Peter was asked a second time, "Are you one of this man's disciples?" He denied it and said, "I am not." One of the servants of the high priest, being his kinsman, whose ear Peter cut off, saith, "Did not I see thee in the garden with him?" Peter denied again (a third time)—immediately the cock crowed.

Out of fear, Peter again denied knowing Jesus. He declared, "I do not know the man."

Scripture in Matthew 26:69–75, Mark 14:66–72, and Luke 22:57–62 recount Peter's denial of knowing Jesus.

> And there arose a great storm of wind, and the waves beat into the ship, so that it was now full. And He was in the hinder part of the ship, asleep on a pillow: and they awake him, and they say unto him, "Master, carest thou not that we perish?" And He arose, and rebuked the wind, and said unto the sea, "Peace, be still." And the wind ceased, and there was a great calm. And he said to them, "Why are ye so fearful? how is it that ye have no faith?" And they feared exceedingly, and said one to another, "What manner of man is this, that even the wind and the sea obey him?" (Mark 4:37–41)

> But straightway Jesus speck unto them, saying, "Be of good cheer; it is I; be not afraid." And Peter answered him and said, "Lord, if it be thou, bid me come unto thee on the water." And he said, "Come." And when Peter was come down out of the ship, he walked on the water, to meet Jesus. But when he saw the wind boisterous, he was afraid; and beginning to sink, he cried, saying, Lord, save me. And immediately Jesus stretched forth *his* hand, and caught him, and said unto him, "O thou of little faith, wherefore didst thou doubt?" (Matthew 14:27–31)

> There is no fear in love; but perfect love casteth out fear: because fear hath torment. He that feareth is not made perfect in love. (1 John 4:18)

Satan is the master at releasing fear all over the world. The spirit of fear is causing people to live unrealistic and untrusting lives. Fear is one of Satan's many invitations. Refuse his invitations; they invite you to his barren playgrounds of gloom and doom. Look at all the misery Satan brought into Job's life because of Job's fears.

> Then Satan answered the Lord, and said,
> "Doth Job *fear* God for naught?" (Job 1:9)

The key word here is *fear*. Job feared his sons and daughters had sinned, eating and drinking, feasting every day without giving God proper thanks. Job feared his children had not remembered to give God burnt offerings and praise. Had they sanctified themselves by not giving thanks to God for their blessings? Job feared they had not remembered to glorify God as they enjoyed themselves.

When we live in the boundaries of fear, we are in Satan's territory. He owns fear; he's territorial and will defend his territory. When we come unto his boundaries, he will attack and claim the intruder. Fear is one of the many territories belonging to Satan; fear is not of God. Where there is fear, there is no trust. Fear is not one of God's properties. Turn from fear, and run into the waiting arms of Jesus. Satan has the authority, the right to come after us when we are harboring, giving shelter to his gifts; he will come to help us enjoy them. Playing his games, receiving his offerings put us at his beckoning call. He will come around to see how you are enjoying his eternal hellish ungodly gifts.

The spirit world has laws and boundaries governing their activity. God, being the supreme law, has all boundaries and powers under his control. God knows what is going on in the heavens and in the earth. God sees what is going on in the depth of hell. Satan knew fear was in the heart of Job. He was the one who placed fear in Job's mind. Don't let fear dictate how we live our lives, domineeringly imposing its power over us. Satan knows the spirit of fear would linger in the heart of man in a very unhealthy way, far too long. After Job blindly accepted the spirit of fear, he immediately found himself inside Satan's territorial grip, and there was a consequence to be paid. Not knowing the payoff fear would bring, he painfully suffered a long time at Satan's hands—read the book of Job.

Don't confess fear. We are not to let the word *fear* come out of our mouth. Fear is avoidable. Let our trust in Jesus rule the day. Jesus said, "Fear not." We do have a way out of fear. He would not say, "Fear not," if fear was not unavoidable. Fear is avoidable if we trust in Jesus. Fear can become a possession if we nurse it, feeding it, keeping it warm and alive in our bosom until it becomes our child. Fear will become a part of us until we feel incomplete without it.

Don't let fear become a permanent part of the life we live. Fear is a hard spirit to ween; it is not going anywhere because it wants to rule over you. If we live in fear for a long period of time, it will rule over every decision we make and, eventually, will possess our souls. We will become fearful over everything, and our favorite words will be "I can't." Without Jesus, we will live with the spirit of fear governing our lives far too long. Like Job, we too will live in constant fear, not realizing we are housing something that is all-consuming, taking control of how we see life.

When fear begins to process our thoughts, we confess, "I am just a fearful person. I can't help it." We can bring into existence what we say. Ask God to show you what is affecting your insight. Understand why you are so fearful. Ask God to give us a different perspective on understanding how to deal with the situations that are being thrown into our lives. We don't have to settle for every ugly distraction that comes our way. Indifference will come into our lives from time to time—that's part of living life. Confront the indifference in faith. Use God's Word. Build faith through prayer. Let our faith become greater than our circumstances. Rest in faith. Trust in God. Praise God for what we want to see come into our lives, and make sure he is a part of what we are praying for.

Peace and joy are just waiting for us to call them into our presence. We can enjoy many blessings by pressing through to God in prayer and praise. Believe God is answering our prayers as we speak. Don't let our prayer request always be "give me, give my family." Think of others; they have needs as well. Don't send up selfish prayers of "me" and "mine." At some point in life, we should come to the realization that our prayers are one-sided. We ask for blessings for "me and my family." We sought God not only for our own selfishness. Wanting God's favor selfishly, we can't see beyond our own wants. We are to see the hurting people all over the world standing in the need of prayer. What do we have to offer God? God asked us to praise him, to give him the fruits of our lips in worship. Singing unto the Lord for his loving-kindness is an offering that is ever before us. Praising our Father is of his asking. All heaven continuously sings and praises Almighty God; it is heaven's delight to praise him.

There is unending worship in the kingdom of God. Faith, obedience, and praise is our ticket into eternal rest. Giving God infinite durations of our love in holy fellowship is beyond our finding out. God is ageless. He is endless love—he is our burning perpetual flame guiding the way. Follow after him. Have we any idea what joy is awaiting us in our Father's kingdom, where his eternal flaming light of love never burns out?

The pounding fear in Job's heart brought him much suffering. Fear caused Peter to deny he was one of Jesus's disciples. Fear kept Peter from walking on the water to meet Jesus. What is fear keeping us from doing? Is it keeping us from walking atop our troubled waters? The Bible says no fear will enter heaven.

Revelation 21:8 reads:

> But the fearful, the unbelieving, and all liars, shall have their part in the lake which burneth with fire and brimstone: which is the second death.[3]

---

[3] Footnotes taken from the King James Study Bible concerning Revelation 21:8:
It is done: The eternal purpose of God to gather a holy, devoted people for Himself, has now been accomplished. Alpha and Omega: Beginning and the End. God is the origin and source of all things. He also is the goal or aim of all things. The water of life represents eternal sustenance and provision—available freely by faith. He that overcometh is the one who has genuine, saving, persevering faith. He will inherit all that belongs to him as a son of God. But sinners, who have shown their rebellion against God by their lifestyle of sin, have already been cast into the lake of fire. The second death is eternal death.

> And death and hell were cast into the lake of fire. This is the second death. And whosoever was not found written in the book of life was cast into the lake of fire. (Revelation 20:14, 15)

Jesus has stilled our eternal storm by his shed blood for our salvation, purchased on the cross of crucifixion, when he said, "It is finished." All we need to do is to accept his finished work. We ought to be loving on Jesus, giving him praise joyfully. Thank God for Jesus—he is closer to us than a brother. He is the very breath we breathe.

8

God's Mercy Imputed

(As it is written I have made thee a father of many nations) before him whom he believed, even God, who quickeneth the dead, and calleth those things which be not as though they were. (Romans 4:17)

Who against hope believed in hope, that he might become the father of many nations, according to that which was spoken, so shall thy seed be. (Romans 4:18)

And being not weak in faith, he considered not his own body now dead, when he was about a hundred years old, neither yet the deadness of Sarah's womb. (Romans 4:19)

He staggered not at the promise of God through unbelief; but was strong in faith, giving glory to God. (Romans 4:20)

And being fully persuaded that what he (God) promised, he (Abraham) was able also to (father a child) perform. (Romans 4:21)

> And therefore, it was his faith imputed to him for righteousness. (Romans 4:22)
>
> Now it was not written for his (Abraham) sake alone, that it was imputed to him. (Romans 4:23)
>
> But for us also, to whom it shall be imputed, if we believe on him (God) that raised up Jesus our Lord from the dead. (Romans 4:24)
>
> Who was delivered for our offenses and was raised again for our justification. (Romans 4:25)

Father Abraham was a man chosen of God, having strong faith in God's leading. Strong faith produces works. Putting God's will in the forefront of our lives builds a divine relationship. God knew he could trust his servant Abraham to obey him. His sins were not imputed against him. God asked Abraham to build an offering altar and sacrifice his son Isaac to him. It is said Abraham believed if he gave Isaac as a sacrificial offering to God, God would give Isaac back to him by raising the child from the dead. Abraham obeyed God. His trust was rooted and buried deep in his love for God. Strong faith is a gift only God can give; it is a precious commodity. Not everyone is granted the privilege.

When Abraham and his son were building a fire beneath the altar, Isaac asked, "Father, where is the offering?"

Abraham replied, "God will provide."

David, while watching Bathsheba bathe, perceived feelings of lust he did not deny. His desires were irresistible, and the lustfulness of it was weakening his ability to ignore this beauty. The feelings were more than his willpower would tolerate. Wanting to take another man's wife in his arms, what was he to do with this hunger for her? The desire to have her grew stronger with every thought. Every time he would visualize taking her in his arms and placing her on his bed, his mind went out of control. *I must have her*, he thought. His urges did not stop on the rooftop. He gazed intently on Bathsheba as she bathed each day. The pain of his longing for her, must be satisfied, aching for her smooth, warm, curved body perfumed so delicately with a gentle fragrance. It was exciting imagining her in his embrace. Craving to possess Bathsheba, holding her to his embrace, ran beyond his mortal control. His intense dreaming of having her rushed over him again and again. This mental picture spun around in his brain, crushing his resistance by the moment.

He cried out, "What must I do to lie with this woman without causing a scandal? I must not disgrace Israel."

Whatever the cost would be, he acted on his lust and fed the appetite of his flesh. He ordered that Bathsheba be brought to him. In defense of this woman, could she have refused to come unto the king of Israel after he ordered her to make an appearance before him?

David satisfied his lustful appetite. Burying his face in the bosom of Bathsheba, he satisfied his deep passion. He took her as if she was his wife. Their intimacy brought forth new life. During their intimacy, Bathsheba conceived. A son was born to David and Bathsheba. David's lust for Bathsheba brought the wrath of God down on David's house. Sickness and death was given permission to enter into the house of David—the king of Israel. In a few years, David's son he had with Bathsheba became seriously ill. David had desired Bathsheba although she was the wife of Uriah. David's lust caused wrath and hatred to rise up in his heart against his good friend Uriah, the husband of Bathsheba. David's country was at war. David, being king of Israel, should have been leading the battle against their enemies. In the days of the kings, it was the king's duty to lead the charge into battle with a loud command, shouting forward—"attack" should have been the cry coming out of his mouth in the midst of battle.

David was thinking Uriah must be killed while in battle. He wanted his hands to be clean, having no connection to Uriah's death. So David had Uriah sent to the front line, hoping he would be killed. If Uriah is killed, it would bring an end to David's worries concerning his love for Bathsheba. Their relationship could move on without scandal.

When David's son took sick, he grieved deeply. On his face, he repented before God for his sins. He asked God to forgive him and save his son's life. "Let my son live," he prayed. His prayers were heard but unanswered. His young five-year-old son would not recover. The boy died on his sick bed. It seemed sowing the seeds of sin took root far too soon, bringing forth the bitter fruit of death to David's house.

The child born from David's adulterous affair with Bathsheba became grievously ill and died. David's love for the Hebrew God of Israel never failed him. The day his son died, he prayed and worshipped before Almighty God with all his might then ordered a ceremonious banquet to be set before him, and he dined sufficiently, rejoicing before the Lord God. When he was questioned about his joyous state of being, he said, "When my son was alive, I would call to him, and he would come running to me. I'd hear the joy of his laughter and could feel the warmth of his body when I held him close in my arms. He was taken from me. Blessed be the name of the Lord God." With this kind of love for God, you understand why it is said David is a man after God's own heart, and his sin was not imputed to him because he loved God.

Second Samuel 12:15–18: David's sin had brought the name of God into disrepute. Such knowledge ought to serve as a deterrent to willful sin on the part of believers.

David's sin would surface in renewed warfare. His house was disgraced throughout his life.

> Even as David also describeth the blessedness of the man, unto whom God imputeth righteousness without works, saying, "Blessed are they whose sin is not imputed. Blessed is the man to his iniquities are forgiven, and whose sins are covered—whom the Lord will not impute sins." (Romans 4:6–8)

David's dancing and whirling about with all his might in praise before the Lord God Almighty was the joy of his heart. David loved God with his whole being. Shouting and singing, David gave Jehovah

God praise night and day. In battle and out of battle, David trusted the Hebrew God of Israel. David's faith in God was everlasting to everlasting, and God imputed righteousness unto him. It is written David was a man after God's own heart. David pursued God in love and trust.

The Bible reads:

> What is man, that thou art mindful of him? And the son of man, that thou hast made him a little lower than the angels, and hast crowned him with glory and honor. Thou madest him to have dominion over the works of thy hands; thou hast put all things under his feet. (Psalm 8:4–6)

> Blessed is he whose transgression is forgiven, whose sin is covered. Blessed is the man unto whom the Lord imputeth not iniquity, and in whose spirit, there is no (hatred) guile. I will praise thee; for I am fearfully and wonderfully made. (Psalm 32:1–2)

In his image, after his likeness, tangible man is a product of God's love. All things were created for God's pleasure. Our outward look and our inward being are representations of our creator. We are a vivid conception of our Father, the Lord God Almighty. We are to give him thanks for his mercy and his grace. We were created to be a part of God's holy family. We are his children. We are to bring pleasure to God—that is our purpose. We are to pray like David prayed, sing like David sang, and dance like David danced. With all our might, dance before the Lord God Almighty. Children of God heed my voice.

9

Cherish Life

Invite Jehovah the Lord God Almighty, the giver of life, into your every thought. Ask God to be your strength during this pilgrimage experience called life. Your appearance on this planet was no mistake; it is an assigned period of time. Cherish this cycle of your being; it will end sooner than you think. Your purpose, your task on earth was created just for you. Find your purpose and get into it; it is waiting to be discovered only by you. When you are called from this earth, you will have to give an account of how you handle your earth assignment. Your work will be judged. Before you were introduced to this system known as the world's system, God looked into the immeasurable unending eons of boundlessness. He saw you amid the vastness of nothingness. Your spirit was then and is now. We are old souls that always have been and always will be. God has purposed each one. Your purpose is the plan God has in mind for you and is to be carried out for his glory by you before the beginning of earth life, this is the only life you recollect because you are experiencing it. We are very old souls, and this is the life we are now experiencing. Maybe we are only allowed to know the life that is set before us as we live one life at a time—God only knows.

Is there other time systems, more life to experience? How awesome the thought. You were scheduled to be introduced to this world system at a precise time and on the date you arrived. Before you were an inhabitant of earth's hemisphere, your destination was predetermined, preordained for such a time as prescribed by God. All things are in God's sight. He knows the beginnings and the endings of all manifestations, and there is no existence without his divine substance at work in it. Nothing is living independently of God's power. You are a visitor to this planet. Your spirit being traveled to this solar system on a divine mission. You are living your earthly assignment as a human being equipped in flesh to give God service from this earth.

God's perpetual existence is deposited in you. Your life is a diagram of divine planning. Your greater life is yet to come. Your visit to earth is an assignment with purpose—that is to be filled in a specified amount of time. All life on earth has a God-given purpose to be fulfilled. Did it ever occur to you that it is very important to find your purpose as soon as possible; you have the ability to achieve the assignment set before you.

Start living in your purpose—it will glorify God your Father. All life is by divine appointment. You are part of God's blueprint—for continuous life uninterrupted, you are an extension in the sequence of time, forever ongoing. There is a built-in divine, remarkable, detailed DNA working within you. An assignment was placed in your soul before your eternal soul was placed into your spirit body, and then that spirit being was placed into a temporary body of flesh. Can you comprehend, fathom the depth of the mind of God? Don't grasp at his wisdom, asking, "Why was I born?" You were born because you are a significant part in God's plan—you are a glance in his eternal divine pleasure of creation. God is continuously building a family, enlarging his kingdom. God had a job, a purpose awaiting your birth here on earth, and there is another purpose awaiting your soul departure. It is your duty to prayerfully seek your purpose while you are on earth.

Your life has meaning. It's the very essence of God's will that you be on earth at this time. You are who you are because God so willed you to be who you are for his glory. Embrace who you are. Don't mistreat yourself. Cherish the gift of life. Use what God has put in your heart for good, and you will function in your divine assignment. You are a living element, belonging to a most inclusive family, the holy family. Your life can be an opportunity, an experience that will glorify Almighty God while you are still in the flesh. He has asked us to love him and to love one another. Learn to love thy neighbor. It is a commandment—he wants it obeyed. You will have to obey the law of loving one another before you can become a citizen in the kingdom of God.

There is an ongoing battle in the atmosphere between the warring angels of God and of Satan; they are fighting over who will be the ruler of heaven.

A good soldier is obedient and will fight the good fight of faith and will cherish self-discipline, respecting the rights of others. This kind of living gives glory to the Almighty. Let's encircle one another with the love that strengthen our ability to live a Christlike life. The human life is passing from one life form to another form of life.

The cocoon's purpose is to envelope its assignment, giving a protective covering to the struggling unborn butterfly while it is struggling to be born into this world to carry out its purpose. Divine authority is at work in the butterfly as it struggles to escape the cocoon, pushing forward until its brightly colored wings appear. Once it is free, it will fly into the world, pollinating as it goes.

You also can do something for those struggling—the unfortunate, those in need of kindness. Show concern for the homeless and the shut-ins of society. You can make a difference. Give a smile. Make others a part of your prayer life. Volunteer whenever or wherever you are needed. Engage with people, expressing compassion when opportunity presents itself. Be there for someone. Let kindness be spontaneous, knowing your effort to show love will not go unnoticed. Your good deeds will be rewarded by the all-seeing eyes of God.

As you travel through your daily routine, be one with the Lord. Ask him to let his presence overtake your being.

May your stay on earth be continuously developing, maturing in divine growth. Having an intimate relationship with your creator keeps you growing in purpose. Understand purpose is something God set up for you to obtain during this life through Jesus Christ, who is one with Jehovah God. Know that God is the mighty force. He is the light, giving everlasting strength to the world. He is the inevitable, the cause of all seen and unseen worlds. Cherish life—it is all around us. Be at peace with God, and you will be at peace with life's interweaving purpose. The tunes, the rhythms of living in God's great orchestra of life, the symphonies, the living complexity of life is functioning all around us. Ask God for wisdom, and above all, ask for understanding.

10

The War Room

During our prayer time, unwanted thoughts may rush into our minds, interfering, prevailing against our trend of thought, our desire to be spiritually alone with the Lord is interrupted. What's causing the mind to become such a battlefield, a real battle to concentrate on the Lord? We are our minds. Control the mind—you control the person. A person without a mind is living in a state of vegetation. Where the mind goes, the flesh will follow. The mind embodies the person. That is why the enemy is after the mind of man. The devil is putting the mind under constant attack, with opposing thoughts during prayer time, daydreams running amok, even vile imaginations. Satanic interference is striking at the very soul of man. Satan does not have carte blanche, complete freedom over our lives. He can't do whatever he pleases with us. The enemy loves playing mind games, trying to destroy the peacefulness man wants to enjoy. While we are in prayer, the replays of life keep returning.

What are we to do? Pray. When we are trying to concentrate on Jesus, these invading hindrance come, bringing confusion to our concentration. Mentally we fight the invasion; the fighting brings weariness to the soul sapping our strength to continue to fight back. Try as we may to pray, to meditate, wanting to reflect only on God's Word, but our wandering mind is in full operation. Spiritual entities keep trying to separate us from the Lord; wanting to disconnect our ability to focus on the Almighty is their aim. When the enemy is assaulting the mind by shortening our attention span, the mind is in warring conflict. Fatigue can set in; however, the battle of priority begins. Opposing spirits are trying to stress us out. Prayer is the only answer in defeating the enemy. Jesus's presence is always near to help fight the good fight of faith. Jesus knows the enemy's tricks of causing old memories to flood the mind, making it impossible for concentration during prayer time. Opposing spirits are consistently trying to keep us from becoming single-minded on God.

Fight to stay focused on God while in prayer; the battle will not be easy, but fight on. Training the mind is a hard task; however, keep praying. Never stop even if we have to pray out loud. Pray aloud until we feel we have the victory over his interfering attacks. Disrupting images will not stop trying to press through. Remember to fight the spirit with the spirit—that is what the Bible tells us to do. The devil will display his best efforts to keep us from having a peaceful prayer time with our Lord. The enemy wants to take our ability to stay grounded in prayer. Keeping Jesus in the forefront of our minds during prayer time is a must, so plead the blood of Jesus over everything that is coming into our minds. Spiritual intrusion into our prayer life is a lifelong battle, and some of us don't realize it. Everyone needs to have their prayer time without interruptions. The desire of our hearts is to focus on the Lord Jesus when communicating with him.

Jesus said, "My peace I give unto you." During silent meditation, the enemy will rear its ugly head. The battle of concentrating begins. Even the grocery list invasion, memories reruns vividly trying to take charge of the mind. The enemy wants us to run out of patience and quit praying. Don't stop the fight for a free mind. The feeling we can't control our minds is unacceptable. The feeling to stop praying—this thought is not from God. The enemy would like to see his intrusions cause us to desert our prayer life and just give up. He wants to destroy our sacred time by possessing our concentration, keeping our minds busy with every thought he can throw at us. We fight back by listening intently for the voice of God. Ask God to keep our minds concentrated on him. We need a one-track mind that is stayed on Jesus.

During this life span, we find we need protection not only from our physical enemies, but also from the unseen spiritual entities that want to devour our souls. They are sneaky because they are unseen and know we can't see them. The unseen world is very much alive, greedily working in the earth, seeing how many souls they can savagely devour. The mind controls the person's behavior. Take away man's mind—you have a body without light. The darkness of the enemy is eating us alive when he is allowed to control our minds, making us one of the walking dead. There are many dead souls walking on this earth. The enemy is in pursuit of souls; God is still in the soul-saving business, so stay in tune with Jesus. God's breath maintains life. Satan's breath inflicts agony and death. The evil one is always lying in wait for our souls.

The soul is a life-giving source, the energy causing life to continue. Our enemy is a distorted spirit being that wants to twist the human mind until it becomes distorted like his. He has a real zeal for the souls of God's children because he hates we are made out of God's love and in his image and in his likeness. Satan is waiting eagerly for our arrival to his chambers of regret, where we will mourn the loss of heaven forever. If we want a fertile, resourceful mind, keep it on Jesus so Satan cannot regard our souls as one of his favorite treats. The evil one's business is capturing God's beloved children, keeping them off guard, wondering and thinking about what if all I heard about God is untrue.

Satan has intense hatred for those bound for God's kingdom. Don't become one of the devil's possessions; he too would like us to be one of his family members. When we are unhappy, severely impaired spirits will approach, trying to enter. They cause spiritual, mental, and physical fatigue to come upon us. When our lives are functioning at their lowest point, just ebbing along, we have allowed the wrong spirit guide to guide us. The wrong spiritual guide has made our lives a very unhappy place to inhabit. The enemy's job is to attack mankind at every point of opportunity. No part of our spiritual, mental, and physical being is off limits. This evil buzzard comes in like a flood, destroying if he can our loved ones—from the cradle to the grave—everything in his sight is fair game and must be destroyed. He will go after our finances to the very last penny. He will strip us to the bone. To whom are we listening? There is death beyond the grave. Be careful to whose voice we are allowing to guide us through this life.

Rather, we see a figure, a shadow or not. If we are feeling something in our presence that makes our skin crawl, plead the blood of Jesus. Say, "The blood of Jesus covers me." We are to ask the Lord to keep us covered in the blood. Rely on God's faithfulness. Know that God lives within the human body; he is the soul of man. Walk with Jesus, praising him every step of the way. Praise draws God's ministering spirits to us.

God did not create hell for man. God created hell for Satan and all his demons. If an individual prefers to live in the elements of sin, making wrongdoing their alternative lifestyle, not regarding the will of God but expressing, I just want to do what comes natural to me. The consequences for living the sinful life could ruin our chances of a fruitful God-fearing life while on earth. Choose this day which master we will serve; do we just want to have the pleasures of sin for the moment, or would we like to have God's holy peace throughout eternity? God sees the future and wants nothing but the best to come into our lives. Let him be our guide, guiding us in every decision. Life is a gift and a privilege. Live life according to God's plan of salvation, respect God's will, and live forever in his kingdom. God gave us the gift of eternal life. When someone gives us a gift, we thank them and keep the gift in a place of safety. Show we appreciate the thought, and let the giver know we are grateful for their kindness.

While we were still in eternity, Jesus was thinking about the plan he had purposed for us. Before we showed up on planet Earth, we were in his mind. He selected the day he would send us into this world with purpose. Lift him up. Let the world see the personality of Jesus through us.

The Lord Jesus, on the cross, has defeated the last enemy, death. He has smitten death upon the cheekbone and has broken the teeth of the ungodly deceiver. Our enemy's appearance may look aggressive, brutal, rude, and loud; pay no attention to his noise. This ungodly, corrupt spirit is rotten to the core and can never be cured of his decaying state of being. Satan, the man of death, has been defeated, a toothless roaring foe of man, is a mere figure of strength. He knows he's on a clock that cannot be rewound or stopped. Satan is a fugitive running from God, but he will find no hiding place. He wants to escape the wrath of Almighty God's judgment, but that is not in God's plan; it is written judgment has been pronounced upon him. He can be intensely loud, rude, showing fury, but look closely—this dark monster is toothless; he has no bite. God gave Satan a blow to the jaw, broke his face, and knocked all his teeth out. He can't rip you to death—not anymore—the best he can do is to bluff and try and gum us to death. He may look like a lion, roar like a lion, strut like a lion, but he has no teeth, no power to back up all his roaring. He is putting on a show, trying to frighten, scare us to death.

> Submit yourself, therefore, unto God. Resist
> the devil, and he will flee from you. (James 4:7)

Satan cannot lead us into sin if we are not willing. He will pressure us with everything under his power, trying to break our will. Prayerfully stand, expecting from God. Satan is doing his job, offering tempting enticements. If that doesn't work, he will try his fear tactics to persuade us. Yield not to temptation. Ask the Lord for deliverance from evil deceitfulness and the mischievous master of lies, the great pretender will flee from you for a season. When we are trusting in God, the ministering angels of the Lord has us hedged in. Satan has limited access to God's children. When he wants to use his powers to test us through temptations, he has to get permission to go beyond his boundaries. Where God's children are concerned, we are beyond his boundaries; we are sealed in Christ Jesus. There are spiritual laws governing the spirit world; they take their laws seriously, not wanting to pay the price for spiritual disobedience, for the retaliation is punishment with laser energy.

Once I saw this warfare being fought out in a dream. God has watchmen hedging in his faithful. Satan is skilled in using vengeance when going after human resistance. God knows Satan's desires. God knows Satan will never give up, trying to deceive the world's inhabitants. He plays unfairly. He is the inventor of trickery, playing crafty games with the lives of men. He is the master of deceit; his greatest game is entrapping the souls of men. He is the Grinch sending messages of fear, giving gifts of deceit tied nicely wrapped with big bright bows that reflect lights of beauty. He will offer us these gifts until his lies are believed and we accept them. His weapon is his endless perseverance, trying to wear us out. He will never give up, trying to outwit those in resistance to his deception. He is a troublemaker, offering disgusting immoral habits that will change the lives of mankind. He has the tendency to turn those close to us against us. The spiritually blind can be turned against those they love. Satan is a master at representing evil as good. The great pretender can disguise himself as an angel of light, so beware—all that glitters is not gold. His strategy is to keep us in spiritual bondage. He is always looking for our weak spot. If we deal with the man of darkness, he will lead us deeper and further under his control until he claims us as his own. He aims to win by weakening our faith; stopping us from praying is his strategy. Unbelief is a dangerous masquerade, a spiritual tranquilizer being fed to us by Satan. Unbelief is a drug of precipitation, leaking false persuasion with hypocritical promises that seduce and diminish our ability to resist Satan's intoxicating trickery of unbelief. Stay away from that guy; he is a dangerous killer. He is death dressed in evening tails with a tall top hat to boot. Look closely—his tuxedo is full of tiny moth holds. The guy is bankrupt. He is a debtor with nothing to offer but hell.

 Here are a couple of Satan's mind games: he likes playing the game of hatred and the game of unforgiveness. They are his signature games because unforgiveness blocks our way into heaven. Satan's deceit lures us to sleep, giving a false sense of security, and we find ourselves resting in his soothing voice when he is encouraging us to feed our flesh. His obscene ambition is to occupy us by renting a little space in our hearts. When we allow the enemy to occupy space in our minds, know that he will be busy engaging, intrusively intruding, digging into the psyche, stealing our mental health and our willpower to the point he thinks we have lost our way to reality. We may come to a point we will not be able to recognize our thoughts from his. He is convincing and will practice his indecent filthy logic through us for his kingdom.

The children of the living God have in their arsenal the equipment to love and restored peace of mind. In our arsenal, praise is found, and worship is always on the menu; triumphantly we range over the deceiver's efforts to stifle us. He will use crafty trickery to keep us from loving our God. Fellowshipping in song and in praise, telling Emmanuel how much we love him is our real joy. Faith and praise will knock out the enemy for a season, but like stormy weather, he keeps returning. We are to give God praise in every season; never stop worshipping. The presence of God is always with us. God is always in season; never is he out of season. It's always a good time to worship God.

There is a heaven to gain, a hell to shun. Escape hell's fire by accepting the Word of God; it is our road map to eternal life. We are to immerse ourselves in his presence. Can we see ourselves seated at Jesus's knee, listening, communicating, being transmitted in his presence? Exchanging thoughts with Jesus while there in his presence, we receive from him the awesomeness of oneness which cannot be explained. When our love for him has become enthroned in his love, our holiness transcends, rising above human limitations through powers of divine love. We receive joy unspeakable.

We are never alone; God's spiritual guidance lives in us. We are to build a relationship with our spiritual guide; he resides within. The Holy Spirit is the core of our totality. The Holy Spirit baptizes in the Word of God; it is an immersion in the water of the Word. Water baptism is the outward symbol of an inward change. The Holy Spirit speaks to us only what he receives from Jesus; never does he speak of himself. The Holy Spirit is a gift of impartation from God through the essence of Jesus. Jesus is the one who imparts the Holy Spirit into our inner man—referring to our souls, our real selves.

Jesus told his twelve disciples, the inner circle, and his followers,

> I will not always walk with you. I will pray
> the Father, he shall send you another comforter,
> that he may abide with you forever, even the

> Spirit of truth; whom the world cannot receive, because it seeth him not, neither knoweth him: but ye known him; for he dwelleth with you, and shall be in you. I will not leave you comfortless: I will come to you. (John 14:16, 17, 18)

The Holy Spirit is a person; he is one with the Father and with the Son. The ministry of the Holy Spirit is to guide us. He is promised to all believers. He takes permanent residence within the saved child of God. "If a man loves me," Jesus said. "He will obey me and come and make his abode with me."

Our eternal spiritual existence is above human understanding. Our earthly goal is to obtain heaven through Christ's finished work. Awake, O my soul. Where will you spend eternity? Feed the spirit man with the Word of God. Be God conscious at all times, recognizing his presents.

We live in a war zone of global extremism, turmoil, and bigotry. Constant confusion and insensitivity is on the electronic runway. Intolerance, untrue accusations are growing larger every day, spreading their judgments like a wildfire raging through the earth. Many believe the Internet lies until we have become the object of their lies. We have come to rely, depending, respecting the Internet as a source for knowledge. The network connects us to one another, supplies information that is not always truth, yet some of us will take what we read and run with it as the naked truth. Many capitalized on the ignorance of others, having a tendency to force-feed our bias to the general public and watch them trying to digest the lies.

To what voices do we listen—the voices of the Internet or the voice coming from within? Can we tell the difference? Our big concern should be "Is the word forgiveness layered on the fibers of our heart?" Forgiving is a must to gain entrance into heaven. Humbling oneself before the face of God is a privilege and is necessary, a requirement to all whom shall enter heaven's gate. Every knee shall bow; every tongue shall confess Jesus Christ is Lord. We must come to God humble; it is a requirement for entry into God's kingdom. Jesus was humble. Are we greater than him? Be humble and filled with love, forgiving one another as God has forgiven us. We deprive ourselves of productivity and happiness in this life when we are unable or unwilling to forgive. We are being held prisoner in Satan's custody when we say, "I can't forgive." There is no room for forgiveness in Satan. He can't forgive. Do we want to be like him? Forgiveness is of God. Obedience, obeying the voice of God, is possible. We who have the advantage of having the indwelling Holy Spirit have an inward guide. Learn to listen to him. The Bible tells us, "Do not grieve the Holy Spirit." Making decisions that put us in a struggle against the guidance of the Holy Spirit is not a healthy thing. The Holy Spirit and God are one. The Holy Spirit is one with God, and God is one with the Holy Spirit. They are the same spirit, having different assignments—they are functioning, working together for the kingdom of God.

God is awesome; his wonders to be performed, his power throughout the universe is on display. Appreciate the wondrous works of his divinity that are beaming throughout the earth. God's wonder-working power of love will never cease.

God has defined the meaning of his transitive powers. His direct will is open to all who has a spiritual eye. Let them see the wonders of his work. Lord, you have hidden the mysteries involving your performing fulfillments from the knowledge of man. Open the eyes of those who are searching your Word to learn from you. Bring us into a knowledge of *agape love*—the deep calling the deep, searching, looking into divine creation. I am seeking your response in the spiritual awakening of my soul. As your Word grows within my heart, my mouth will speak of your glory.

When our earth life expires, we immediately come into new life; your presence will overshadow our souls as we travel faster than the speed of light to our destination. When we arrive, we will see you as you are, for we shall be like you.

I will not even try to describe the loving experience awaiting our arrival in heaven. Certainly it is an amazing fact to realize earth was not really our home. We were strangers in the earth, foreigners journeying through a human life with a divine appointment on earth for a divine purpose. We are not to be distracted by the vicious storms that must come to bring our lives into purpose. Tribulations will come to make us stronger in faith. We are on a work assignment; God is with us as we work out our earthly purpose. We are to examine what comes into our lives then take our complexity before God and reason with him when we are confused. He loves reasoning with his children and wants to leave his peace in our hearts. When we talk with God, he gives us the insight we need to carry on.

Sometimes blessings are concealed in the struggles that invade our lives. Who has lived their lives on a flowery bed of ease, all scented down with sweetness, on a cushion in a palace built high upon a hill, feeling like they haven't a care in the world? Whom do we know is living that sort of life? Trouble will come no matter how high we live. Understand there is a price to pay for coming to planet Earth. We can buy into spiritual blindness by listening to the wrong voices. Life on this earth is no picnic, nor was it meant to be. God didn't cover the earth with only the beautiful green grass and the little white flowers with little yellow faces—there is more to life than the fineries of nature. There is a price to pay for living in this world. Jesus's visit to earth cost him his physical life. There are two kingdoms vying to rule; they are contending for man's innermost being—his soul. Be not confused about which kingdom you are serving. Both kingdoms are fighting to possess and hold as property the human soul. Pray to God; his way is the only way leading to eternal rest. By far, life is no dream. We live in a world of sin. We are to examine, inspect our motives—are they concealing who we really are? Are we actors and don't know it, just acting out life? Do we know who we really are? What spirit is leading, guiding us? Do we say one thing and find we are doing another? Do we want to do good but finding there is something keeping us from doing what we know we ought to be doing?

We are to critique our motives. What is causing our decisions, our source of action, our behavior? Did it arise from a derivative that is from heaven above, or was it from hell below? Who are we? Do we really know who we are and to whom we belong? Whose voice are we obeying? We must know the answers to these questions before the Lord calls us into accountability when we are called to appear before him.

11

Spiritual Jealousy

Before the downing of time, there was spiritual jealousy in heaven. Satan was zealous to take over heaven; he cherished the reign of God. God's authority appealed to Lucifer (Satan). He wanted to sit in the seat of the Almighty. The compelling truth—Satan wanted not only God's throne; he wanted to be God.

Marvelously, Isaiah describes the fall of Lucifer (Isaiah 14:12–17)

> How art thou fallen from heaven, O lucifer, son of the morning! How art thou cut down to the ground, which didst weaken the nations! (v. 12)

> For thou hast said in thine heart, I will ascend into heaven, I will exalt my throne above the stars of God: I will sit also upon the mount of the congregation, in the sides of the north. (v. 13)

> I will ascend above the heights of the clouds; I will be like the most high. (v. 14)

> Yet thou shalt be brought down to hell, to the sides of the pit. (v. 15)

> They that see thee shall narrowly look upon thee, and consider thee, saying, is this the man that made the earth to tremble, that shake the kingdoms. (v. 16)
>
> That made the world as a wilderness, and destroyed the cities thereof; that opened not the house of his prisoners? (v. 17)

Before Satan's fall, he served as an angel of high ranking before the throne of God. He was adorned with every precious jewel imaginable. He was the model of perfection, full of wisdom and perfect in beauty. He was called the "anointed guardian cherub." Despite Satan's high rank in God's presence, his pride turned him against the Lord God. He said in his heart, "I will ascend to heaven, above the stars of God. I will set my throne on high. I will sit on the mount of assembly in the far reaches of the north. I will sit above the heights of the clouds."

He was persuasive enough to convince one-third of God's angels to join him in his rebellion to take over heaven and dethrone God. His jealousy, his rejection of God's government, and his pride led to his fall from heaven. The eternal fallen tormentor is the ruler of hell (Revelation 20:10).

Satan originally was created as one of God's highest angels, possessing all angelic attributes. Satan ("Adversary") led angels in a rebellion against God. He is described as the originator and chief practitioner of sin (1 John 3:8), "that wicked one" (1 John 5:18), a thief and destroyer (John 10:10), a deceiver (Revelation 12:9), murderer and liar (John 8:44), and the accuser of the brethren and his titles "angel of light" (2 Corinthians 11:14) and him that "deceiveth the whole world" (Revelation 12:9). His present-day activities include opposing the will and work of God. He is a counterfeiter of God's work, trying to destroy all that is good. A Christian can overcome Satan when he remembers four basic principles: *First,* though Jesus is greater than the devil (1 John 4:4), a Christian must still have a healthy respect for the enemy; even the archangel Michael did not confront Satan except in the name of the Lord (Jude 9). *Second*, a wise Christian will evaluate his life and avoid those situations where he is most likely to be tempted (1 Thessalonians 5:22). *Third*, he should resist the devil by submitting to God (James 4:7–10). *Finally*, the Christian should always be prepared, wearing the whole armor of God (Ephesians 6:17).

Satan obtains permission to tempt Job (Job 1:6–12)

Now there was a day when the sons of God came to present themselves before the Lord, and Satan came also among them, and the Lord said unto Satan, "Whence comest thou?" Then Satan answered the Lord and said, "From going to and fro in the earth and from walking up and down in it." And the Lord said unto Satan, "Hast thou considered my servant Job, that there is none like him in the earth, a perfect and an upright man, one that feareth God and escheweth evil?" Satan answered the Lord, and said, "Doth Job *fear* God for naught? Hasth not thou made a hedge about him and about his house and about all he hast on every side? Thou hast blessed the work of his hands, and his substance is increased in the land. But put forth thine hand now and touch all that he hath, and he will curse thee to thy face." And the Lord said unto Satan, "Behold, all that he hath is in thy power; only upon himself put not forth thine hand." So Satan went forth from the presence of the Lord (*to afflict Job*). Job emerged from the severe testing with a fresh appreciation of God's sovereignty and sufficiency for the believer's life.

"Sons of God" refers to angelic beings. Satan is considered one of them though fallen from his original sinless state. His name means "Adversary," and he lives up to the meaning of his name. This passage showed that Satan has access to God's presence. His final casting out from heaven is described in Revelation 12:10, where Satan is described "the accuser of our brethren."

12

Intimacy with God

Where is this influence coming from—man's refusing to obey God? Is it coming from the spiritual underworld? Subtle animating disembodied evil spirits have the ability to invade, penetrate man's thoughts. They can infuse man's mental power of obedience, telling us sin is a matter of one's opinion. When we are contending with sinful temptations, our behavior can become a product of our thinking; wrong thoughts may affect our psyche concerning God's will.

It is evident we were born with a sixth sense, giving us higher intelligence than we display. Man does not use his mental capacity to its fullness. The sixth sense—it seems many seldom try to use or even bring into discussion. ESP (extrasensory perception)—having nonphysical contact but having the faculty of perceiving a flash into the future. Many have never tried to cultivate using the sixth sense to make it a part of their debates in life. Sentient (sen-chi-ent) forces have an effect on human behavior more than we would like to think. Believe disembodied intelligence has an effect, an influence by making impressions on the physical embodied intelligence. This interaction happens to us more than we know.

At some time or another, we are moving under spiritual influence, wondering, *Why did I do that? Why did I say that?* At some time or other, we have realized, "I was just thinking about you, and you appeared. You came to mind, and the telephone started ringing. I answered, and it was you." We may ask ourselves, "What on earth is going on? Did our spirits connect?" At times when we are alone, we may perceive unexplained activity happens, giving us an eerie sensation, a mysterious spine-chilling moment seemingly for no reason. We wonder, *What on earth is going on?* These strange circumstances may make us nervous. *Jeepers-creepers, why are these weirdies happening?* we think.

A strange awareness may linger in our hearts while our flesh is crawling and our consciousness frozen; are we expecting something frightening to happen? We stand, listening to the rhythm of our heart beat. In silence we wait, wondering what spooky thing is going to happen next. The ability to perceive spiritual activity is common for some. Many can see future events. When the unexplainable is occurring, we hear ourselves saying, "What is that? Did you hear that? Did you see that. It's weird, the strangest sound." We transmit to the spirit world through thought. Other times we may have visions. Even verbal communication could come into play. We might hear someone calling our name—"Did someone call me?" When we answer, we are interacting with something we cannot see; "I thought I heard someone calling my name." The ability to see and hear the disembodied transcends our five senses, and the unexplainable can be frightening if we dwell on it.

We are not accustomed to using our sixth sense, and when something out of the ordinary happens, we find it concerning. Spiritual energy is a force we live with daily. It's a higher intelligence, transmitting its activities through living source. For various reasons above our comprehension, it can work through us. For good or for bad, all throughout the earth, this energy is working. It could be a guardian angel from heaven above or from hell below. Spiritual influence is undetectable especially when we do not have intimacy with God. The Holy Spirit will let you know when you are under attack by the enemy. We are to fight the spirit with the spirit. We think all the moments we spend making decisions are under our control—that's not necessarily so. Human logic is often spiritually influenced. Sometimes we wonder, "Why did I do that? Why did I say that? I didn't mean to say that to you—it just came out of my mouth—I am so sorry."

You say, "For some reason, I feel so confused. What's the matter with me?"

God is a spirit. We are to call on him when the mind is embattled, engaged in messy disarray, and we can't think straight. The devil is a vicious aggressive spirit being, bringing intense pain and regret into our life. The devil tries to hide from the face of God. He runs but finds no hiding place. When we have just come from the presence of God and his impeccable light is still engulfing our being, the enemy must flee from this glorious light glowing on our being. The spirit that comes out of the eyes of God can burn the evil spirits until they scurry from your presence. Whose guidance are we living under? Which spirit has their hook in our flesh? What spirits are we allowing to animate through our lives?

We think because we are embracing the golden rule, salvation is automatic—think again. Treating others like we want to be treated is very good practice. The world has always been in need of people with the consciousness of kindness, showing consideration and respect for others. What does the world need? Is it love? Never let go of love; it is a healing ointment. The mystery of love—where is it coming from? Showing generosity to others, letting no vile thing come out of your mouth—these humanities do not give us carte blanche to enter heaven. God wants us to be neighborly; good deeds are blessed and added to our heavenly account. The Good Samaritan loved God. God blessed the Good Samaritan with the spirit of meekness. Humbleness was carved in his soul. It was his nature to show kindness to the suffering. The Good Samaritan's deeds were recorded in the Bible to be studied by generations, showing true motivation and kindness by helping the helpless in a time of need, when no one was watching. Our good deeds are our treasurer. They are being laid up in heaven. The Good Samaritan pleased God, his unconditional love, his concern for an abused stranger who had been a victim, afflicted, and lay helpless on the ground. The Good Samaritan was not concerned that the man had no means of repaying his kindness.

Having a personal relationship with God through the shed blood of Jesus Christ is our open doorway to God's heart and favor. Salvation through the blood of his Son Jesus is the only way, the only passage of entry into eternal rest in God's kingdom. The spirit of obedience is a God given privilege that is given to few. The highway to hell is wide and broad, and many find the way to it. The gate to heaven is narrow, and few can find the way through it. Come to God through obedience; obedience is the narrow gate that leads to heaven.

When God tells us to do something, do it right then. Don't wait to see what others may think. Don't give fear time to creep in and overrule the divine request. Don't wait for human approval. Obedience is the key to God's heart. He said, "If you love me, you will obey me." It matters not what man thinks about what God tells us to do. We are spot-on when our character is sharpened by obedience to God's will. We are tested daily. Choose to pass the daily test, and obey the voice of God. Many times God is whispering to our hearts, and we think we are thinking when we are actually listening to the voice of God. We who say God is our Father are tested and tried, not the naysayers, who refuse to believe God is and with their seared conscience are still telling people there is no God. The skeptic denies the power of God. Don't suffer the consequences of disobedience because of what people may think of you.

God's ways are not the ways of the world. People finding fault with what God is telling us to do—It's okay we will be judged by our walk with God, not how others see our walk. Our faith and our prayers will combat evil until it flees. We are to tell God all about any trouble that comes into our lives, have a deep conversation with the Lord, listen to his advice, and obey. It is through God we try the spirit by the spirit to see if they are from God. Stay in tune with Jesus, know obedience, and love is dominant in heaven. Love is chief; love the Lord thy God with all thy heart; obey him with all thy mind. His ways are high above the inquisitive busybodies who envy and have resentment, giving their criticism when they see someone obeying God. The spirit of jealousy lives in many and will boldly speak out against the things of God.

When we are in obedience to our heavenly Father, some may call us Miss Goody Two Shoes, and that's all right. When God assigns us a task, men may view it unfavorably, saying, "That's silly. I don't believe God told you to do that." Remember we are dealing with

God's will, not man's will. If God said, "Do it," obey. They were critical of Jesus and jealous of the way the people loved him and followed after him—praising and obeying him. Our cooperation with God is not a private affair; it should be open for all to see. We are not to keep our relationship with God to ourselves. Put it out there. Spread the good news around. Let the world see whom it is we serve.

There are many who walk with God, straddling the fence of righteousness, hoping no one will notice his walking with God while winking at the devil—they are what we call men pleasers, having a foot in both worlds. Obedience is having a pure relationship with God. Obedience is the riches of heaven. Jesus obeyed his Father; it was his nature to live in obedience to the will of his Father. When we are doing God's will, people will evaluate, analyze, and criticize whatever God tells us to do. God is talking to you, not our criticizers. The devil will try to hinder our obedience to God by using men as road blockers making it difficult to obey God. The enemy will come against the spirit of obedience. He does not want us honoring God through obedience. Know from whence our troubles come. They come from the pits of hell, trying to deprive heaven of souls.

There are those who are duped by the devil, giving judgments in ignorance against many people, whom God has called to preside over certain ministries. God-given understanding is a precious jewel, and everyone will not understand what God is asking them to do. The Bible tells us to get wisdom, but above all things, get understanding. Know what, thus says the Lord. Do we think we are the only beings leading us into action, we are making all our decisions for our lives? Think again? Receiving criticism is a part of life. Constructive critiquing—okay, we can accept that. Opinions can be given in a very ugly way, making the criticism hard to digest. Take it as a teaching in forgiveness and patience. We will learn patience in this life, or we will live in an unhappy state. God chose us to do a work. Obey. Refuse not the will of God—the sin of disobedience will be on us, not on our critics who may laugh at us for doing the will of God. The critics interfering with God's work will be judged for meddling in God's affairs. There is a consequence to be paid for every behavior. We are to do what God tells us to do regardless of others' disrespect and scorn for doing the will of God. Above all, remember God's ways are not our ways; his ways are high above our ways.

"Do you love me more than self?" Jesus asked Peter. That question is still relevant today. Do we love Jesus more than self? If the answer is yes, then obey him. We are to show our love for God in all our ways. Love is more than words. Love is something we do. All must bring sacrifices to the mystery table of love. Love is a mystery. God sacrificed Jesus that we might live with him forever. What a mystery. Was this act of love beyond human understanding? Which one of us would give our son that someone else could live?

Let's let our light so shine that the world may see we are the children of a living God. Don't hide the light God gave us under a bushel. We wouldn't want God to hide his light from us. Don't play the game of hide and seek with the gifts of God: I love thee, I love thee not, I obey thee, I obey thee not. Our salvation is at stake; if we want to play games, go and buy a toy. Don't play with God's gift of salvation. Are some of us ashamed or fearful, feeling threatened to show our love for God to an angry world? The world is fickle. It does not know the stability and the patience love brings. The world is erratic and changeable. God never changes. He is the same God today as he was yesterday. His love and faithfulness never will lose its power.

The Holy Spirit has infused—permeated—our souls into his presence. Praise Almighty God for eternal life in his endless, ageless kingdom of love.

Recognizing God's presence is key. Jesus draws near to us when we give an ear to hear his calling. He knows the purpose of our lives. There may come a time when Jesus allows us to see him in the spirit. Think that is impossible? Jesus appeared five times to me. He has allowed many to see him. Remember the upper room when doubting Thomas questioned Jesus's appearance in the upper room. After the resurrection, in John 20:17, Jesus said unto Mary Magdalene, "Touch me not. I have not yet ascended unto the Father."

On the road to Emmaus and the ascension into heaven, Jesus showed himself at will; remember the spiritual transformation on Mount Hermon in Matthew 17:2; Jesus shows himself when he so wills. Obedience is what Jesus wants from us. He is obedient to his Father, and we are to follow his example and be obedient to God our Father as was the Son. When God opens our eyes of wisdom to absorb his will, divine understanding has come. Listen intensely. Discernment is one of the manifestations of the fruits of the Spirit. Determination to be obedient is what God wants us to practice. He will show us the way to obedience and how we are to do his bidding. When we accept Jesus into our lives, it is not about us anymore. We are now representing Jesus. Our lives are to reflect the teachings of Jesus. Mirroring Jesus, no more do we image the world. We are in the world but not of it.

The moment I received the impartation of the Holy Spirit, I remember it was electrifying; and incapable of being explained, it was an unforgettable experience.

The Holy Spirit is the expert in our lives; God sent him to us. He has an ongoing effect on our lives as he leads us into life that is to come. He influences our inner man, guiding him to obey God's will. The Bible said, "Stir up the inner man by the way of remembrance for all the good God has done in our lives. In all we do, do it unto God, remembering God's faithfulness. Glorify the master with praises, asking him to let the mind that was in Christ Jesus rule over you." The Bible said, "Let this mind of *obedience* be in you that was in Christ Jesus." We need a Christlike faith so we can walk on top of troubled water. By faith, Jesus walked on the troubled sea. His faith kept him walking on top of the water, for there was no doubt in him.

Do we visit healing services, hoping, looking for a miracle to happen? There are intercessors who petition Almighty God's favor on our behalf. The intercessor cannot heal us. The Holy Spirit is working through the intercessor for God's glory.

In God, there are three divine persons, equal peers; they are one unit: God the Father, God the Son, and God the Holy Spirit are one. They are coequal, having equal standing with one another, belonging to the same Godhead. The Trinity functions in different positions that contributes one another for the glory of their divine nature—God the Creator, Jesus the Savior, and from the intimacy of God's bosom came the breath of God the Holy Spirit. The Holy Spirit is a gift from God, of God—the third person of God. The blessed Trinity is the unity of God, Jesus his Son, and the Holy Spirit, his breath. These three Spirit Persons—they are one. They are the united Godhead. (God is a threefold being.) God the Father, God the Son, and God the Holy Spirit are one and the same person.

> And I saw a new heaven and a new earth; for the first heaven and the first earth were passed away; and there was no more sea. And I John saw the holy city, new Jerusalem, coming down from God prepared as a bride adorned for her husband. And I heard a great voice out of heaven saying, "Behold, the tabernacle of God is with men, and he will dwell with them, and they shall be his people, and God himself shall be their God. And God shall wipe away all tears from their eyes; and there shall be no more death, neither sorrow, nor crying, neither pain: for the former things are passed away." And he that sat upon the throne said, "Behold, I make all things new." And he said unto me, "Write: for these words are true and faithful." And he said unto me, "It is done. I am Alpha and Omega, the beginning and the end. I will give unto him that is athirst of the fountain of the water of life freely. He that overcometh shall inherit all things; and I will be his God, and he shall be my son." (Revelation 21:1–7)[4]

God will tabernacle with us. The presence of God will be with his people, and he will forever dwell with them. *It is done the eternal*

---

[4] A description of the eternal state (following the Millennium and the final judgment), centering in the new Jerusalem as the eternal habitation of the saved. The first heaven and the first earth are replaced by a new heaven and a new earth.

purpose of God to gather a holy, devoted people for Himself, has now been accomplished.

> And I saw no temple therein: for the Lord God Almighty and Lamb are the temple of it. And the city had no need of the sun, neither of the moon, to shine in it: for the glory of God did lighten it, and the Lamb is the light thereof.[5]

---

[5] There is no temple in the city since both the Father and the Son will be present in their fullest manifestations. Its light will be provided by the Shekinah glory of God and of Christ. God's saints will serve him forever. The greatest blessing of eternity is that we shall see his face. Amen means "truly" or "so be it." The believers' simple response is "Come, Lord Jesus."

13

You Are Infused in My Being

My child, you are infused in my being. My accessibility to others is working through you as you allow me to work through you for my glory. The Holy Spirit knows my mind and my timing—for we are one and the same spirit.

Go often into the inner sanctuary of your soul—where peace awaits.

Enter the indwelling. Absorb the goodness of God's presence that is always there, waiting to be tapped into. Ask God to humble you to the very core of your being "that you may get an understanding of my will. Learn how it is to be eternally grateful for my everlasting faithfulness."

God's presence is divine essence, a detectable spirit being—no other joy and peace can be experienced like having an infusion from the Lord. Let your soul cry out to the heavenly Father to assist you in your determination to please him. You need to know how to make the separation between a good performance and a bad performance before deciding to act on what is coming into your mind; give the message forethought before acting. Know when God's spirit is working through you and when a demonic spirit is trying to get you to work for him. Learn to discern the spirits by the spirit, detecting, sensing the difference between the actions taken in love or taken in selfishness. Give deep consideration to what you are about to say or do. Someone's peace of mind may be determined by your words and your actions. Before arriving at and executing a decision to speak, try to distinguish by separating the voices that are urging you to put your thoughts on display. Be still; wait on God's presence. Give God time to speak to your heart then, and only then let your conscience be your guide before you make the decision to give someone a piece of your mind.

You have God-given powers to rightly process your free will, rightly divide whatever comes to mind—question the proceeds that are blooming and unfolding in your mind. Satan may be trying to make you show a side of yourself you would not want anyone else to see. Through a sense of love, use your mechanism (machinery) of peace given to you and working through you because of your association with the divine nature that lives within your being. You have become an overcomer for the kingdom of God through obedience to his will. Depending on years of acquired learning, prayerfully studying the Bible, going to Bible studies, learning and listening to the voice of God, you have become an enlightened child of the living God. The quiet tranquility through this oneness with the Creator, being at peace with yourself in God, you have a growing reservoir of godly built-in behavioral patterns. You will act on them because it pleases God to see you on the job, working for his glory. You are able to sense right and wrong through your godly association of the Holy Spirit. The unfolding joy, the love you are experiencing—share it with others. Combining the elements of biblical teachings and lifelong learning, these ought to be deep-seated; look inward, search within, explore self—your inner sanctuary—a place where God is always available.

Truth is provided and is obtainable at the altar of your God-given soul; visit there often. Recognize the voice of God. His presence is beckoning to you to come unto him. God has long patience, awaiting the precious fruit of the earth. You are the one he has been waiting for. You are a precious jewel in God's sight. Blessed is the man that endures temptation, for when he is being tried and when he is an overcomer, he shall receive the crown of life, which the Lord has promised to them which love him. Tragedy is not always a curse. Victory over trials bring God's blessings into view. The guidance of the Holy Spirit is a gift to God's children that love him. Do you know who you are? You are one of God's chosen. You are standing in divine favor. Seek the desires of God's heart. God is patiently waiting for his chosen to realize they are a chosen generation, a royal priesthood, a holy nation, a peculiar people, that ye should show forth praises to him, who hath called you out of darkness into his marvelous light (1 Peter 2:9). Speak to God in songs, listening for his voice as you sing. Be an overcomer. The Father is anxiously awaiting your arrival at the end of your earthly journey.

The antagonistic enemy of your soul goes around, seeking whom he may devour. There is a hostile force invading the atmosphere, living in the midst of man, invading and influencing every mind with his thoughts.

The enemy is out to genocide God's chosen—deliberately trying to destroy souls by turning them away from worshipping God. Spiritual warfare is being fought on this earth ever since God had him overthrown, driven out of his kingdom, and banished from all his heavenly duties. Satan's forces are combating the forces of God. They would like to wipe out our names from the book of life. The enemy of man's soul would like to infringe, encroach upon our heavenly benefits. This being can't ever again obtain any heavenly benefits; neither does he want you to receive what God has for you. You can experience all the blessings God has your name on—just keep trusting. You can be successful, thriving. Keep praising him in every situation and see prosperity grow through faith in Christ Jesus. Praising God should be our signature movement for life more abundant. The enemy wants to keep you from eternal rest, disputing with your mind, enticing you to abandon your faith. This is his way of stopping you from eternal peace. When life brings you a challenge larger than life, don't feel defeated. The challenge came to make you stronger and wiser. God has the last word on what happens in our lives. Trust him, and see the outcome. God is multidimensional; it's impossible for us to fathom in our mental perception of human comprehension. You cannot grasp nor do you have the language, the intellect to give a definition of divine life, so please keep the faith. Things of God are far beyond the understanding of man.

We are living in a world within a world. Our two worlds are thriving together. The seen and the unseen worlds are very much alive; they are active, vying for the soul of man. These worlds are evolving together, working against each other, and it will be that way until the thousand-year millennium begins and the worldwide peace agreement comes into effect.

We are living in the greatest grandeur imagined—God's symphony of life is thriving. Every living thing should be engaging in its purpose, giving glory to God. God's will shall be done on earth as it is in heaven. Even the scented flower gardens are doing their job, sending out their scented perfume for the world to enjoy. The bumblebees are making sweet honey, gathering nectar from the flowers that are growing across the meadows and fields, showing the wonders of nature working together in harmony, doing what God purposed them to do. When all creation is doing what they were created to do, what a symphony it creates. Obedience to God's laws brings glory to the magnificence of the Creator.

Never will we be able to fix God into our little boxes though we try to put all his grandeur into our finite limitations. God is bigger than our greatest imagination. God knows our thoughts before we even receive them from spiritual input.

In the aspect of supposing, suppose there was no time zone on earth. Suppose there had been no plan of creation, no scheme of purpose. Suppose there was no sun to shine and there would be no daylight, the absence of the moonlight that lights the night. Suppose there was no earth to light and what we call earth had to continue in endless blackness. Suppose God had not said, "Let there be light," and had left the unknown in utter blackness. Suppose the thick darkness was a moment in infinite extending indefinitely. Suppose mercilessly the deep hue of night was the plight of eternity, no light ever at all—could there be any life? Suppose men were created without purpose. Suppose nothingness was all man could ever expect out of his eternal existence. Yet our souls would exist obliviously in the voidness, of nothingness, and there would be no death, the sounds of crying souls that fades not away in the darkness of an unending night. The thought of supposing brings tears to my eyes. The moon that could not shine light on the endless night brought tears to the eyes of the man in the moon as he looked down on the blackness engulfing all that was not. The unformed voidness could not do anything to bring light because there was no light to bring. Just supposing—what if God had not created light?

> In the beginning God created the heaven and the earth. Verse-2, And the earth was without form, and void; and darkness was upon the face of the deep. And the Spirit of God moved upon the face of the water. (Genesis 1:1, 2)

> And I saw a new heaven and a new earth: for the first heaven and the first earth were passed away; and there was no more sea. And I John saw the holy city, new Jerusalem, coming down from God out of heaven, prepared as a bride adorned for her husband. And I saw no temple therein: for the Lord God Almighty and the Lamb are the temple of it. And the city had no need of the sun, neither of the moon, to shine in it: for the glory of God did light it, and the lamb is the light thereof. (Revelation 21:1, 2, 22, 23)

There is no temple in the city since the Father and the Son will be presented in their fullest manifestations. Its light will be provided by the Shekinah glory of God and of Christ.

In the new creation, there will be no need for a sun or moon to shine in it. God the Father and Jesus Christ will be in full Shekinah glory. They will light the Jerusalem. Their light is the most beautiful radiant light that can be.

14

Fan the Flames of Love

Experience the sense of unspeakable joy—by fanning the flames of love, our good behavior outweighing our wrong behavior. Look to love; love can outshine the darkness of all our yesterdays. God's pleasure is to create. His creations bring him pleasure. For his pleasure does he create. God's creation has a built-in purpose. Some species are defined and will thrive through their existence without having a choice to be anything else. They cannot make themselves different than what they were created to be. A daisy is a daisy and cannot become a tulip. It must live out its divine purpose as a daisy. A daisy cannot say, "I am trapped in the body of a daisy, and I am going to change my situation. I will find more happiness as a tulip." The daisy was not given free will. The purpose of the daisy was to shine as a daisy all the days of its life. God wants us to love ourselves as he fashioned us. God gave man both purpose and free will to choose whether or not he wants to obey what God has purposed for him in this life. A man may think at birth my gender was unjustly identified as male because the outside of my body are genitals that had nothing to do with my inner self. I've never felt like a man. I feel like a woman trapped in a man's body. I have to do something about my outward appearance; it's an invasion of who I really am. I have a legal right to live my life as a woman, and I am going to take care of my situation in court. Transgender may be an option for many. Be confident. God is the answer to our fulfillment. God loves us just the way he created us. God loves us with all our disenchantment. He loves us with all our feelings of imperfections. The perfection of the soul is what's important.

As yet, Satan has not been imprisoned, but he is on his way; he will be held prisoner in a prison God has created for him and those who obey him. In God's appointed time, Satan, the god of the underworld, will be imprisoned.

When the Antichrist is sent by Satan to fool the people, some will believe he is the Messiah. He will be sent to declare war on believers and to persecute the Jewish people. He will rule for three and a half years, and then he will be revealed to the world; Jesus will return with an army of angels. Satan will be bound for a time. The earth will be in such terrible condition. All things will have to be made new. The millennium age will bring peace on earth for a thousand years. During this time, Satan will be imprisoned, cast into the bottomless pits of hell. He will not be permitted to use his cleverness to harass and entice mankind with his skillful temptations until after the thousand years has ended. When the millennium has ended, Satan will be loosed on earth to contend with mankind. He will inflict havoc on man with a vengeance, knowing his time to torture man is short. He knows he has a rendezvous with destiny at some precise assigned time and a place where he will meet his fixed and final fate.

When the white throne judgment takes place, Satan the fugitive will come before Almighty God to receive his final judgment. He will be judged and sentenced for trying to overthrow the sovereignty of God and for tormenting and deceiving the inhabitants of the earth. Satan will be sentenced to his kingdom of darkness. Never will he nor his angels be allowed to leave the presence of the damned, a place that had been prepared for him and his prostrate angels.

If we want a joyful life, we cannot let the enemy get comfortable, cozying up to us by letting him have residency within our minds. His job is to conquer the mind of man then mount the conquest over his fireplace as a mantle that boasts another human soul added to my accumulation of souls, an addition to my trophy collection—my, how it grows.

Fanning the flames of love is what God is all about. The divine spirit of God lives within man. God is love. We are to let love rule victoriously over our lives. May the love of God be cemented, unmovable within man's heart. Enter into a moment of quiet serenity. We will find calmness waiting there. Let's dress ourselves in the garments of tranquility and love that our souls may find peace as we go along life's way.

When we realize who we really are in Christ, our confidence will never again fail by fleeing out of sight into the endless night. When we feel life has come crashing down around us, go talk with friends and loved ones. Don't curl up alone in self-pity. A confused mind breeds a troubled life that can easily lead into deep depression. Even our strength to pray can fail. Know that God sees and feels what we are going through. Time is passing us by. We are losing hope. It is an effort trying to find peace of mind. It is of great importance not to waste time by doing nothing to strengthen our plight in faith. Cry out to God in Jesus's name; he will show the way out. He will help us to propel our faith to greater heights. Don't stop asking God for wholeness. Don't stop believing. Hold onto faith even if we don't feel any better while praying. Don't look at the circumstances. Pray until the forsaken feelings have left. Know recovery has come.

Circumstances affect the way we see life. Subtle remarks can creep ever so quietly into one's psyche. Don't let life put us down. Life is continuously changing, and that's how life will exist. Change is inevitable. Our lives are made out of many changing events. Our fate is in God's hands. Faith is a gift and is given to us by measure. Not everyone will receive the same measure of faith. We can claim abundant life when we are receiving, and when we haven't received very much, using the gift of faith, we can find happiness with what God has put in our hands. No more assumptions—don't assume the changing seasons of time that must take place in life are robbing us of happiness. When change appears to be taking us in unwanted directions, bring faith to the table. Pray. Stand in faith. Watch God work on the behalf of the believer waiting in faith.

Reflecting, meditating on God's faithfulness has powers that are hidden from the nonbeliever. Prayer will set a soul free. Kindness is something many can give. It will lift the morale of others, helping them travel through life. As we are journeying to our new home on high, may we give a helping hand to a weary traveler.

Satan is inviting the world to his underground spacious playhouse. He has enlarged his welcoming halls and rolled out the ceremonial red carpet. Each invitation bears his engraved signature requesting the presence of anyone who is willing to accept the autographed invitations to his festivity below in his flaming imposing palace of lodging. Welcome to all is the call. Sin has a wide exciting entrance, and many are attracted, enticed to go in to see the mystery of the call. Once behind the doors marked "pleasurable times awaiting," the doors are locked. There are no doors marked "exit" in hell. No escaping this hideous everlasting eternal dankness. We have chosen Satan's offensive smelling dungeon, with its odors, to be our new home; through our many years of practicing a life of sinful pleasures, we have inherited the right to this endless nightmare. When we leave our human existence without repentance, asking God in Jesus's name for forgiveness of our sins, we don't want to enter the spiritual world with unforgiven sin. Unforgiven sin will enter the doors of hell and will come before Satan for their reward. Our souls will experience life in chambers that inflicts anguish and torture. The soul lives forever with the damned. In utter darkness, the soul will never die. Death never knew God. The inhabitation of the dead will begin new life in the scent of hell burning fire and brimstone, having everlasting anguish in the pits of no escape.

15

Soul Highly Valued

Experiencing what we call death is the spiritual flight of one's true self. Our spirits have escaped this body of flesh. When the soul separates from the body, the life-giving breath breathes no more through our physical presence. When the soul leaves the body, the body has no more life in it. The soul continues to live in its spiritual habitation. The spirit embodies the soul. Both soul and spirit live together through eternity unless God chooses to separate them. When the intelligence that is animating life departs and is no longer entrapped in a body of flesh, it is freed from its confinement. The body in which the soul had dwelled, without a soul, is now pronounced dead; the body has lost its engine, its energy. There is no more life-giving power. Our existence has ended. Not our consciousness; independently the consciousness goes back to the God that placed it in the body. The spirit being embodies the soul. The soul is highly valued; it sustains life. When the body no longer has the power to breathe, it is pronounced dead. When the soul has departed from its assigned assignment and its existence is no longer required on the assignment, it goes back to its generative force. The soul is the breath of God passing from one assignment to another assignment—or should I say from life to life.

> And the Lord God formed man of the dust
> of the ground, and breathed into his nostrils the

breath of life; and man became a living soul. (Genesis 2:7)

The soul is the part of man that shows his real character. Man's true self is a reflection of his spiritual image. The soul has incorporeal existence and does not have to have a material body to exist, neither does the spiritual existence need to be embodied by human flesh. Only God can separate, disconnect the soul from the spirit; the spirit could become a wandering spirit if God so willed it to be. The soul belongs to God and will return to its source. Adam was formed from the dust of the earth and laid helpless on the surface from which it came. God breathed into the form, the impression of a human figure, received life from the breath of God, and the image of a man began to breathe. God named this breathing being Adam. God's breath is the principle that gives life. Death is described when the departing breath leaves the body, when God calls his breath back to its origin. He will send the soul on another assignment. The soul will always be at work. God will always be creating. However, this old world will not keep spinning on its axis forever. We are going to get a new earth. This old earth will pass away.

In our new lives, we will recognize those we previously knew. We will behold God's Lamb as he really is, for we will be like him.

Derived from our choices we made during our human experience, our souls will pass from life to life, carrying the human remembrance of who we were, not who we are. Thank God, Jesus set us free, our earth debt no longer in existence. We should choose prayerfully what we put on our human agenda. Our agendas speak to who we are, and who we are goes into the spirit world, for it is the real you. The essence of our being is the hidden man that lives within. Some of us will meet ourselves for the first time.

Time is flying. We are going faster than we realize to the land of the by and by; it's much later than we think. We are living in the pathway of time on our way to our eternal home. We will arrive to our new existence in a matter of time. What's in our hands is our offering; can we offer it to a loving God? Obedience is an offering of love. God said, "If you love me, you will obey me."

Life on this earth is short, but we are given a chance to find our assigned earth purpose and live it out for God's glory.

Our awaking, our awareness, realizing we are always just a breath away from eternal life is astonishing. I ask, "Can we take comfort in knowing that our new beginning, at all times, is nearer than our hands? What's in our hands? Are our lives in order? When we have passed from one life to another, will we be ready to meet our maker? Will we be excited, finding we have answered the call of Jesus?" No longer are we limited to human incapability. There are assignments awaiting our arrival to our new lives. Our souls never die; they go on at the Omnipotent's pleasure.

Many will escape hell and enter a paradise, a state of peace, souls that have been counted righteous because they have been washed in the shed blood of Jesus. Nevertheless, I believe there will be souls in heaven not permitted to clearly see God. Our works on earth will be tried by fire, and many works will be consumed. What is the consequence for those works consumed by fire? Promotions and rewards will be handed out at the ceremony of rewards. If our works are destroyed by God's holy fire, what then is our reward?

I saw in a dream or vision two women who had escaped hell but were assigned to a place hard for me to describe, but I will try. I went to a place in the spirit world. I rang the doorbell. I could see through to the other side of the door. A rotating floor moved the person to the door; the person opened the door without getting out of her seat. She was dressed in what looked like crushed red velvet and was sitting on a crushed red velvet chair with a small table covered with the same red material as her dress. The table was not attached to her, but she was a part of the upholstery. She was attached to the chair. She and the chair were one unit. They were incapable of being separated. They were joined together. She was at peace. I observed a little ways from where she was sitting. She was talking with a woman who was dressed in crushed green velvet, attached to a crushed green velvet chair. There was a small table in front of her. It too was covered with the same green material as her dress. The room they were sitting in was dimly lit. When I entered the room, they did not speak to me. They did not stop talking to each other as I entered. They seemed to be at peace.

While I was in a coma, I saw departed souls floating peacefully through the hereafter. Having escaped hell, many departed souls are assigned to different spiritual existence. My ma died; she came back to take me where she is now living. I heard a voice speaking that caused me to stop, let go of Ma's hand, and return to my body.

If we died today, are we ready for our lives to be inspected and tried by God's holy fire? The testing of our earthly works by fire will come to pass. If they are consumed, destroyed by fire, then what? Will we receive immediate judgment? Is this judgment eternal? Only God knows.

Some souls will not have the realization—the awareness—that they are not seeing the Lord as clearly as other souls are seeing him. They are happy in whatever state they are assigned, not knowing there are other spiritual-dwelling places they are not privileged to be aware of. They are happy in their present existence, not conscious that there is more to heaven than they are privileged to realize. Some souls will sleep in peaceful bliss, undisturbed in their paradise of dreamland, floating with their white gowns flowing as they travel in eternity.

God paid a great price to pave the way for returning souls to return home. He sent his only Son to earth to suffer death on the cross to redeem souls. Don't be one of those Christians still living in sin, thinking "once saved always saved." If we make mockery of so great a gift as salvation, what will our reward be? Will we be able to clearly see God when our works are consumed by his fire? What then is our reward? Yes, we have escaped the damning punishment hell but not likely to see clearly the face of God.

Let go the ego. Listen to the divine Spirit of Truth engaging us with offerings of true light. This earth is only a shadow of things to come. Our souls will experience the unknown. What is unknown today is tomorrow's spiritual experience. Our souls will live in God's eternity in the conditions our reward has inherited. What will that be like? As I aforementioned, earth life is only a shadow of things to come that are laid before our spiritual passage as we go from life to life. We are part of God's omnipresent plan in ongoing life. The saved lives are in him. Ministering spirits are here to assist God's earthly servants who are performing duties for God's glory. They speak to our minds, listen, and discern if it is an internal voice, or is the voice coming unto us?

Know that heaven and earth are working together as a team, working for the glory of God. Living in the flesh is not our souls' everlasting assignment; we are spiritual beings living a temporary human life on earth. We are being tested and tried for a grater life still to come. The battle of the mind is constantly being ruthlessly fought for and brutally challenged by Satan's ministering spirits. They are all around. They are causing a great deal of sickness and trouble in man's life. The evil one is in dispute with divine righteousness, defying man to obey God. Yes, it will cost us something to be in obedience to God's will. Are you willing to pay the price, the cost of going to God's paradise in the afterlife?

Love is supreme. We are to love our enemies and forgive them, do good to them. Be angry and sin not. We are not to let the sun go down on our anger—that's what the Bible tells us. Not keeping these divine laws destroy our peace of mind and eat at our souls until we repent of our anger. We will have to account for the way we treat others and the way we mistreat ourselves. Our life is a gift. Treat it well. You may never come this way again.

Thoughts are exceptionally powerful. Wrong thoughts can be appealing but not giving us a healthy soul. Our free will should always be alert, perceiving. Most thoughts come from the spiritual realm. There are billions of spirits moving through earth's atmosphere, influencing the mind of man. We create our spiritual surroundings by the thoughts we entertain. Our minds can be a spiritual playground. Spiritual pressure causes us to create an atmosphere through the substance of thought. We draw God's Spirit; we draw Satan's spirit through thoughts. Thoughts are powerful, causing us to act or to react in ways that bring forth deeds—both good and bad. We are to examine our thoughts, questioning them to see if we are entertaining thoughts that are from God, or are we entertaining the opposing spirits of God? When people upset us, we are not wrestling against flesh and blood but against spiritual wickedness being fought in high places.

God, in his great mercy, removes much of our past unpleasant memories as we grow older. Let God's ministering spirits be the leading escorts of our minds. The Holy Spirit lives within God's children; however, God sends an army of ministering angels to aid his children in their time of need. God is involved for reasons of his own; his ministering spirits are in our daily lives. Those of us working on God's battlefield of redemption, bringing in heaven's harvest, are indeed God's army. God's angelic army shields us from the fiery darts of the enemy.

We make decisions based on our limited knowledge and interpretation concerning God's will. The angels of the Lord know who we are and what our purpose in life is. Interact with God's messengers; they are sent to help us do God's work. We are to keep our eyes on Jesus, praising him in every situation. God sends angels to earth as helpers. They are awesome in strength, they are awesome in faith, and they are endowed with divine power from the seat of God's throne. They are anointed beings loyal to God in every way. They are extremely fearsome. They will not let sin come near their presence. Angels have the power to defeat the presence of sin by the power that radiates from their being. They are magnificent soldiers, protectors of God's heavenly kingdom. If we ever are privileged to be confronted by a ten-foot angel, the sense of their electrifying godly purity beaming and oscillating from them, the emitting light flowing out from their beings can't be explained. Their holiness, the brilliant white light coming from these angels, flows through their clothing from their spirit beings.

It is humbling knowing you are standing in the holy presence of God's trusting workmen and God allows you to see them. Angels are God's messengers; they are about God's business. It's not for us always to understand the meaning of their visit. I felt they could become spiritual incinerators, burn a person to a crisp with their consuming powers radiating from them. It seems I've always seen them travel in pairs. If God is allowing us to see his messengers, there is a lesson in their visitation. Pray to God while in their presence. The realization they are God's messengers ought to be sufficient enough for us to obey their bidding; however, ask God what is it he wants us to do.

God is supreme. God is love—love is all there is. We are to love one another—this is the will of God. We are spirit beings functioning on various levels of development and intelligence. We are to keep learning; there is more to be learned than we can ever imagine. We will never know spiritual growth if we are always measuring one another's faults. We are incapable of judging accurately. If we see a drunk lying on the ground, we are quick to make a judgment. We judge what we see—just another drunk lying on the ground. Jesus sees the precious soul he died for, and there is an immediate sacred sacrificial bond; a blood-binding covenant is standing in need. The magnificence of his Father's love for humanity is lying on the ground, waiting to be spiritually born.

Jesus can look on a person and, with the spirit that comes out of his eyes, can burn out the dark evil spirit possessing this individual. The drunk is a distinct entity, highly valued, inseparable from God's love by the blood of Jesus Christ. The King of kings will make him whole.

16

In Touch with Spirit Self

We are to energize our whole being—the soul, the spirit, and the body. Examine closely our attitude on life, the way we are using God's free grace. At the end of our earthly pilgrimage, be able to stand in faith, believing there is endless peace, a loving home prepared for those that love God in his kingdom. We are to magnify the Lord with our whole heart, break loose from the symptoms of self-pity, and I am going to get even attitude. Through faith, we can pass through earth's rim and touch eternity, becoming spiritually free from the confinements of human limitations through our immovable faith. Stay steadfast, never doubting God's Person nor his Word; it takes that kind of faith to set us free.

It was God's will to have our souls go through a human experience. We were assigned to live a temporary life on this earth in a body of flesh. Our limited time on planet Earth shows God's mercy on mankind considering earth's atmosphere, its gravitational force that is stretching day by day and pulling at our flesh inch by inch until the human skin loses its elasticity, causing wrinkles that give an appearance of old age. Lifegiving conditions on the human body can brings anguish—the pain of living with arthritis that impairs, disfiguring the human body, the infections, the diseases, and dementia's memory impairment. Time on earth can bring that which tortures, weakens, and make man's stability fragile until we need assistance to sustain our mobility. Thinking about living forever on earth with recurring heartaches, a body racked with pain—the anguish of it all—boggles the mind. Thank God our earth time is limited in this body of flesh made from particles of earth's dust. Dust will vanish in the winds that blow across earth's surface.

In our interrelatedness, our spiritual functioning with God when the deep is calling the deep, the nonphysical revealing its connecting powers. In reality, the unseen thought is substance; it is communication, the exchanged information between two individual spiritual beings. Faith is a spiritual force of unseen substance at work for us and through us. Faith is flowing energy, an active substance being transferred spiritually to God through us, producing the seen, actions from the power of prayer. The universe is spiritually existing through the direct intervention of God's divine power. An individual does not have to be restricted to human limitations. Using the mechanisms of our sixth sense, we can soar beyond man's limitations if we permit ourselves to tap into spiritual reality through concentration on God and his love. Use the measure of faith God has implanted in our hearts; it is adequate to bring us into intimacy with him. We are to use our spiritual ability faithfully and wisely by communication with the Lord; that is the only way to reach his heart—communing with him in love and obedience.

Pause for a moment. Imagine this first social human being, Adam, for whom God created the garden of Eden. His social activity was with the host of heaven. God visited Adam at the close of the day. During the evening, they would walk and talk. Still Adam was desiring something more tangible—he was lonely, he felt unfulfilled—so God gave him someone he could touch and identify with. He gave him a woman to fill the loneliness of his days and nights. God satisfied the longing that had become Adam's burden. God knew the hunger in Adam's heart. He took D and A from Adam's ribcage and made him a helpmate—a woman—named her Eve. Adam said, "This is flesh of my flesh, bone of my bone." In the sight of God, they become one.

There is more to life than a resounding echo ringing in the depths of the thunder that lives in the heart of man, and man doesn't yet understand who he is.

Participate in the freedom of loving-kindness and working through the time that has been assigned to us on this planet. Enter in among life's vibrations that are beyond the thin spiritual veil between the seen and the unseen. Be in tune to the human limitation of our receptibility. There is unexposed life in us to be discovered, waiting to be activated by the faithful who believe there is something more than the naked understanding of man. There is holy visibility for the faithful. There is more to humanity than meets our eye.

As earth's life is paling out, each moment of life should be ripened deeply in the soul of man. Plucking from among the unexplored, studying the hidden secrets of the soul is awaiting discovery. We are to become familiar with our spirit selves, experiencing the unshielded—that is living in the midst of who we really are and who we will always be. Now is the time to discern what is beyond the range of human sight and sound. Faith is our substance needed to tear away the veil, the mystery of the unknown—the life living within—and wanting to be exposed to true life, grasping for comprehension of what is, and what is meant to be will be. We must have patience and forbearance. Wait on God; he will show the way to his heart as we persevere in faith, believing all things are possible. Conceive what is to be will be found in God's faithfulness toward us.

Our spirit will rise from the grave of sin, escaping human bondage. We will receive a risen body that has escaped the confinement of the old man of sin, and we will be like unto Jesus, no longer under the bondage of sin or of the gravitational and electromagnetic forces. What are we going to be like? Who will we be? We have little knowledge of our power to come, our new body without flesh that is like unto the Lord. How will it be being weightless and beyond the gravitational pull that no longer has an effect on our movements? Will we be able to visit the earth to see our loved ones? We know our new body will be fashioned like unto his glorious body. We are one in spirit with the Lord. Can we understand now where we are in God's plan? No is the answer—to the mysteries to come. We forever will be in his kingdom with a body like his Son. Our joy will be in obedience to the Father.

> Although it doth not yet appear what we shall be, when he shall appear, we shall be like him. (1 John 3:2)

> In our glorious, powerful, bodies we as his servants, shall serve him in love, and in joy forever. (Revelation 22:3)

It is a privilege to be given the gift of faith. Faith is a gift. Everyone is not permitted to receive the spirit of faith, to believe that God the Father, the Son, and the Holy Spirit are one divine Godhead.

What a comfort to know, beyond a question of a doubt, there is a heaven to gain and a hell to shun.

In the concept of our imaginary perception, can we behold—perceive the dwelling—where we will live? God has designed for his children a palace. Does that blow your imagination to inconceivable heights?

It is written,

> Eye hath not seen, nor ear heard, neither have entered into the heart of man, the things which God hath prepared for them that love him. (1 Corinthians 2:9)

When our time comes, we will be conscious instantly that we have passed out of this life to greater life. We will know we are experiencing the promise of the everlasting gift of life—with our Creator. We will be with Jesus in a twinkling of an eye, and we shall see him as he is, for we shall be like him. We are his inheritance—now that is good news! There is no pain in death; fear it not. The departing soul is independent of our human effort to keep it from leaving the body. When the time comes for the soul to be set free from its earth-bound duties, effortlessly it will depart. Realize we are passing from one spiritual assignment to another, from our human state of consciousness to greater spiritual awakening. Our spirit beings are never in a nonexistent state; the spirit is imperishable. The soul is the breath of God and will live forever. We will never be a forgotten soul. We are God's breath. Our sin debt was paid before we were conceived in the womb of time. We who are forgiven are the bright shining lights of righteousness. We are the personal property of the Almighty bought back to the Creator by the precious shed blood of Jesus Christ, God's anointed Son. The giver of salvation said, "To whomsoever will, let him come and drink from the well of salvation."

"Surely, surely my word will not fail. I will never leave you. You are my inheritance, shining and bright. I will never let go those of mine," said the Lord, a prophecy given during a Sunday church service.

17

Forgiveness

The drastic effects that come along with our human experience may cause many to be filled with bitterness that can last a lifetime.

I was born during the Great Depression. I was one of those giveaway children. In those days, people suffered many hardships. Many committed suicide—they had lost not only their wealth but their social standing. During the late 1920s and early 1930s, many city people found they were unable to feed their families and sent their children south to their grandparents who lived on farms. They wanted to be sure their children would eat.

I was given away several times before the age of five. I had a lot of young uncles and aunts. They would find whoever I was given to and bring me back home to my mother who had just given me away. Mother would hear a knock on the door. When she opened the door, there I stood like an unwanted puppy she could not get rid of. I failed to tell you my grandmother had seventeen children that knew every inch of their neighborhood. When they went on the hunt to find me, they found me. Some of my aunts and uncles were just a few years older than I was. Believe me, they would always find me and bring me back to my mother.

When I was about four years old, mother gave me to a lady by the name of Mrs. Lacy. Mrs. Lacy was an elderly woman who had a daughter that was a prostitute by night, so she slept late into the day.

I remember once Mrs. Lacy's daughter told her mother that I had wet the bed. After working all night, she said she was tired of getting in a wet bed. Mrs. Lacy was ironing, and I was squatting underneath the ironing board, playing with a cigar box, a gold paper cigar ring, and an empty toilet paper roll. There were two men sitting at the kitchen table; they were having a conversation. They had given me some pennies. I made a game out of them; again and again, I would drop the pennies through the empty toilet paper roll. When Mrs. Lacy's daughter told her I had wet the bed, she stopped ironing and doubled the ironing cord and began whipping me as hard as she could to punish me. I was screaming and crying as she gave me a thrashing—I can still remember the pain of it.

The two men said, "I can't take this any longer," and they left.

Shortly after my fifth birthday, one of my aunts found me and took me from Mrs. Lacy back to my mother. Mother said, "It don't do me any good giving her away. Someone will find her and bring her back." It was suggested I should be taken out of town and given away. Later I was taken to another city and given to a great-aunt. She was my grandmother's oldest sister who was sixty-five years old or thereabout. She did not have a kind bone in her body. The moment she saw me, she found fault with my facial appearance. I was "too blue-collar looking." I was not a pretty child in Ma's sight.

At a very early age, I felt insecure. I was made to feel I was an ugly child, that I looked different from people she considered handsome. Whatever I did was wrong in her opinion. Ma made fun of my persona for years. "She looks like she's Chinese"—she'd make that statement because my eyes were almond shaped.

Ma's favorite daughter-in-law would say, "Put her hair in bangs. The Chinese wear their hair in bangs," then she would say, "She ain't got no eyebrows. She's gonna have to make herself some brows when she grows up."

I was put to shame because of my big nose. Ma said my nose was spread all over my face. I have a dimple in my chin. Ma said I had a cleft chin; she didn't like it. I said I didn't have a cleft chin; I said I have a dimple in my chin. I didn't know whether to like my dimple or not—maybe it too was ugly. I found it hard to look up at people. It was paralyzing. It was painful for me to show my face. I wondered what people were thinking when they looked at me. As a child, I was unwilling to look up. When talking to someone, I always looked down; I didn't want people to see my funny face. I felt I had a frightening face like a deformed monster. I thought I looked like the hunchback of Notre Dame. I never felt good enough to be accepted because of my looks. I wanted so badly to be accepted; I wanted to be included. I was always trying to please people, hoping they would like me. Feeling unwanted, inferior, and unloved for years, I tried to stay in the shadows as if I was a ghost, not drawing attention to myself. Wanting to be loved and trying to be good enough to please Ma was the dominating factor of my young life. For years, I lived in fear of not being good enough to make Ma happy. I felt incomplete. Something was missing, but I did not know what it was. I was raised in partial obscurity. I was not allowed to be friendly and mingle with people very much while in Ma's sight.

Ma didn't like anybody. No neighbors came to our house. In the 1930s and early 1940s, we lived near Ma's small farm; we referred to it as "the other place"—it was located on the outskirts of a small town in Ohio. Jesus was my only friend, but I didn't tell Ma how I felt about my Lord. I could talk with Jesus about anything, tell him all my heartaches. I thought of Jesus as my protector and my brother.

Many times Ma told me, "You'll never amount to a hill of beans." I thought Ma may be right; I was just a walking joke. I hated myself. I spent my young life wanting to die. Many times I tried committing suicide before the age of seven. I felt death was my only option out of the misery I was experiencing. I was seven years old when I started school. I did not legally belong to Ma; she had no legal papers showing how she got me, so it was hard for her to get me enrolled in school.

In school I swapped daydreams for studies. Daydreams were my escape mechanism—imagining I was someone else who live with someone else. Ma was never a part of my daydreams. When my mind took flight, I escaped Ma's reach. I pretended I was very beautiful and exciting to be around. I was someone else in another land, living another life. I was happy and loved. Ma would not help me with homework, and I could not concentrate or keep my mind on schoolwork. I wanted to free myself from my surroundings, so I would go off into another existence. I would escape my body. I was not there anymore. I did poorly in school. I was just a daydreamer, having all kinds of vain imaginations. I was always getting into fights at school. Kids poked fun at me because I stunk like cow manure and had sores on me, so I was bullied. I never had a toothbrush until I ran away from Ma. I had bad breath.

From a young child, I felt overwhelmed. I had no control over what was happening in my life; I felt alone, unloved, unwanted, and very fearful. I was living in danger all my whole childhood. I didn't like myself. I was ashamed of how I had to live and the way I looked. My poor performance in the school curriculum kept me feeling inferior. I felt my life was a mistake and I was an outcast. I knew I was a part of the human race, but I wondered why I was ever born into this world; I have asked myself that question many times. I didn't know where I belonged—in heaven or hell—I knew I didn't belong with Ma. I longed to be somewhere other than where I was. I lived in shame and in pain. All the while I lived with ma, I became a pretender, dreaming my young life away. Pretending was my only means of escape from my prison.

I grew up spooked by the darkness of our creepy old house. I was living a life in a state of fear, terrified by unexplainable sounds that sent shivers through my body. During the night and sometimes in the day, I could hear something walking through the house when there was no one there but me.

At an early age, deep in my soul, I felt the weight, the heaviness of life fate had dealt me. There was a war going on in my psyche. I stood in the balance of the unknowns and the balance of love and hate. A wise man said, "To err is human. To forgive is divine." I acquired the art of forgiving at an early age. I traded my desire to hate for the need to be loved. Under every rock I searched for love, but my search was in vain.

Reed's Chapel is where I went to Sunday school. I liked going to church. Sometimes Ma would let me stay after Sunday school to attend church services. Ma did not go to church. She felt the black church was too emotional. "Them n——are always whooping and hollering." She called them holy rollers. Ma's father was a freed African escaping through the underground tunnel, running from the state of Georgia to find freedom in Canada. He was a six-month-old infant escaping slavery in his mother's arms. My great-great-grandmother fled the USA with my great-grandfather in the late 1700s. Ma's mother was Irish, born in Ireland. Ma's parents, as far as I know, met and married in Canada. They had thirteen children. They lived in Canada during the 1800s and in the early 1900s.

Ma's ethics were very European. Ma passed for a White woman in the work place and was a Black person at home. For a romantic partner, she preferred a man with a dark complexion. She married a man from Tennessee. She and her husband had two sons. She said he was the finest man who ever stepped in shoe leather. When Ma was young, she would wear many hats. She could be mean as hell. She could be nice as pie. She could be White when necessary and Black when she wanted to be. She was whatever met her fancy in the moment of opportunity.

At age ten, I was teaching Sunday school to younger children in our little church that was sitting on the hill. I could not read very well, but I would read the heck out of pictures. The power of my imagination would kick into full gear. I presented the front of the lesson cards with vigor, in a way that appealed to the senses of the children and me. I remember one of the Sunday school cards had a picture of Jesus knocking on the door. I read the picture to the class.

I said, "Jesus is knocking at the door. Open the door for Jesus. He wants to come in and talk to you. Jesus loves you. He wants to come in and play with you. If you give him some food, he will eat supper with you."

The children loved for me to tell them stories about Jesus, and the older people of the church listen to every word I said. They thought I was pretty wonderful. I loved Jesus and loved talking about him. People would say my love for Jesus showed in my face. I taught with passion. I was happy when I talked about Jesus. I would forget about my unhappy life. When I did return home from church, I'd go out on the porch, get up on the banister, and preach to the chickens.

I would preach until the Spirit of God came over me. The chickens would cackle, turning their heads sideways. They would look up at me as if they understood that I was talking to them.

Ma would yell out to me, "Stop that—making a mockery out of God—before he strikes you dead." Her words scared me, and I'd jump off the banister, run in the house, and try to be friends to Ma so God wouldn't beat me with a rod of iron.

There was an elderly White couple, a man and his wife whose goal was to bring the little children to a knowledge of Jesus Christ. She had a harelip but wore a smile all the time. She had such a sweet, soft, friendly face that was lovely, and I so loved her. Despite the fact she had a deformed mouth, she kept loving Jesus and did not fault him for her disfigurement. She never was embarrassed about her looks. She would not let her disfigurement stop her from telling people about the love of Jesus. She loved teaching the school kids about the wonders of Jesus, how he loved the little children. We would run as fast as we could to get to the elderly couple's home before the second school bell rang. She always had hard candy waiting for us. The candy was stuck together because it was hard Christmas candy and the heat of summer would make it stick together. She could make that candy last all year long. She'd pinch off one piece of candy at a time to give to each one. Oh boy, we looked forward to that piece of hard candy; it too was one of the reasons we kept coming back to her.

I would leave her home so happy I forgot I was an unhappy person. I fell in love with Jesus because of that old lady who was teaching out of her love for Christ. She and her husband relied on the love of Jesus to keep them strong and healthy. Because of the elderly couple, I started believing God was my father, the blessed Virgin Mary was my mother, and Jesus was my big brother. I was always told Jesus loved me, but if I was bad, I was told God would beat me with many stripes, beating me with a rod of iron. I would say, "Jesus, don't let God beat me with the rod of iron." I felt Ma's beatings were enough. I was told God would beat me forever and ever. I was afraid of God as a child. I said if God comes after me, I will hide under my bed. I know now about God's mercy and his grace and that he created me out of his love. I've come to learn that God is love. He is not standing by the wayside, waiting to beat me with a rod of iron. He is not an electric paddling machine beating us forever and ever without end.

I am remembering my life as it was in my youth. Once upon a time, a very long time ago, although it was like last night's nightmare, it was my reality—remembering the realities of my life.

Many were the cold, dark winter mornings, about 5:00 a.m. At age six or seven years of age, I walked alone for a few miles to a small farm we referred to as "the other place"—that's where our farm animals were kept. We had three cows that had to be milked twice a day. Milking the cows was one of my chores that needed to be done before and after school. These old cows did not want to be milked. When I would milk them, sometimes they would slap my face so hard with their tail. It was painful and would sting for hours.

To get to the other place and take care of our farm animals, I walked through a field next to a barbwire fence where wild horses grazed. Their grazing area was about three hundred acres of pasture. I feared the horses. I thought one day one of them might jump over their barbwire enclosure. In time, my fears became a reality. The horses had seen me passing by day after day for years, and in time, one horse decided to make the jump and jumped the barbwire fencing. He had me on his mind. He lay on his side, in the tall grass, biding his time, waiting for me to pass by. He knew what time I would be coming, and on schedule, here I came. He must have gotten impatient, restless, waiting for me to appear, so he raised his long neck and turned his head in my direction to take a look, to see if I was coming.

He saw me approaching. Quickly he dropped his head. He had seen me. I had seen him too, surrounded by the tall grass. The feeling of danger went all through me. I had been told, "Never turn your back on an animal. They like to sneak upon you when you are not looking." So I backed—back to the road instead of cutting across the field that made my journey shorter; I felt safer going the long way around and take the road where there were a few houses. I kept looking to see if the horse was coming after me. He stayed, lying on the ground, thinking I would soon appear close enough for him to jump up, take his head, and knock me down then trample me to death.

When I got to the cow barn, in the dimmest of the early morning, I could observe the horse's movement in the field that stood between me and the him. I kept low to the ground, almost a crawl, hoping the horse could not see me. There was some distance between us. I knew I could not have gone back to Ma without bringing the milk home.

One day, I was told to go into the pasture to get ma some crab apples. There was a (sour) crab apple tree in the horse pasture. Ma liked to use crab apples when making apple jelly. She thought the sour apples gave a sense of balance, a specific flavor she tried to capture that offers a uniqueness to her taste buds. She wanted her palate satisfied with a flavor others could not acquire. Her apple jelly was to present a taste of superior over any other apple jelly could offer her taste buds.

I dreaded going into the pasture. I knew if the horses saw me and thought they could reach me before I could get away from them, they would come after me. In my imagination, I could see them trampling me to death and could hear their galloping hooves pounding the ground with thunderous sounds. The thought of this was frightening. I told Ma if I go into the pasture, the horses will come after me. They will kill me.

Ma said, "If you don't go get them apples like I told you, I'll kill you." I was fearful of the wild horses, and I dreaded Ma's punishment. I was just a little kid, and fear was my constant companion. I lived with it. Fear—we had a great relationship—it went to bed with me at night and was there to greet me each morning. Fear was my best buddy. We couldn't exist without each other.

I remember that day. I was crying and praying while heading for the pasture. When I reached the pasture, I rolled beneath the barbwire fencing and started running toward the crab apple tree. From afar, I saw the horses. They were looking my way. A big black horse was the leader of the pack. The leader, with his head held high, started galloping in my direction, the pack following after him. I kept my eyes on them, praying as I ran to the tree. I ascended the old apple tree and felt safe. I watched the horses stop near the tree, acting as if they were paying no attention to me in the tree. They kept their heads down, eating the grass nearby. At times they would drift a little farther away as they kept eating putting a greater distance between the tree and them. That was a good thing. I wanted them to keep moving back.

Every once in a while, the lead horse would look up to see if I was still in the tree. I was waiting for the distance to grow greater between me and the pack of horses. I had no time to waste. I kept busy picking apples—filling my burlap sack. Ma kept me on a time clock. She'd watch to see how long I was out of her sight, how long would it take me to do this chore. I kept my eyes on the lead horse. He was the one that would look up to see if he could see me. Each time he looked up, he would drop his head and keep on eating. It seemed he kept his head down a little longer and moved a little farther away from the tree.

I knew the lead horse was baiting me. He thought he could catch me no matter the distance between us. I said to myself, "As soon as I feel there is enough time and distance between me and them, I will make a run for the fence." Although I didn't want to give the horses an opportunity to kill me, I knew Ma was waiting for me and watching the clock. I needed to get out of the tree, get home, and show Ma I had not been lollygagging, wasting time. Pleasing Ma was most important. I had to live with her and I wanted her to be proud of me and I worked hard to that end.

I filled the bottom half of the sack, put a knot in the middle to split the weight of the apples once the bag was full. The knot would rest on my shoulder, so the sack would hang even, front to back. Then I filled the upper half and put a knot at the mouth of my burlap sack, closing it. I threw the sack across my shoulder, ready to climb down from my safe place. The lead horse had dropped his head for about the seventh time. He had kept his head down a little longer each time. He looked up to see if he could see me. When I felt it was safe to leave the tree, I jumped, hitting the ground with all the power God had given me. I ran for the barbwire fence. Running faster than I had ever ran in my life, I ran. As soon as I thought I was close enough to the fence, I threw the burlap sack, watching it fall over the barbwire like a flash of lightning crossing the midnight sky.

I too hit the ground about the same time the burlap sack dropped to the ground. Rolling beneath the barbwire, I felt free. Once on the other side of the fence, I kept running as if my life depended on it. I knew the horses could and would jump the fence if they saw me. When the horses looked up again, they wouldn't see me. I would be out of their sight. When I got home, I stood facing Ma, hoping she was not mad at me for taking so long. I handed her the sack of crab apples. She never knew I had to hide out in the apple tree to keep the horses from killing me. She knew she had put me in harm's way but didn't care.

Many times, Ma has ordered me to place my life in jeopardy. Farm animals kill people every year. The records show they kill thousands of their handlers each year. Animals can become very dangerous and unruly during the time of propagation—their breeding season. There are times when the animals do not want to be bothered, going through a breeding process, and they let you know it—get out of their way—when they don't want to be romanced by a potential breeding partner. Once our cow injured a bull. We had tried to breed her with him. She refused the bull's affections. She fought, horning him until he backed away from his date. Our cow said, "No date tonight buddy." The owner took his bull back home with his head bowed low from the beating he took from our cow. Dealing with unruly animals while they are in heat is no pie-in-the-sky kind of job.

Many a time while milking our cows, they would slap me across the face so hard with their tail. The sting was lasting. My face would turn red for hours. They'd try horning, and kicking me, and if I was pinned between them and the wall of the barn, they would enlarge their belly, trying to crush me, squeezing me until I was able to push them away. It seemed they knew I was a child; they had no respect for me. They would look at me as if to say, "You little squirt. I'm not letting you boss me around."

Ma owned three milk cows, four or five pigs, even a blind pig named Molly; there was old Charly, our horse, a young bull named Billy. We would kill our bulls when they reach nine months of age for veal. We had many chickens, guinea hens, ducks, and other feathered fowl walking about the yard. Ma raised food for all her livestock. We planted fields of soybeans for hay. It was a good food product for feeding the cows and horse. We also planted corn and other vegetables and grew most of what we needed for food.

At a distance, the grass always looks greener. One time, Ma thought her neighbors' cabbage patch looked good enough to be in her backyard. She could not pass by these cabbages without wanting to treat herself to one. I was told to steal a particular head of cabbage. Ma had seen this cabbage earlier in the day and desired to ascertain the taste of it. Why she picked this one out from all the rest of the cabbages, I don't know—they all looked pretty much the same to me. She knew the row the cabbage was in and how far down the row it grew.

The neighbor's garden bordered our property. I did not want to steal that cabbage. I thought, *When I die, I'll go to hell and burn forever for stealing this cabbage.* I knew God was watching me. He sees everything. I did what she told me to do—go in, get that cabbage—I had to do it or get a beating. Ma always told me I'd go to hell for lying or being dishonest, yet she is making me steal. We knew stealing was a sin. I was asked to do things that made me feel shame—what if I was found out? I felt so guilty when I looked that neighbor in the face.

If I did not lie when Ma wanted me to, she whipped me for disobeying. Ma would beat me for things I did and for things I did not do. There were times she'd say I did something, knowing I did not do it; she would then beat me until I would say yes, I did it, to get her to stop beating me.

I was fifteen, nearing my sixteenth birthday. On my way home from school, Ma had decided to meet me. She had part of a tree branch in her hand. She was going to beat me with it for no other reason but to embarrass me in front of my friends. She liked embarrassing me. If I'd start to run from her, she'd say, "Don't run. I'll give it to you good when I get you home." So I would stand in front of my friends and take the beating. While beating me, she would always say, "Stop your crying, and stop that sniffling before I really give you something to cry about."

If she thought I was working to slow, she'd hit me with whatever was in her hand. My friends knew Ma was mean, and sometimes they would say, "Mrs. Brown is so mean."

All those years I lived with Ma, I felt my life and health was in grave danger. One of my jobs was to clean the overnight chamber pots that contain urine and defecation. I had to carry the open chamber pots downstairs, through the house, out to a field behind the barn, and dump their contents. I carried out all Ma's assignments whether I liked them or not. I performed my duties, fearing Ma's retribution; she was desensitized when it came to dealing with my physical and mental well-being. As a young girl in her care, she did not care about what happened to me. I wanted something or someone to come and rescue me from my destiny of doom and gloom.

I really wanted to die. I thought that was my only way out. I did not want to live out the hand fate had dealt me. I was suicidal. I hated myself and my life. I tried committing suicide more than once to get away from Ma. Mr. Lee and Ralph, Ma's oldest son—they were thorns in my side. They caused me so much pain and suffering. They robbed me of my childhood.

Come journey with me through the early years of my development into womanhood. An incident happened which I will never forget. I was about seven years of age. I attempted to end my existence in this world. I saw a funeral procession coming up the hill near the house. I cut through fields to get ahead of the funeral cars. I ran all the way to the graveyard. I jumped into a freshly dug grave. I thought I would not be noticed; somehow they could let the casket down without seeing me. Remember, I was about seven years of age at the time and mentally depressed. Lying there six feet in the ground, I could see old flowers sticking through the dirt from the grave next to my face. When the workers came to get things ready to lower the coffin, they saw me and yelled so loudly; they carried on so badly they almost fell in on me. They scared me. I panicked, jumped out of the grave, and ran like crazy into a nearby field.

I lived with such anguish in my soul. Suicidal tendencies were beckoning me, "Come." Haunting, relentlessly death kept calling to me. I was living with spiritual, mental, and physical heartache. At any given moment, I was willing to try anything to get away from the binding shackles life had placed on me. All I could think of was getting away from the horrors of my life. Life was my greatest adversary; a life where I had no power to escape my tormentors. I was living in unimaginable conditions, but most of all, I was unloved and craved to be loved. I was starved for affection. I needed to be shown kindness from another human being. I had seen my friends who had mothers that loved on them, gently stroking them on the head. I would think how special that is. How precious some children were to their mothers—I wanted some of that affection. To live in their shoes for one hour and receive some of that loving tenderness would be a dream come true.

I was introduced to unhappiness at a very early age. I was five years of age when I was given to Ma. When I take observation of the life that once engulfed me, my past experiences come alive when certain words are spoken—words we call slip of the lip. In seconds, the tongue can trigger the painful past. Memories from our youth linger in the subconscious and may resurface when triggered by certain words—as freshly as if the joy or the pain was inflicted only yesterday, causing us to relive our past.

Early memories have a way of sticking in the memory bank. Our longtime memory seems to have a hold on us we tell our story over and over again. Our longtime memories lives on; it's the short-time memory we can't remember that don't seem to catch root. I wonder, had I had a healthy childhood, today who would I be? What mystery had I not been allowed to live out? What untold stories will never be born? What purpose was left unaccomplished? For years, I thought my quest for peace and rest lay in suicide. During those tender childhood years, I wanted to get away from the only life I knew. I was living a very stressful and painful existence. I lived in hope of a better life to come. I had a very confused, disoriented understanding of life; and what life is really all about, I did not know.

In my search for happiness, trying to get an understanding of the nightmare I was living, I was born to suffer is what I figured out. I've lived under terrible stress, there was an unseen force that was deliberately crushing the light of life out of me, but I keep on living.

I know there are many people living very unhappy lives; I was never the only one. Some suffer more than others—for what reason, I do not know.

Look around. What do you see in the eyes of people? Learn to read the faces—they read like books, many telling the stories of life unfulfilled. They have never reached the pinnacle of happiness. Their dreams too are perishing from the lack of attention, affection, and loyalty—the three things many are starving for. The world is hungering for kindness. I find suffering is the fate of mankind because of the lack of love. Think about Jesus and his disciples—did they suffer? Yes, because man has never learned to love one another. Where there is no love, there is no real life; we merely exist.

Think back on the history of man's early civilization and development. Their story of day-to-day survival was inhumane. The continuation of human life over the last few thousand years until this present date is filled with savage inhumanity to man. Living under the control of the Taliban, a fundamentalist Islamic state, or any aggressively militant group in operation brings suffering to the human race. We know there is suffering in this world—always was and always will be. What can we do to rectify this situation? We don't have to be a part of building a painful society. We can treat our fellowman with kindness. You and I can make a difference in making this world a better place in which to live. We too can be kinder to one another. We should listen to others. Everyone has a story to tell. Listen to what's on people's hearts. Put your anger on the back burner for a while. Don't use anger as a weapon of defense. We do not always have to keep defending ourselves. Walk away from unfriendliness, and get a breath of fresh air. It will improve the quality of our response.

At age five, I was sentenced to a deplorable existence. Unthinkable to many were the conditions in which I was to grow into womanhood. I was given to a great-aunt. She was my grandmother's oldest sister. This old soul seemed incapable of showing love. She was on a mission. Determined to keep me oppressed, ignorant, and fearful was her goal. She wanted to keep me under her control for as long as she had breath in her body. Fear is life's greatest enemy, and I was full of it. Her weapon of choice in deciding how to deal with me, to keep me under her foot, was the technique of fear. You can train a five-year-old kid to be fearless or fearful. She wanted me mentally handicapped—she saw to it. I became paralyzed with fear, and she wanted me fearful of her. She wanted me to have to depend on her throughout her life, the fear of what would happen to me if I didn't have her to point my way. Ma wanted me to believe I was insane. At times I thought she's right—I am a lunatic.

There were times Ma would sneak up behind me in the darkness of night when I went to the backyard to use the outhouse. When Ma would catch me alone, she'd try to instill fear in me by appearing out of nowhere with her piercing eyes looking straight at me. She deliberately wanted me to learn to be fearful at an early age so I would be in remembrance of what punishment was like at her hands. I would not have the mental stability, the strength to wonder about the what-ifs; my memories of her punishment would never let go of me.

Our staircase was a good place to drudge up fear. It was closed in, walls on both sides, and the absence of light—you were in total blackness after you close the door behind you; you could not see your hands before your face. Ma sometimes unexpectedly would creep up behind me while I was ascending the darkness of our staircase; she would make the most dreadful screaming, startling sounds that paralyze me with fear; the pain of it would run up and down my spine. I would jump, scream out, and cry but had to keep on moving up the dark staircase as if nothing happened. I was crying inside most of my childhood, but I had to act like I was happy. I would laugh and say, "Ma, you scared me to death. If I acted like I was unhappy and cried, Ma would say, "I ought to kill you. You're worthless."

When I could cry. "Now what are you crying about?" she would ask. I silently cried and prayed walking through the darkness of our staircase. I could see things—different colors of moving lights. I could feel and hear things. I had to go upstairs to get whatever Ma had sent me to get or take the consequences of disobedience. I once saw the spirit of a little girl that looked a lot like me. She was standing in the darkness of the staircase. She was looking at me and had on a red dress designed with little animals. I told Ma what I saw. It made her so mad she grabbed me by my hair and the seat of my pants and threw me up the stairs into the darkness. Now I was not only fearful of the dark and the little girl that was standing there, looking at me. I was hurting and crying silently. I dare not make a sound. Ma would come after me again.

Ma's behavior was absolutely inconsiderate of my feelings or the pain she caused me; I was just an object in her sight. When I think back, Ma could have been living with dementia. She would tell me to do something then ask me, "Why are you doing that?" I would say, "You told me to do this." She would say, "You are a barefaced liar. I told you to do no such thing." Ma was possessed with the thought she was high class. People who had to have an encounter with Ma found her uppity, with an attitude most distasteful, and self-serving, but they said nothing to her face about her conduct. With a smile, they would put up with Ma and buy her eggs, butter, milk, and buttermilk. During the hog-killing season, they bought meat from Ma.

Ma told me I had clubfeet. My feet were not twisted; they did not show any deformity. They were short and fat. Ma could be hot. She could be cold, unpleasant when she wanted to be unpleasant, and she liked life the way she played it. She was the master of her ship. Ma was very resourceful, clever, and quick thinking. When Ma decided to like you, then that was a different story—you could do no wrong. In our house, Ma only liked three people: number one herself, her youngest son's wife, and the granddaughter by her oldest son; his wife she did not like.

Ma's granddaughter came to live with us when she was about three months old. At that time, I was eight years old. Ma knew how to be courteous, how to show politeness, and high-quality manners that she could put on display when she wanted to. She has a sister that lived in another state. She came to visit every August. The house had to be spic and span; new wallpaper had to be put up, new curtains, and the outdoor toilet had to be spotless. She would take away the old newspaper we used and put out store-bought toilet paper to accommodate her sister's desire. Ma would buy special food and drinks, even bottles of beer and a few cigarettes, and wore her best house dresses to accommodate her sister's stay. Ma's sister put a smile on Ma's face the whole time she was in our house. Ma would smile and laugh; she carried on a civil conversation that could last all day and half the night. Ma made a good impression on her sister, who was known to be high class. These two old ladies had a good time talking about what mulatto beauties they once were and the fun they had in days long gone by; their longtime memories kicking in and working overtime.

It was wise to stay on Ma's good side. You did not want to ever clash with her and get on her bad side; she could become your worst nightmare. A woman secretly killed and ate Ma's pet chicken. I went looking for the beloved beautiful cocky chicken named Brown Boy, a rooster that went strutting about the backyard with a pompous stride, crowing and chasing the hens about. Brown Boy liked bacon and eggs for breakfast. If you would coo very softly to him, he would coo along with you and look you in the face. Drop a few grains of corn on the ground, he'd follow the trail of corn until there was no more corn to be found.

I found Brown Boy's feathers behind the privy that belonged to the lady living across the street from us. I told Ma where I found Brown Boy's feathers. She said, "I'm not putting up with no chicken thief around here." Ma said, "She's one of those Louisiana n———. They are superstitious. They believe in witchcraft. They think you can put a hex on them. Voodoo is like their religion. I'll make her think those Louisiana darkies done found her and have put another hex on her. I know how to get rid of a chicken thief. I'll conjure up something. I'll make up a couple small black fuzzy bags, fill them with lard, mix in a little coal dust, and put some dog hair on top, put it in pouches, sprinkle a little red pepper on top of the mixture. When she opens 'um up, the red pepper will make her sneeze and tear up. She'll think the voodoo spirits have found her and are working her over."

Ma told me, "When it starts getting dark, I want you to hang a bag on the front doorknob and the other bag, hang it on the back doorknob." As dusk dark was approaching, Ma started putting all the lights out in the house. We watched from our living room window. Ma wanted to see the woman's reaction when this young mother saw the bags hanging on her doorknobs.

It was getting time for the woman to come home from work. She always had her little boy by the hand. The child looked to be about four or five years of age. He had a very large head. Ma said he was a water-head baby. The young woman had told Ma she left Louisiana because she believed someone had put a hex on her and voodooed her child, causing his afflictions. Ma's antic worked on the young mother. In the dusk, the dimmest of early evening, the woman could see something hanging from her front doorknob and did not try to open her door. She went to the back of her home. Seeing something hanging on that doorknob, she did not enter her house. She took her child by the hand and left in a hurry. In a couple of days, the weekend came, and she moved. We never saw her again.

I recall Ma telling me some years ago each morning, she and a group of people were standing at our local bus stop. This particular morning, like every other morning, when the bus finally arrived, the scene got frantic. The crowd got anxious for a seat. A White man became uneasy, wanting his wife to get into the bus first to get them a seat. He put his arm across the open door to block the people until his wife reached him and went through the open door to pick a good seat. Ma thought, *Who does he think he is? I want to get off my feet too. Not this morning, not on my dime, mister.* She said, "I went under his arm. When I got on the top step, I kicked backward, striking him in the face. I never looked back. I found a seat. When he and his wife passed by me, he said, 'I wish I had you where I came from.' I looked up and told him, 'Suck it up. I've got you where I belong.'" Ma said his face was bloody. "I had kicked him in the mouth." Ma said, "White folks are used to treating Blacks any kind away and getting away with it."

Ma not only planted fear in me; she knew how to plant fear in the lives of many others as she often said, "I'm hell when I get started." She'd look at me sometimes and say, "I've forgot more than you'll ever know."

The mistreatment I received during the eleven years I lived with my ma were the scariest and most dreaded years of my life. I lived in pure hell—enough hell to possess my memory forever. Ma wanted me to be scared of her, and I was. I wanted a life without having to have Ma dictating me. Ma thought I would be unable to function in life without her stern guidance. She wanted me to be extremely unintelligent and would tell me, "You don't know beans when the bag is open." Ma wanted me to be ignorant to the bone, and I was. She raised me, stripping me of all self-confidence. I did not know the meaning of the word *self-esteem*, having no self-trust or worth; I was like a puppet on a string, controlled and influenced by my owner, and that was the only world I knew.

In my formative years, I lived in mental and physical slavery. I was Ma's slave in every sense of the word; she was my slave master, and I obeyed. From age five to age sixteen, she kept me in bondage. She felt secure, feeling she had someone who was dependable, afraid to disappoint her, and would serve her all the days of her life. She worried about not having someone to depend on and trust in her old age. She would say, "When I get to the place I need someone to hand me a drink of water, I'll be depending on you to hand me that glass of water."

I felt Ma despised me the way she looked at me and raised her hand to strike me across the face; she had what she wanted—an unenlightened work horse—that's all I was to her. She had a lifelong hook in me for her own selfish concerns. She wanted me to be a mental cripple, disabled, and stripped of all my abilities to know how to live without her. I was to be deprived of knowing what life was like outside of Ma's domination. She never considered how I'd live after her death. Maybe she thought I would take her place and become Mr. Lee's mistress. She showed no regard, no thought of my future welfare after her death. Ma lived in the moment, counting on my youth to last as long as she needed it. I had become her permanent live-in house servant and farm hand, performing duties for her until her life was ended. There was about a sixty-year age gap between our ages.

Slaves are always looking for the chance to run away. I knew I too, somehow, someday, would run away from Ma's plantation of grief. When that time came—and that day did come for me to run—I ran.

Ma's brother, my uncle Jack, told me that he told Ma "As soon as that gal got big enough to do you some good, she ran off." He told me Ma said to him, "She don't owe me nothing"—that was the truth. If Ma has ever told the truth, she told it then. Ma had extracted her wages out of my hide both through labor and mental stress. She too had extracted from me, pound up on pound of human flesh with the rod. I paid my debt to her, living eleven years under her hands. She used the whip on me the same way the old White slave masters did on their Black slave. When a slave got their freedom, they owed their slave master nothing; neither did I owe my slave master anything. She owed me a childhood; I felt I owed her respect as one human being to another, and that was all I owed her.

Like the old slave owners, Ma beat me because she could, because I was there. She ruled over me. She could handle me as she pleased. There was no one to stop her, and at that time, there was no law against child abuse. When I got to be sixteen years of age, I needed to be free, for my sanity was at stake. I needed freedom from Ma knocking me to the floor and kicking me in the stomach while she'd tell me, "Get up." When I got up this one particular time, she threw me against the wall behind the cook stove, still beating me. For some reason, in my last year with ma, she started going into uncontrollable rage, tearing off my clothes. I was developing breasts, and I needed a brassiere to keep them from moving up and down. When I was walking fast through study hall at school, my breasts would bounce. The boys were waiting for me. They would make cat calls. They would say, "Here she comes." They would stand up and laugh and shout at me because of my bouncing breasts.

Ma's daughter-in-law had noticed my breasts in motion and say, "Missy, you are in need of something to hold you down." She brought me a brassiere. She only brought me one bra. I would wear that bra day and night; I never washed it because I did not want Ma to see it. Once a week, when I took a bath, I would hide the bra under the cook stove while I bathed.

Ma did not know I wore a bra until she started ripping off my clothing. During one of my beatings, Ma knocked me behind the cook stove, ripping my clothes in two. She saw the bra for the first time. Ma let out a scream and ripped the bra in two. In that moment, I lost my only protection I had against the boys' laughter. How could I face the boys at school when they watched me rushing through the study hall because I was running late as usual. My protection was gone. I wanted—I needed—my bra.

My grief festered in the moment. My brain enflamed. I grabbed Ma under both her arms, lifted her up. Coming from behind the stove, carrying ma under both her arms, I sat her on the stove. The stove was not hot, but I think it may have been warm.

Ma said, "If you put your hands on me, I'll kill you." Ma was trying to put on a brave face. I was crying. I turned from Ma and walked away. I do not know how Ma got off the stove. I went upstairs and went to bed, crying in my grief. I knew then I had to get away from Ma before something worse happened. I am unable to reprocess the memory of that evening. I cried myself to sleep. How would Ma and I coexist after that confrontation? My memory is not too clear. This I do recall—after that night, I was not afraid of Ma anymore. We did not talk about what happened that night. As usual, I treated Ma with utmost respect. I obeyed. I did my chores, breaking large chunks of coal, bringing in firewood to make a fire in the old cook stove and on cool nights making a fire in the dining room stove to heat up the house overnight so in the morning Ma and her granddaughter could get up in a warm environment. Milking the cows, doing the chores was expected of me, and I did my jobs faithfully. I told some of my friends, "When school starts in September, I am going to run away. Will you help me find a place to stay where Ma can't find me?"

September did come and I did run from Ma and my friends found a place to hide me. They found me a room; it cost them five dollars a week. They put their allowances together to pay my rent, and each day they would split their lunch, saving part of their lunch to feed me.

Knowing there was nothing I could do about Ma's bullying ways, I still feared her a little. I remembered her laughter, often laughing at me, saying she didn't believe I had good sense. She would say, "I'm going to get the men in white coats to take you to the insane asylum. You need to be put away with the rest of the cuckoos."

I believed her. For years, I had been sticking pens in my arms. I slit my forearm and my wrist. I would hurt myself. I punished myself—for what reason, I don't know. I found fault with myself. I didn't like the person I was. I would sit on the floor and bump my head against the wall. Ma would say, "Keep on knocking your head against the wall, you gonna knock out what little sense you got." In my bed, I'd lie in a fetal position and rock myself to sleep. I was overweight, felt ugly, and thought I was as ugly as Ma kept telling me I was. Ma and her favorite daughter in-law would have fun making fun of me and laughing at me because of the way I looked. Ma said my nose was spread all over my face, that I looked a mess. Unloved, unwanted, nowhere to turn, I kept my tale of woes in my heart. I didn't want anyone outside the house to know what kind of life I was living. I pretended to be happy go lucky; I was the great pretender. I wanted people to think I was happy. I would go skipping down the road. I'd talk to myself and tell myself, "You are the dumbest, ugliest person in the world." When Ma started telling me how disgusting I looked, she would make me stand and look her in the face for what seemed hours. She talked to me for such a long time I would have to shift my body weight from one foot to the other time after time. I had to listen to her telling me I was brainless, dimwitted, a halfwit, had a thick skull, was not able to learn anything.

I was an unwanted dunce that had been placed in her life without her consent. Like a mushroom, one day I popped up in her life, out of nowhere. Ma and her favorite daughter-in-law had fun making fun of me throughout my childhood. I can still see them laughing, looking at me. I felt my face was disfigured. I was their joke, and they took great pleasure in making me feel stupid and ugly. I did not know how to make them love me; they had not taught me to know what to do to make them happy. It all started when I was five years old. The sad thing about Ma's degradation—I believed I was what she described me as being. I was not a human being. In those days, it was very hard for me to want to keep on living. Sometimes I acted crazy; I would make faces to make myself look even uglier than I was because it seemed to please Ma seeing me make ugly faces and looking crazy. She would say, "If your face freezes like that, you'll be a frightful sight."

The dumber I acted, the more she believed she had pegged me—just right. I was a kid with no sense. Psychologically, Ma felt I was already mentally disabled, incapable of ever leaving her side. Before I came to live with Ma, I was a brisk little kid, running and playing, full of life. I was a child full of laughter and very joyful. I was not afraid of the dark, nor was I ashamed to show my little dirty face. I would look up at people when talking to them. I was always looking up and smiling—it was my nature. I had young aunts and uncles to play with. They made me feel approved of and loved. I was playful; it showed in my mannerism.

Ma changed all that. She did not want me to have a free spirit; she wanted to dwarf my spirit, and she did. I came to the point of being numb to the feelings of approval. I felt dumb, unfit to go into society to make a living on my own. I was fearful of life. Ma thought she had made me her mental cripple, and that's the way she wanted it to be. I felt I would never find my way out of her grip. Ma would tell me I could not find my way out of a paper bag. Emotionally and educationally, she thought I could not exist without her domination, her telling me what to do and how to do it and when it must be done. She felt she had done her job well. In her sight, I was totally unfit. Depending on her was my only survival. As long as life was in her body, I would be there for her—she would see to that.

God only knew what would happen to me after Ma's death. We never talked about my inheritance or if I had any. There were times when I hoped Ma would die; I wanted so badly to get away from her. Ma used to tell me, "The Lord don't want you, and the devil wouldn't have you." I thought, *Maybe that saying goes for you too*. I thought she'll live forever just to keep dictating my life, just to keep her foot resting on my neck. I had a hate-love affair with Ma. I hated the way she treated me. I loved her. Ma was the only mother I had—what would I do without her? I needed to stay in Ma's good grace.

When I would put my arms around Ma and say, "I love you, Ma," I was hoping at least one time she'd say, "You're a good girl."

That never happened. When I would show Ma love, I so badly wanted to receive some love back. She never once showed me love. I would cry inwardly for the love I never received. I felt unwanted when Ma did not show me love; I felt she detested the sight of me because I was fat and she said I was clumsy. I was not an obese child. When I ran away, I was about 125 pounds, five feet two inches tall, but I was embarrassed and self-conscious of how I looked.

How often would I say, "I love you, Ma," she would always say, "Get out of my face. You don't mean it. Get away from me before I knock your fool head off." Ma could be brutally insensitive. She knew her words cut deeply—everyone in the house knew what Ma was capable of doing and tried to stay out of her way and in her good graces.

What Ma brought to the table of discussion was God's laws as she interpreted them. God only exercised judgment and punishment was her harsh reality of who God is. He beats you with a rod of iron and will send your souls to hell to burn in the everlasting fire with the stinking odor of brimstone. She would say, "You don't want to run into the vengeance of God." Ma's eyes were very cruel. You could not look into her eyes without feeling a threatening icy cold chill—they could speak volumes to you, making you feel defenseless before her. She did not have to say one word, just give you that look—her eyes said it all. You wanted to get out of her sight. Ma's eyes could chew you into little tiny pieces and spit your flesh to the wind. She could crush your souls with her piercing eyes, penetrating. They tore you into itty-bitty pieces. She would fling the pieces back into your face with laughter.

Ma's glare was beyond penetrating. You wanted to escape her presence, wanting to turn your back from her staring to get away from those intensely cruel cold glaring eyes. A feeling of death came over you just meeting her gaze.

I was in grade school. I always came home for lunch. I had finished eating and was running to the back door on my way back to school. Ma caught me off guard. I didn't have time to duck. She had an old round lead glass mirror that was embedded in a dark mahogany frame. She had grasped the mirror by its wooden handle; she hit me so hard across my face. When the mirror connected with my jaw, the force of the blow broke the wooden handle off the mirror. Instantly my face had swollen so big. Ma looked at me and said, "You won't be going back to school."

That afternoon, Ma kept me home from school. She did not want anyone to see me and ask, "What happened to you?" I would tell them, "My ma hit me across the face with a wooden mirror." She often told me, "One of these days, I'm going to knock your bloody head plum off your shoulders"—that day I think she really tried knocking my fool head off with the mirror.

Talk about Hitler—Ma was a Hitler. There were times she'd look at me and say, "Why are you standing around doing nothing? I ought to knock your fool head off. Get out of my sight. I can't stand the sight of you. Get out of my sight. Go find something to do." I would hear her saying under her breath, "I can't stand the sight of that young 'in. She gives me the willies—always crying at the drop of a hat. What's she crying about?" Ma often told me, "When this African and Irish blood gets stirred up, I'm hell on wheels. You'd better get out of my way. You better look out—here I come. Get out of my way. Hell is a coming."

Ma was nosy, had an opinion on what was going on throughout the neighborhood. When the mailman drove up and put mail in our box, ma would send me out to get the mail. She watched me every step of the way to see if I was going to look and see who got mail. I would hand her the mail. She'd look through it if the mail was not hers, and she wanted to know what was sealed up in the letter. She would steam the letter open and read it. If there was money in the letter, she would keep the money, seal it back. If there had been mention of money in the letter, she'd throw the letter in the old cook stove, burning it up, no evidence. No one was the wiser, they had no knowledge of what Ma was doing. She didn't care if I stood there looking, I knew better than to say anything.

When I look back at the years I spent with Ma, I am convinced she was a very insecure and unhappy person. She was miserable and wanted everyone around her to be miserable. She was a cunning slippery old soul, devising misery for others to taste. Inventing unhappiness was a game she loved to play. Ma could tell me stories about ghosts that were headless that would stand my hair on edge then say to me go upstairs, go to bed; there's school tomorrow. I would start crying.

The ghost stories were still fresh in my mind. I could see the ghosts she had been describing. They were standing there in my imagination. They were looking at me. I could see them with their heads cut off and dragging their chains across the dungeon floor. Getting my mind ready to go upstairs was hard for me to do. I stood looking into the pitch black as images danced before my eyes. I went slowly up to bed through the stairway that was engulfed in pitch blackness. Full of fear, I felt my way up every squeaking step that cried out to me.

In our old house, the stairway was very cold, barren, yielding no light. There was no electric wall switch. It was a total blackout; I could not see my hands before my face. I had to go up to my room, feel around in the darkness for a string to pull on the light.

Ma disliked all my school friends. She didn't want me to have friends. As a matter of fact. Ma never had anything good to say about anyone except herself (and Haile Selassie; she said he was the only real royalty there was. He was the emperor of Ethiopia. His lineage goes back to King Solomon and the Queen of Sheba. He was a Christian and adhered to the tenets and liturgy of the Ethiopian Orthodox Church).

One day, Ma was looking out the kitchen window. She saw a woman walking down the street. Ma said the woman was a trollop and a strumpet; she didn't know the woman but didn't like the way the woman was dressed. The lady was wearing her husband's trousers. She had his hat on. Ma laughed and said, "Look at that old woman. She looks like a drunk with those men's clothes on."

When I was out of Ma's sight, she would call me. I can still hear Ma calling my name. Once I remember her saying, "Come on in here. What you doing out there? Stop your lollygagging. Get a hustle on you—hurry it up. There is something I want you to do. Get in here—Johnny on the spot, do you hear, young lady, when I tell you to do something, come running as I speak before I knock your bloody head off. When I tell you to do something, do it right then. I want to see you jump when I speak, do you hear? Don't let me have to call you twice. Don't let it take you all day to get in here, you big old clumsy ox. You're worthless. Get on with it. You're sickening to look at. Look at your shoes, they are all ran over. I guess I'll have to buy you another pair."

In the kitchen on Saturday nights, I took a bath whether I needed it or not. In our old farmhouse, we used a round tin tub for bathing. You could not immerse your body in the tub; there wasn't room enough to sit in it, so you stood. There was a space in the kitchen near the old cook stove we used as our bathing spot. An old man in his fifties or sixties lived with us. Ma said he was a twenty-year boarder. Every time I took a bath, he would come into the kitchen to pump himself a glass of water and watched out of the corner of his eyes as I bathed.

I'd cry out, "Ma, get Mr. Lee out of here. He's looking at me." I would bend over, trying to hide my private parts from the old man's seductiveness. Ma would yell from the dining room. I can still hear her voice coming through the swinging door between the kitchen and the dining room. Ma sat every evening at the dining room table, reading the evening news paper and listening to the evening news on the radio. She would answer me, "Aw, that old man ain't thinking about you." She acted as if she didn't have a clue—that that old man was watching me bathe every Saturday night. I put up with Mr. Lee's weekly evening trips to the kitchen sink to pump himself a drink of water as he watched my naked body developing into womanhood. He tried to rape me from age five until the day I ran away from home at age sixteen. Only by the grace of God did I escape that old man's assaults.

One day I was on my hands and knees, scrubbing the back hall floor. I had to polish the floors good enough to pass Ma's white glove inspection. That day, when Mr. Lee came through the back door, seeing me in a vulnerable position on my hands and knees scrubbing the floor, his eyes did not deviate; he walked straight to me, jumped on my back, and tried to insert his penis into my body; but by the grace of God, that day God delivered me from that old man's strong grip on both my wrist.

When he noticed my breast growing, he would try to run his hand down my bosom to feel my breast. One time when Mr. Lee's hand went into my bosom, I threw hot water in his face to make him get away from me. There were times he would aggressively seize my wrists. I would struggle to loose myself from him. He has scratched me, tore the skin off my wrists, trying to keep me from freeing myself from his hold. There were times I had to punch him hard in his face. I fought him violently as if I was fighting a mad dog. I was a harden farmhand, strong as a young stallion, and I could fight like an angry bull.

It was only by the grace of God I prevailed against that old man. That old man was strong as hell. I would close my teeth together, burying them in the old man's face. I fought him hard until he gave out of breath and was glad to back away from my teeth. I dare say, "How could Ma not have ever been suspicious of that old man's attraction toward me?" I think Ma suspected all along what that old man was trying to do to me. She wanted to substitute me, sacrifice my innocence to Mr. Lee. Instead of having him bothering her for sexual favors, she was willing to sacrifice me. She would rather see him come after a child rather than have him come after her. She never let on she knew Mr. Lee was trying to molest me throughout the years of my stay in that house. She had turned a blind eye to his lewdness because she didn't want to be bothered with him.

When he was caught in the act of harassing me, he'd always made excuses as if it was my fault we were fighting. He wanted Ma to think I was a troublemaker; I was causing him to have to struggle with me. Sometimes she'd catch me struggling with the old man and say, "What's going on around here?" Right away, Mr. Lee would answer—because I could not stop crying long enough to tell my side of the story—"I was trying to show that gal how she ought to do this job." He painted my picture as if I was rebellious and out of control. He always put all the blame on me for any angry consultations I had with him while I stood crying, thinking Ma hated me. I was afraid

Ma was hating me more and more every time she caught me in a tussle with that old man.

Mr. Lee was Ma's boyfriend. As a youngster, I did not know anything about Ma and Mr. Lee's cuddling. I could not imagine in my wildest imagination seeing Ma hugging and kissing any man. I thought she was too mean to let a man get close enough to be called her boyfriend. Ma said Mr. Lee was there taking room and board—I believed her. When I think back, Ma has often said, "Watch your mouth, young lady. That old man pays the bills around here. This house belongs to him. That old man had this house when I met him." I've also heard her say, "That old man can't be trusted. He is after every skirt he sees."

Ma would beat me for protecting myself against Mr. Lee's aggressions, and all the while, she knew he was a villain and a scoundrel; he was after every woman he saw. He was bent on having his way with any female he could get his hands on. Mr. Lee tried raping me every chance he got. I would not stand still and let Mr. Lee have his way with me; I fought him off until the day I ran away from home.

Ma had two sons. Both sons, at some time or another, with their wives would come and live with Ma. Her oldest son with his wife and child lived with Ma for years because he couldn't get work. Ma's only granddaughter was raised with me. We were like sisters. She lived with Ma until Ma died. Ma showed her much love, thinking, *She is my only grandchild*. Ma's oldest son was the same age as my father and mother. He too was a scoundrel, a sex deviate. He was just as bad as Mr. Lee, maybe even worse.

He was not worth his salt. He wouldn't work; his wife worked. He was too trifling to keep a job. He thought he was God's gift to women. He thought he was good looking and a lady's man. He was a known sex maniac, a womanizer. All the family knew his reputation as a woman chaser. He had a ferocious ungoverned appetite for sexual pleasures. Like a hound dog, he would pursue any female he could get a scent of. If there was no witness to give evidence against him, he would try his luck at getting any woman he could. The females didn't come too young or too old for his aggressive sexual appetite.

I was just seven years old when he started getting the desires to sexually assault me. He saw me as an unloved child, having no parental protection. He knew I was there in his mother's house because he was the one who placed me there without asking his mother's permission to do so. Ma had no say-so in my coming to live with her. It was Ma's son's suggestion to take me from my mother and give me to his mother—a decision he alone made.

I remember having a life before I was brought to Ma. At age five, Ralph brought me from one city in Ohio to another city in the same state and placed me in his mother's home; she was my great-aunt. Ma was on vacation in another state when I was brought to her home. Ralph left me there with his younger brother, who was about twenty-three years old and single, but he had a girlfriend. The younger brother took me to his girlfriend's apartment. I remember him and I standing and knocking on a door. When a young woman opened the door, looking at him and then me, he said, "She is not mine. I did not know what else to do with her."

The woman looked at him then down at me. There I stood with a doll that had her clothes painted on her. Right away, he had told his girlfriend, "She's not mine. I didn't know what to do with her. Ralph brought her to my mother, and she's on vacation. She'll be home in a couple days. Can she stay with you until my mother comes home?"

Ma was surprised when she returned home, she found she had a five-year-old girl to raise. I don't think she was too happy to take on the job. She could not send me back. Where would she send me? No address was attached to me. Ralph had left town. Ma was in need of farmhands. She would skill me in the art of farming. In time, the situation could become very lucrative—an extra body to work her farm. Ma wanted laborers. She needed extra hands around the farm. She would train me to farm, so she kept me. Also, Mr. Lee had the right to claim me on his income tax because I was living in his house. He earned the money that bought the food I ate.

The two men that was now living with Ma liked having a little sex toy in the house. Ralph, Ma's son, fell on hard times again; he had no money and needed a place to stay, so he came to live with Ma. He knew I was there and a couple of years older than I was when he brought me to his mother. I was just ripe for the plucking. He was determined to regard me as a sex object. He did not think of me as a person; I was just a tool by which he could relieve himself. From age five to age sixteen, while I was developing into womanhood, the men of Ma's house were noticing my body changes and desiring to explore my innocence. These men thought they could take me by force—the innocence of my childhood was there for the taking, and no one would care what was happening to me. Ralph, Ma's son, was more corrupt and grizzly than old man Lee. Having Ma's son in the house was an increased risk of my being raped. He felt he could use any behavior he desired against me—no one would care. From the early age of seven or eight, Ralph saw me as a potential sex object living at his fingertips. Ralph was always trying to insert his finger or his penis into my vagina. He tried using whichever part of his body was easiest or quickest for him to use against me when and if the moment presented itself. I never wanted to be caught alone with him.

Occasionally on Saturday, Ma, with Ralph's child and his wife, whom she did not like, and her youngest son's wife, whom she did like—they would go downtown to shop. I recall one particular Saturday that will always burn in my memory. That Saturday, only Ralph and I were in the house. I was upstairs in Ma's bedroom, vacuuming her nine-by-twelve rug. The vacuum cleaner drowned out sound. I was always singing as I worked. I did not hear Ralph approaching. He sneaked up behind me. He threw both his arms tightly around me, imprisoning my arms against my body. Holding me in a secure grip, he pushed his finger into my vagina. I think he broke my hymen. Blood began to run down my legs. In pain, I screamed so loudly, crying and cursing. Later I thanked God I did not experience the pain and agony of rape. He had turned from me giving out frightening piercing inhuman hideous sounds as he descended our old staircase. These sounds were incapable of coming out of a human being—only the spirits from the pits of hell could make such sounds. He was one of them, so they could speak through him. His master, Satan, was jumping with joy while Ralph was attacking me. Ralph got his deviant orders straight from hell's chambers of torture. He carried out Satan's orders because he belonged to

Satan. He was the property of satanic powers. He was possessed. Evil owned his soul.

A few years later, I came back to Ohio to attend Ma's funeral. I was told Ma had joined church before she died. Ma died when I was nineteen years old. Ma was seventy-nine or thereabout. She died without ever revealing her age. About four years after Ma died once Ma spirit came to take me to her spiritual dwelling. Somehow her spirit connected with my spirit. I could see my spirit hovering over my body. I was waiting on Ma's spirit to reach me and take me with her. I could see Ma running down the sidewalk, looking right and left through the houses as she looked for me.

When she got to where I lived, she ran through the closed door, up the stairs without touching a step, coming into my bedroom. She got me by the hand. We both ran down the stairs and through the closed door. We crossed the street and ran down the sidewalk to the corner. At that point, we turned right and started to ascend into space. A voice spoke, saying, "When you were young, she was mean to you. You ran away. If you go with her, she may be mean to you again. You may not be able to run away."

I stopped. Ma had to keep going. She did not look back; she could not force me to go with her. I felt it was God's voice speaking to me. I returned to my body. I had been Ma's faithful, obedient servant while she lived on this planet we call Earth. Ma felt she could use me to perform duties of labor again while in her present spiritual assignment. I believe she is lacking, in need of something while in her present habitation; otherwise, why did she come after me?

There are some things we do not know about this life nor the life to come, so be wise; be increasingly diligent in the Lord's business.

Our souls transfer this life experience from one habitation to another habitation. God knew all the time what was going on in my life when I lived with Ma and the men that were living in her house. I called it the street of no return. Those days were frightening, a place of nightmares. God allowed me to go through that life experience for unseen reasons. Blessed is the name of the Lord God. My life is in his plan. He did not want me to bear the pain of being raped, so I was not raped by the men in Ma's house. They never did succeed in their attempts to ravish me. For his divine purpose, God prevented rape from happening in my life at that early age.

God gives purpose to life—he gives each one's life purpose. Whom among us have the authority to question God's reasoning? He is so high above our finding out, yet he lives in us and is one with us. That's a mystery.

Carefully considering, can we describe what happens in life and why? What happened to Job, and why was it permitted? Why was Job tested? What did it prove about his character? Satan was permitted to lay a hurting on Job, but Satan was not permitted to take Job's life. Job lived through his testing with prayer, and he worshipped God for bringing him through the nightmare that he had to live through. The evil spirits came to oppress him, trying to cause him to lose his faith. Job's faith and love for God never lost its power; it strengthened his faith.

We learn patience through forbearance. Despite the difficulties of life, know that difficulties must come to show growth in how we learn to handle our trials. We gain knowledge while developing spiritually; while we are bearing the pains of patience and of forgiveness, we grow. During our seasons of difficulties, we become the sons of God, for all God's children are tried; Jesus was tried. God's beloved goes through something and learns to forgive.

> Forgiveness is a virtue, and virtue is divine power from on high. Don't curse the test, your salvation may be wrapped in your testimony. (Revelation 12:11)

Testing is required and is very necessary for spiritual growth.

Thank God for his patience and forgiveness toward us. We too need to receive the patience of others especially forgiveness from those whom we have hurt. Become aware of the importance of treating people with kindness. Kindness, patience, and forgiveness are divine jewels; they are precious stones adorning God's kingdom.

It is hard to forgive the hurts, the cruel things others have done to us. Although years have passed, we tend to hold on to those cruel twists of fate that has been engraved into our memory. Unto this day, they may have an unconscious effect on our quality of life. However, when we are able to let go of the past and forgive—not necessarily forget but forgive unconditionally—we will lose the pain that once intruded deeply into our psyche and robbed us of our peace. God, with his love, will fill the holds that were bore into our souls by the treatment of others.

I have forgiven all those in my past for all the spiritual, mental, and physical sufferings I endured at their hands during the time my young life was under their control. I can now truly say I am free—at last, I am free. Great God Almighty, I am free to live and love.

I shared a part of my testimony, hoping it will be helpful to someone. We need to know even if there is harm going on in our lives, even if the inhumaneness is being done in secret, know that God sees all things. We are never alone in our suffering. It is being watched closely by the seeing eyes of Jesus, and he weeps over us in the presence of our God. We are living in a world of the hurting. Let's try and make the world a better place. The suffering of the innocent has always been with us. Let us keep an attitude of trust, faith, and dependence on God's mercy through his grace, for his mercy is renewed every day in the heart of man if only we believe. Blessed be the name of the Lord God Almighty. Remember, Jesus suffered for us. We too can endure, remaining firm in faith. We are buried and sealed in Christ's finished work. We are to forgive all matters of hurt, for we to are guilty debtors set free by Jesus's finished work on the cross of forgiveness.

18

He Called Me Servant

For over eighteen years, God used me in street ministry. During those years of ministry, I served as a volunteer chaplain in the original Detroit General Hospital and made the transition from the old (original) hospital to the newly built Detroit General Hospital. I also ministered in nursing homes as well as private homes. I was a standby speaker for "Sing a New Song Ministry" and a standby speaker for "Women's Aglow Fellowship." Whenever I was asked to address an assembly at a college or appear on TV to witness for the Lord, I would accept. If a church was losing its congregation and invited me and my partner to start a revival, we would do so. God gave my partner the gift of discernment and would direct her to a person that had a spiritual, physical, or financial need. She would whisper in my ear the needs of the individual. While praising God in my heart, I would approach the person, lay hands on them, and pray for the healing of their circumstances. God heard my prayers always, and he answered them. God called me to a threefold ministry—the ministries of *intercession*, the ministry of *praise* and *worship*, and the ministry of *healing*. These three ministries needed my complete dedication as a servant to Almighty God.

I was invited to minister to inmates incarcerated in the Wayne County Jail, located in downtown Detroit, Michigan. The prison ministry gave me access to many troubled souls. I listened to their testimonies, paying close to the soul crying for help. These were some of the youngest and most talented individuals you could ever hope to meet. Some were unschooled but had an innocence about them yet not completely blameless of what society was expecting from them. They want to be a part of society again, accepted without scorn of their past. These young citizens try to live out their lives in a crippled, sick, capitalism-greedy society where private corporations are making money off their imprisonment. There is so much creativity—creative talent warehoused—in our prisons for capital gain. The correctional system would do the country a tremendous justice if they turned our prison system into educational institutions. Trained individuals bring with them hope and encouragement. The prepared inmate being released back into society will bring a blessing to our society. When a member of society is returned back to us, there should be a rejoicing. People released from imprisonment should have the skilled jobs they have been trained for waiting for them.

One inmate's story remains vividly in my memory. I was studying the gospel of St. John with a twenty-five-year-old male who happened to be incarcerated in the Wayne County Jail, awaiting trial. He had been arrested and convicted twice before for the same type of crime—rape and indecent exposure appeared to be his pitfall. Now again, he is facing another rape charge. This would be his third rape conviction if convicted. In a few days, he would be going before a judge to receive an indictment. He had been in jail nine months. My job was to minister to this young man in such a way he could find solace. In his grief, he needed to meet and get acquainted with that quiet peace within himself. He needed to come to the knowledge of God's saving grace and come to believe God loved him right where he was and loved him too much to leave him in his same condition, carrying the sin load of rape in his soul. Believing Jesus died on the cross for his freedom from Satan's firm grip of sexual sin, I wanted John to come to know divine peace and love through the finished work of the cross through the blood of Jesus Christ. All John needed to do was to ask God's forgiveness, repenting, desiring to turn from sin in Jesus's name. This young man's soul's salvation was my primary concern. I wanted him to know God loved him now just the way he was but loved him so much he would not leave him in the sin he was in.

God meets us where we are and can expunge our souls from sin. With the spirit that comes forth from his eyes, he can burn out any unclean spirit within us.

This young man told me, "Last night, I asked God to deliver me from this terrible weakness that plagues me day and night, or let me die. I have no more strength left in me to fight against these demons."

These angels of darkness came unto him to occupy his life and bring destruction to his soul. Their assignment was to capture and control this young man's soul, and they were. These evil spirits were assigned to the young man before he emerged from his mother's womb. He wanted to be delivered from the pain and misery of being a rapist. He was sick and tired of having to live his life enslaved to Satan. He hated the life he was living. He realized he was being used by the power of darkness, but he did not know the way out of their powerful grip. He was tired of being in the clutches of these sexual demons; they were drawing him deeper and deeper into their domination and their spiritual filth. These dominating spirits were using their supernatural powers on John. They had the ability to overrule the young man's will by opposing him with their continuous battering.

John knuckled under their abusive hammering and was submitting to their controlling force. He wanted to stop their attacks against him but felt powerless under the death grip they had over his life. He dreaded their demonic visitation and desperately feared their retribution if he did not obey. They would torment him day and night until he submitted to their will. He told me these evil spirits would come to him as often as seven times in a day. After inflicting torment on him all day, they would jump on him during the night until they twisted and wrenched his endurance. His ability to think straight had diminished. His mind so clouded from the lack of rest. He was in no shape to fight back. His thinking was distorted—warped, blind sighted by fear of their satanic powers, believing they would never go away. The devil would not permit him sleep until they had indulged their appetite for the tasty taste of sexual sin was satisfied.

This particular day, he told me, "Last night, I told God, 'If you can't heal me, kill me. I don't want to live like this any longer. If I can't stop my sexual activity, I want to die.'" He talked to God with a repenting heart, humbled by sin and full of sorrow and shame; he called out to God to show mercy and deliver him out of the hands of these spirit creatures from hell. He did not realize he had enhanced his struggle in spiritual warfare by asking God to enter into the battle. The war was on. His spiritual warfare has been brought to God's camp because this young man put his plight in God's hands. God is able to destroy all our enemies as he so wills in his timing.

We are to cast our cares upon him, for he cares for us. Let the war games begin. The Bible tells us to fight the spirit with the spirit, and that's what John was doing when he asked God to come into his life and to help him.

That day when our visit was over, something supernatural happened. God showed his presence was with us. When our study period had come to an end, the young man, as always, called for a guard to come and take him back to his cell block. He stood in silence at the iron gate, waiting for a guard to come and fetch him. While he was waiting, he leaned back against the concrete wall. I was sitting on a small iron bench that was bolted to the concrete floor. I was facing the jail's wide corridor, looking through the iron bars, waiting for a guard to remove the inmate.

From the corner of my eye, I could see a small angel, about the size of an open hand, coming through the concrete wall on my left. The angel was dressed in a long white flowing gown that went down to its feet. The angel had long flowing white hair and moved quickly past my face to the young man that was leaning against the opposite wall to my right. I saw the angel enter into the forehead of this young man. God allowed me to see this divine spiritual impartation. I give God all the glory, for all the glory belongs to the Lord. I knew then God had answered this young man's prayers. God had let my eyes see an angel entering into the forehead of this young man. I took it as confirmation, confirming this young man had been freed from the spirit of rape. I told him, "Young man, you are no longer a rapist. You are a reborn child of God. The Spirit of God has just entered your forehead." John had not seen the angel of God, nor did he feel the angel enter his forehead.

As I think over what God had permitted me to witness the day an angel sent by him, on an assignment to enter into a young man's being, that young man stood in a prison cell, unaware of the presence of God. God let me watch this angel carry out its assignment of communication, an answer to John's prayers through impartation of the Holy Spirit. I witnessed a miracle, the divine work of Almighty God in action—his angelic being carrying out the divine will of Almighty God.

> Lo, the heavens were opened unto him, and
> he saw the Spirit of God descending *like* a dove,
> and lighting upon him. (Matthew 3:16)

Had I been standing there that day with the others, under the open sky, looking up from a distance, would that little angel, with its flowing white gown and its long flowing white hair, appear to me to be a flying white dove? God said he is the God of all ages. The God of yesterday, today, and forevermore, he is the same God. He never changes. The Father is still giving assignments to his angelic beings. They are still on their job, ascending and descending from heaven to earth. The power of God is alive today as it was that yesterday—a long time ago and for all the tomorrows that are still to come. God's work on earth is not done. He is not finished with us yet. He is still handing out assignments in answer to our prayers.

Relish these words. Know that the harvest is plentiful, but the laborers are desperately few. Obeying God during our struggles is key. Struggles hold secrets to everlasting life. Obedience to God is the way to keep growing in a deeper fulfillment of purpose. Obeying God shows our spiritual strength. The strong level of love we have for him shows in our obedience to his will—obeying, having trust and a dependency on his Word, believing in his faithfulness.

There is an inner eye at the center of our being placed in us before we came into this world. This spiritual eye is equipped to perceive the activity of every thought. The all-seeing eye is a life force we cannot get away from—not in this life nor in the life to come. This spiritual eye influences our being. Its assignment is a link between right and wrong. Although we continually fight against the Holy Spirit guidance, it will continuously be with us because it's embedded in the mind of the individual.

God will never leave us nor forsake us. Know there is always a spiritual being watching over us. We can run from God, but we cannot hide from him. No matter how far or fast we run nor how far we may fall—he is already there, waiting to soften our fall. Be still and look within. God's love is mind-blowing, immeasurable. I am convinced love is not to be measured; we can't put a cap on love. His love is the secret weapon holding our fragile world together. Love and life always respond to one another through the Creator.

Throughout life, we will come to realize more and more our words matter. They are substance, affecting both the giver of the words and the receiver of them. Love can start a ripple effect that can spread through the world. The spiritual rim is affected by our behavior more than we have the ability to grasp. Spiritually we are what we speak when we speak from the heart. The day will come when our enlightenment will be opened, our true self will be revealed, that hidden self must show itself—oh, what a time that will be when we are exposed to who we really are.

Psychologically speaking, we should take inventory of our words before we spit them out for the whole world to deal with. Think of the damage words have caused. Is our tongue our friend, or is it a foe to all mankind? The tongue is a wonder, a powerful instrument, and could be used to encourage, bring hope, spread love throughout the world. Tame the tongue. Let it be used as a meaningful tool of blessing. As we bless, we too are blessed. Our lives will spring up before us in new birth.

This world has become environmentally toxic and is an endangerment to this generation's health and the health of generations to follow. God knows exactly why he is allowing man to be so destructive. One day God will show us the answers to our questions. God is saying, "See only me. Focus on my love, not the surrounding storms that occur on earth's surface. Timing is everything. I will interrupt the storms in due time," sayest the Lord. Faith in God's love is our strength. Our empowerment depends on our faith as we wait upon the Lord. Share the good news of the Gospel, proclaiming the excellency of the kingdom's message of salvation. Love is the only way to eternal survival. To live forever with the Creator, we must live in love.

Say to the Father God Almighty, "I will serve thee, Father, in this world and in the worlds to come." When God tells us to do something, be faithful and do it with joy. When answering his call, answer it joyfully that is pleasing to the Lord. When we are not obedient, we are unyielding and stubborn, the Bible calls it being stiffnecked. If the Holy Spirit cannot persuade us to obey the will of God by wooing us to comply, God will get someone else to do the job he intended us to do. I've been there, and I regret it to this day.

One Sunday in church, God wanted me to lay hands on a woman standing at the altar; he wanted to heal her. I thought, *What will people think?* She went to the altar for the preacher to pray for her healing. I was afraid to obey. I felt the power of God swelling my right hand until it pained. Still I did not move. I knew people would think, *Who does she think she is?* I've asked God's forgiveness for the fear that gripped me. I ask forgiveness for my disobedience more times than you can imagine. I know I am a forgiven soul, yet for years, I kept asking forgiveness for that moment of disobedience. I am so sorry I did not obey his prompting, the wooing of the Holy Spirit.

I would love to be given that assignment once again. I feel I am stronger, but I know I would need his help for whatever he asks me to do. That day it was fear that held me back, kept me from obeying God. I pray no more is fear part of my life; let my fear be replaced by faith. Lord, you strengthen Peter. You never stop loving him for denying you. After that, Peter lived all his life for God. He sacrificed himself to bring God glory. At the end of his days, he hung upside down on the cross to show he was not worthy to die in the same position on the cross as his Master Jesus Christ.

Day by day, we need the Lord to strengthen us in every way. I thank you, Lord—you did not cast me away in my disobedience. You have kept me through all my faults. I've always been a long way from perfection; imperfections appeared to walk beside me, yet you hear and harken unto my prayers. Thank you, Lord Jesus. I am covered, sealed with the shed blood of the Lamb of God. Jesus, the only begotten Son of God, is my strength. Jesus has done a finished work on the cross for all my sin. Jesus has taught me to have endurance in season and out of season. I call unto God's presence that resides deep within my being. He hears and answers my prayers.

He never sleeps nor does he slumber. He's the watchman on the wall of my soul. I give him praise and glory for resurrected life. Thank God I will never have to live this life again.

19

Divine Plan

The constant flow of divine nourishment to the soul will give greater life and understanding to all that yield to its supernatural strength. Experience the pruning away of sinful elements clinging, trying to enter the soul. You must experience the flourishing faithfulness of God, showing his divine relationship with our souls. Think of what Jesus went through in his obedience to the will of his Father. Despite the unwanted pain of pruning away the undergrowth of sin, that must be pruned to remove all undesirable spiritual growth from the branches of life that we may bear greater fruit as we walk this journey into the newness of life. We need God's perpetual care to remain resilient and stay strong in our faith walk. We need to live an existence that does not change nor diminish our loyalty to God. Our old man is not dead; he is only dying. We keep feeding him with our fleshly desires, so we have to try and bury him again and again. He keeps resurrecting because we keep feeding our old man the flesh. We should always be on guard, watching and examining our thoughts. Are they from the old man or the new man? Where are our thoughts coming from? Where are they leading? Let us put God in the forefront of our minds, asking God to be our vanguard, guiding, leading us through all life's challenges. If we face the coming years in strong faith, not doubting but leaning on Jesus, who is our safety net, we will find that life is worth living in his embrace.

Practice and honor the principles of love through faith in God's Word. Through prayer and forgiveness, we tap into God's gift of learning how to give of self. God is the power that gives and keeps on giving through love a gift that is thriving through us to others by his grace.

We can enjoy the sense of being grounded in faith even when the world is spinning out of control all around us by every ill wind that is blowing.

Accept our spirituality, the sensitivity of our divine attachment to the nature of God. Our religious values will make a statement about who we really are. Our acceptances of self will show our character, our mental stability, and insight into who our inner man belongs to—does he belong to God, or does he belong to the world? Concerning the works of our inner man, our spirit man, the Almighty seeks to bring him through human life with a deeper relationship concerning the will of God. Learn to be still, listen, and heed the whisperings of divine wisdom as it whispers to our souls. Many times we ignore the voice coming from within. We call it our first mind or our second mind. Pay attention to the quietness of the soul when it speaks softly into our being. The Holy Spirit will urge, direct, but not force his divine will on us. The Holy Spirit is our defender in the time of battle. Don't resist him. He lives within our being for God's glory.

Make time to volunteer, to enrich someone's life. There is no better way to nourish our spirit of love than to lift the spirits of others. Remember, unforgiveness is a disease coming from hell's laboratory that brews the fermentation of hostility, hate, and unforgiveness. Unforgiveness is not of God. Kindness is a good medicine. It nourishes the soul and puts a smile on the face of God.

Whenever we do a favor, do it wholeheartedly, no hesitation. Be earnest in all that we do. Never be lukewarm when giving kindness to others. When the need comes, be sympathetic with understanding. Most of us have a story that needs to be told. Listen to what others have to say; give an ear of compassion and understanding to every man especially when we are supposed to be helping them enjoy a better life. We are to let people know that we are concerned and sensitive to what is happening in their lives. Ask what has made them fearful, feeling like they no longer have any control over their affairs.

Give them an ear—hear what they are really trying to tell us. Try to understand what they are going through. Be a blessing; a little smile may be the gift they needed. Showing a little empathy, the kindness we give away may come back to rest on us someday.

The wages, the cost, the price of holding onto resentment blocks our true happiness, giving us a payoff of heavyheartedness. Resentment keeps divine light from flowing through to our inner man's prosperity and growth. Divine light gives infinite life to our innermost being. Remember how important it was for us to feel God's forgiveness for our past? Should we be committed to forgiving those who have hurt us and maybe still hurting us, show them the same mercy we would like to receive from God?

May God's love always shine through us whenever we interact with others. Practice no criticism; we all have our faults. We all stand in need of being understood and forgiven, for we all have sinned and came short of the glory of God. Purpose is the reason for our earth journey. We must find our purpose and get into it. Each of us are unique. There is not another person on earth that is exactly like who we really are. You are priceless and uniquely made. You are special in God's sight, particularly critiqued in God's image, and we should be a representation of God's love.

Love is essential to life. Practice the gift of love. Don't let this God-given gift lie dormant. We are to show love and compassion to the world. It is the will of God that love flourish luxuriously throughout all creation. God's love is flourishing—look around, take it in, and enjoy the ride. See the love in the way animals protect their young. Watch mama bear; see her loving protection when danger comes near her little ones. We also have that built-in capacity to love and be concerned for the welfare of others. Accept God's great gift of love and watch it as it works for our betterment. Don't leave such a precious gift as love in a suspended state of automation hanging on the nothingness of life. There is a starving world out there starving from the deficiency of love. We will give an account for neglecting love—such an esteemed gift of God. It is our earthly duty to show love to one another. Ask God to awaken our souls to his divine will that we may learn to love our fellowman as the Father has loved us unconditionally. Be quick to show kindness; it draws spiritual healing, which is so important to our physical, mental, and spiritual health.

Some describe their emotional need dwindling until they let go of a toxic relationship. Getting freedom from a bad relationship illustrates mental strength and reduces the stress that has caused mental and physical health issues. The need to free ourselves is crying out, telling us separation is the way out. Look inward. Our hearts are packed with the treasury of God's gifts from life's hard-earned, hard-learned, inconceivable wisdom that lives within each of us, wherein infinite immeasurable love grows and awaits to be set free. Can you hear love calling out, "Set me free. Turn me loose. I've got work to do."

Stop, think, recognize the magnificent adventure of aging. Our life is a story book of the many choices we made. What a glorious gift it is to be able to write out the story we have lived.

With every breath we breathe, dear Lord, give us the power to choose good over evil. In our conscious mind and in our unconscious mind, let goodness reign. May wisdom from on high be our guide, leading us to choose the path paved in holiness. (Be holy as I am holy, sayest the Lord.) Holiness leads to eternal life. What is holiness? Obedience to God is holiness. Our obedience shows our love to God. Holiness is wrapped in obedience.

The Bible said each of us has been given a measure of faith. Let us use our measure of faith to its fullest potential, bringing glory to Almighty God. When God commits a talent to our care, he wants valid return. Remember the story of the talents of gold and silver in the Bible? The owner of the vineyard gave talents to be invested for him. Some workers used their talent more wisely than others. They brought back profits. One man buried his talent, afraid to engage with life's risky unpredictable investment market. We too are to be profitable, for we are workmen. Winning souls for God's kingdom is our great investment in future life. Believers should always be in the soul-winning business, investing the Word of God into the world, working, reaping, bringing in the harvest from the fields of sin, for the kingdom of God is at hand. There is no time to waste; it is later than we think. Now is the season for gathering and reaping so that the harvest may be plentiful and wisely used. Our God-given gifts are to be used for the enlargement of his kingdom.

Life's most-sought-after element, in the human experience, is to reach the pinnacle of God's inner peace. It abides patiently within his children. The fundamental desire in man's heart is to walk in peace. Man longs for peace. When we have no doubt of a better life to come, we stand on the solid ground of faith, believing God's Word is for today. Where there is no doubt in our belief of a better life to come, then there is no pursuit of haunting shadows bringing us despair. Unbelief is the darkness of despair. Never doubt the existence of God nor his love for us. If we doubt (we are skeptics), how can a doubter achieve true inner peace? If we are uncertain in our faith about God's faithfulness, what then is there to look forward to? Through faith, we gain heaven as our reward. Faith is the substance of things hoped for, the evidence of things not seen. We say we believe there is a God; the devils also believe and tremble when they think of him. The devil know they cannot possess heaven, yet they have enough sense to tremble at God's power. Some of us will not tremble at God's awesome power. When we are in the business of satisfying the flesh, some will forget to show respect to God's will. (Read James 2:19.)

We are spirit beings living in a physical human state of existence. We are not free from the human consciousness nor its unconsciousness. We have two spirits assigned to us at birth. Both spirits are working in our presence. These spirit beings are able to live within or without our being. Some of us live with the awareness of their presence, knowing they are always crouching nearby. God and Jesus are within us—Satan is not. He's the one crouching, standing nearby, waiting for a chance to transgress our souls and dishonor them, bringing to shame God's children. Our lives, our decisions are greatly influence by spiritual beings. We are to live in a prayerful state of mind. We are not the only intelligence inhabiting this planet. Unseen intelligence has a great effect on human behavior. There are ministering spirits assisting and attacking the mind of mankind, whispering into our consciousness day and night. There are guardian spirits (angels) sent by God to protect and support us, strengthening us when necessary from unseen spiritual danger as well as physical danger.

Many of us are enraged with life, confused, even frightened by the many disastrous events that are taking place in what we call our space, where we are living our lives. After every storm has faded away, there is a calm, a tranquility. The unrest has passed. Hope is being restored. God is providing a peace as we begin knitting our fractured lives back together. My beloved, storms will come. They are a part of life's journey. They are our passageway to greater life. Did Jesus go through something on the cross? Was that not a stormy time in his earth life while he was giving himself for us?

When we live a life of service, the giving of oneself, working with and for others will help us avoid times of self-pity. When situations get stressful in our lives, look for an opportunity to help others. We will get our minds replenished through reaching out to others. Pay attention to how others deal with the horrors of life. Working with and for others helps us to keep a pleasing disposition because our mind is no longer just on ourselves. We should learn how to give of ourselves without overcommitting and getting resentful to the point Satan can come in and say, "You are doing far too much for others, more than they are deserving of. They don't appreciate you. Stop it. You deserve to keep all your stuff, and all that time you are giving away, you could be using it on yourself." God gave his Son. Can we inconvenient ourselves and give a little of our time to someone else?

Vanquish the nonredemptive imaginations that cause extreme imaginary visions on the mind and can never be a part of our real life. We are to see only the life we would like to have for our betterment. Work and live toward a godly end. We are to anticipate only good coming to us. God will bless us and make us a blessing to others.

Our five senses give us the ability to confront truth. Ask God to help us confront his truth. We are to perceive our purpose, our responsibilities in life. Take charge of them; we have purpose. We were not put on earth just to do the boogie-woogie day and night; God wants us to understand we have accountability to him and to our fellowman. We are not an island unto ourselves. We were given purpose in this life. We are to find our purpose and get into it.

Every day of our human existence, we are determining where we will spend eternal life. We have the choice of two kingdoms. Our behavior will choose which kingdom we will spend eternity in. One kingdom is for the saved souls; the other kingdom is for the damned souls. Which of these kingdoms is our behavior choosing? If sin is motivating our lives, we are working toward the kingdom of the damned. Our lives mirror our souls. O my soul, awaken to the light that is revealing the extensive anointing power of God and is flowing through my being because of the life I have chosen to live.

Through the Holy Spirit, our loving Father desires to work through those who love him and are willing to work with him. The Holy Spirit is the gift of God through Jesus Christ. Jesus told his disciples, "I am going away. I will pray to the Father, and he will send you another comforter—the Spirit of Truth. He will come to you and will live in you and be with you always." Impartation of the Holy Spirit is the placing of the power of the Holy Spirit into our innermost being, creating a new man, giving us new life through Jesus our savior.

God's breath gives us life. The soul is that part of us that will never die; it's the breath of God. The soul is incorporeal existence. The soul is the real spark of life indwelling man. The intangible living breath of God came to dwell in man. Death is described as the soul departing from the body, causing the body to become void of life. The body goes back to the dust from which it came and, eventually, fading into nothingness. The soul lives forever; it goes back to the God that gave it. The body of flesh without God's breath has no value. Its support system is gone. What remains will soon vanish.

> And the Lord God formed man of the dust of the ground, and breathed into his nostrils the breath of life: and man became a living soul. (Genesis 2:7)

> God said, "Let us make man in our image, and our likeness." (Genesis 1:26)

Man was created in both the image and likeness of God. An image may be similar but not necessarily identical to its original. The likeness is used as a gauge of comparison. When man fell (into sin), he retained an impaired image of God. Regaining a likeness of God is one of the accomplishments of our salvation. Our spiritual likeness is restored in justification. Our character likeness is being continuously developed in the process of sanctification. We will be like Christ when we get our glorified body. When Jesus returns for his people, he shall change our vile bodies that it may be fashioned like unto his glorious body. The power by which God is able to subdue all things to himself is the same power that raised Jesus from the dead—to know him and the power of his resurrection, according to the divine spiritualization of God's workings, whereby he is able to subdue all things unto himself and to transform believers to new life in him.

20

Death Is a Comma, Not a Period

Death is not a period. It's not the period that ends who we are. Death, as we know it, is only an end to a body of flesh made from the elements taken from the earth. Death is a projection projecting us into the greater life we must obtain. Flesh had a death sentence before it was formed in the womb. When the life-giving intelligence and energy of the egg and the sperm engaged, the mammal's flesh begins to develop. The days of flesh were created to be few. The life of the flesh is much like the petals that form the flowers; they were born to have a short earth appearance. Their few days bring great pleasure to God, for they are functioning in their purpose. Death, as we understand it, is not inflicted on our totality. We are three-dimensional beings—breath, spirit, and flesh. Let's be clear—death is only a period to our flesh. Flesh is only the visible dimension of man, the dimension of man we are capable of touching. Our flesh came from the dust of this planet, and what the dust produces nourish and maintain our lives because we are one. We came from the dust of this planet we call Earth. We are returning back to the earth daily through our consumption of earth's vegetation, by eating and depositing the digested eliminations back to earth.

The human body is very restricted in its limitations. This body of flesh is a temporary residence for the spirit and the soul. Our spiritual being is intangible form we are not capable of seeing. The spirit will live on and does not need an earthly residence in order to keep functioning. In time, our human state of being will fade away like the floating mist floating into nothingness. Only the soul and spirit will live forever. The soul is the eternal breath of God; it is unending.

Whatever relates to earth life are things we are able to see and touch. They are temporal, and in time, they will diminish from sight. Even the sequence of time, as we know time, is temporal. Flesh's appearance has been given an allotted amount of earth time. Each passing moment, our assigned appearance on this earth is running out of time. The body of flesh was not built for an unending existence—thank God for that. God's eternal plan is always in full operation. Our spirits must be set free to go on their journey that is without end. Flesh was created for a purpose—that is serving God's eternal plan. Our period on planet Earth speaks only to the physical, flesh to flesh, eyeball to eyeball you might say; our external appearance is only necessary while we trod this planet. Our flesh body is living in the only world it was created to function in. We are to come to understand, find our purpose while living in this human form. This life is the only life we as humans know and understand. It is the only life we are allowed to remember. There is more to our being than we comprehend. We will let go of flesh in order to attain the greater life that is awaiting us. We ought to be very concerned about our decision making while on this earthly journey; our decisions eternally define us. When we reach the other side of the comma (*death*), we will, through eternity, have to face the decisions we are making. We are now living between the comma and the period of our earth's appearance.

While living in the physical, we are functioning in two totally different worlds. We are communicating in both the spiritual and the physical worlds. I know there are many that do not believe there are two coexisting worlds operating in our lives. We are governed by a two-world system, both having the authority to challenge man's free will. The spiritual and the physical existence defy and confront each other; they bring completion to who we really are as God-fearing beings. God created humanity to be engaged in his work ethic. He sends angels to walk among us to help us to overcome the works of the devil.

God formed our temporal body from the dust of the earth. This form lay lifeless on the ground. God desired friendship with his image. God gave the form life so that they could have communication. They would walk and talk in the garden God had planted for food, and God explained to Adam what he should not take to eat.

The human being, in time, will speak out, saying, "I was once young. Now I am old." Our bodies react to time. Our spirits defy time because it is one with eternity where there is no time. The Bible tells us God knew us before the foundation of the earth was laid. The spirit houses the soul. The soul entered the dust form that laid lifeless on the ground in the garden that laid east of Eden. The dust received the breath of God and became a living being. God walked and talked with the being; he named him Adam. In the cool of evening in the garden east of Eden, God would call to Adam, and they would walk together through the beautiful garden east of Eden.

Are our lives reflecting souls that are unfed? Are our souls living in a desert place? There is an unseen fire burning within the soul of man—feed that fire. Let not our souls go starving, thirsting, consumed by the lack of divine knowledge, leaving the soul dress in pain, scantily clothed in truth, naked because it has no acquaintance with the Word of God. His word is our covering. There is power—wonder-working power in the living Word of God. God's Word is alive and on the job. God is faithful to keep his promises—trust, obey, walk with him, and when he tells us to do something, do it right away without complaining.

> If I shut up heaven that there be no rain, or if I command the locusts to devour the land, or if I send pestilence among my people: *Keep the faith, then*... If my people, which are called by my name, shall humble themselves, and pray, and seek my face, and turn from their wicked ways; then will I hear from heaven, and will forgive their sin, and will heal their land. (2 Chronicles 7:13–14)

> But his word was in mine heart as a burning fire shut up in my bones, and I was weary with forbearing, and I could stay. (Jeremiah 20:9, *he kept the faith*)

> "For I know the thoughts that I think toward you," saith the Lord, "thoughts of peace, and not of evil, to give you an expected end. Then shall ye call upon me, and pray unto me, and I will hearken unto you. And ye seek me, and find me, when ye shall search for me with all your heart." (Jeremiah 29:11–13)

Only God can give man the grace he needs to endure to the end. If we walk by faith in a sacred way, being in obedience is the way we will come into harmony with his will. "If you love me, you will obey me," says the Lord.

Can we remember that defining moment when God turned our lives around for his glory? Could it have been when we came to understand that salvation was through Jesus Christ's finished work on the cross? Jesus the greatest debunker of evil? Pray to receive wisdom from on high to face the challenges that will come as we journey toward our eternal home. Believe prayer has great value, knowing that prayer should be divinely inspired. See your prayers approaching the presence of God, and see the Father as he receives them unto himself. Prayer is divine communication with our heavenly Father; it brings him great pleasure as his children talk with him and listen to his voice.

Showing humility as we live life can be hard for some, letting go of pride and becoming as little children in the eyes of God. There is a division between ego and humility. Submitting, yielding oneself to another is hard. Humbleness is God's priority and is a must do for his children. Pridefulness is why Satan was kicked out of God's heaven. We all need freedom from the spirit of pride (being all puffed up, thinking we're so such a much).

God hates pride. "Pride comes before the fall." We are to give God credit for all our good fortune. Don't say, "Look what I did all by myself. I am self-made." We are colluding with the devil when we make that kind of statement. We are not to leave the Lord God out of our equation of life. When adding up all our good fortune, give God his glory. God is affecting every complex element in life. Give him credit, for he is due all credit and all the glory belongs to him. God said, "No flesh will glory before me."

From the bosom of our Father God came Jesus Christ, his Son, to rescue mankind. He came from heaven to earth to shed his blood and die for our sin. Jesus walked in humility, showing us the way to his Father's heart. Jesus spoke to us only what he heard the Father speak. His innocence made him worthy to be offered up for our sin; he did not try to defend himself from the shame of death on the cross. He was judged by insincere sinful men who made a mockery out of the courts of justice. He died among the guiltiest of men; those who found no guilt in him put him to death. Our Lord was crucified, hung high upon a tree for mankind's sin. His journey was not in vain. Salvation has come unto us through his shed blood, a free gift for whosoever will let him come and drink freely from the well of salvation.

Let us awaken from our slumber and sing unto the Lord a new song of hope and joy. Dark days will come, but the Lord is living among us—whom then shall we fear, knowing God is with us? Let us deliver unto the Lord genuine prayers in faith. Doubt is not a spirit from God. Doubt comes to us from the kingdom of darkness. We will be tempted by the devil and enticed by the world's system. Hold on. God is not finished with us yet. Be an overcomer, for the Lord is with you.

Remember, Jesus is the light that gives life. There is no darkness nor was there found any spots in him. Jesus is the only true light that brings eternal life to men.

Let us be an inspiration to one another, drawing from our internal love deposits, and spread his joy and kindness to the world. We are laborers of the Lord. Focus on the things pleasing to God. There are missions waiting for our prayers and our hands to come to their aid. There is nothing like the supernatural gifts of God that he gives his people when they stand in unity of faith through the Holy Spirit. We have been grafted, spiritually pulled into the family of Almighty God by faith in Jesus's finished work, a work designed by God for our salvation.

Our new heavenly bodies will look much like our earthly bodies but will be endowed with life everlasting, fashioned like unto his glorious body. Our appearance will undergo an outward transformation with the effervescence of youth glowing through us. We will move at the speed of light. We will be forever healthy and energetic. We will sparkle brilliantly—brighter than the celestial stars.

We will experience an inward transformation—a new perfect nature—like unto our Lord and Savior Jesus the Christ. Come, draw from the promises of God. The Lord wants us to let the Holy Spirit guide our way to and through his will for our lives. The Holy Spirit is the working will of Almighty God working through us for his glory. We are to give the Holy Spirit dominance over our lives by letting him show the way to God's will.

Death is not the period we think it is; it's a punctuation mark in our continued existence somewhere else. The comma is a break, a pause within the life of our earth sentence. We are living in the comma. The period only ends our earth's existence. We must escape this present life for an eternal life assignment that is awaiting our arrival. Death predicates, expresses, and affirms a change has taken place in our existence. Our spiritual passage from one life to another life induction did take place. Our assignment to human life was only for a short length of time much like the flowers of the earth. Spiritual life may present itself in cycles, reoccurring to reflect life as God so wills. They say our lives' history will open before us when we are leaving this earth, flashing before us like a dream. A comma is a punctuation mark, not death; the soul and the spirit will live on. The period makes complete the whole sentence to life as we know it; we are now on a new journey. The comma applies to spiritual freedom, letting us know we have more life to be lived on the other side of the comma. We have no period. There is the beginning of new life. When the time has come, fly with me. We have life yet to explore in the kingdom of our Father.

21

My Journey in a Coma

I had an out-of-body experience; I would like to share it with you. I found myself in a tunnel. I don't remember entering this tunnel or my journey to this place. I was running. I remembered being so tired. When I came to the realization, I felt as if I had been running at a rapid speed for a very long time. I did not want to go on any further; I was exhausted. The realization of what was happening in that moment was strange. Was I fleeing from something, or was I fleeing to something? I could not see anyone. I do not know when I had started running or why I kept running. What was I running from? I asked myself. I knew I was running and looking to see if there was anything else in this big hollow space.

I wanted to see signs of life—any movement would do. I kept running faster than I had ever ran. I could not stop running and looking and wondering about this unfamiliar place. I was on my way somewhere, on a journey to where I did not know. I realized I was tired enough to drop to the ground and never move from the spot. I was drained of strength. My feet had gotten so heavy I could hardly put one foot before the other. I knew I could not go on much longer. It seemed I was running through a grayish misty unending tunnel shaped like a cloud, and I was in its belly. I did not see any signs or hear anything indicating life. I was thinking I am all alone.

"Perish the thought," a voice came to me; through this foggy, dense light, someone had spoken. Out of nowhere, from the grayness that was surrounding me in this hollow structure, came a voice that echoed in the silence. How was I hearing this voice? Where was it coming from? *Who is there?* I thought. I sensed this presence knew I was coming and was there, waiting for my arrival. It was there to encourage me to keep going. The voice seemed to know how tired I was and wanted me not to give up. I felt it understood the nature of my journey. This intelligence knew who I was.

As I ran, I realized I could see myself. I was observing myself outside my body. I was shorter in stature. My size seemed unimportant. I was moving at such a rapid rate of speed, like a bird on the wing, running as if being chased by hell's fire. I kept running as if my life depended on my ability to get where I needed to be and be there on time. I did not ask myself, "Why can't you stop running like the winds are pushing you without mercy?" I just kept running, and my eyes kept searching the enclosure. It seemed I had been running a lifetime. I was thoroughly tired—worn to nothingness and at the point of collapsing.

I said to myself, "I am going to give up. There is no end in sight." I had been looking straight ahead as I ran. I could see I was surrounded by the dull grayness of the tunnel walls. I can't make it any further. My limbs are too tired to keep moving on, yet I ran. As I ran, I kept looking at the endless tunnel walls. I thought, *To keep on going makes no sense, but if I stop, then what?* I kept looking into the dark grayness that enclosed me to see if I could find a way out or even understand the situation I was in.

I looked up. Seeing through the dimness, there was a break in the cloudlike tunnel. I could see the sky. There were people out there. They were many, many people above the tunnel lying flat on their backs. They were outside the tunnel, free to travel. They seemed to be asleep. *They are resting throughout eternity,* I thought.

I cannot go on any further. I've given my best efforts—that's it. I am going up there and join them and get some rest. I'm so tired; I too want to float throughout eternity. I could see their faces as they lay stretched out on their backs; it seems as if they were lying on some invisible support. Their clothes stayed in place. The winds did not blow their clothing about as they travel, floating effortlessly. They were asleep, looking angelic and peaceful. I thought I will join them. I would like to be in that restful state of existence. I'm so tired. I was so worn out from running, I was extremely anxious to rest. I wanted to become as peaceful as they looked to be. I would join them and float throughout eternity. I felt so weary—too weary to move one more step. I was about to surrender to the mystery of the tunnel, give up, stop running. The hopes of floating with the sleeping souls, who were dressed in long white gowns—it was very appealing to my weary soul.

I no sooner got the thought than again I heard the hidden voice say, "There is light at the end of the tunnel." The voice had power to instantly increase my energy, renewing my strength. I was strengthened, given the power to keep running, and I sped off like I had hind feet; I had been given the swiftness of a young stallion, and I was on my way (Psalm 18:33). The voice had promised light at the end of the tunnel. I ran until a light came into view. I could hear voices. My eyes opened. I was in the recovery room—back on earth and in the flesh. I could hear and see. All my senses were working as they did when I was in the spirit and was running through the tunnel.

It seemed as if more than one person was handling me. They were throwing me around, handling me roughly, and there was nothing I could say or do. I tried to say, "Stop being so rough with me," but I could not talk. I wanted to defend myself. I was young and ready for a good fight, but I did not know where I was, and I could not figure out what was going on. I was helpless to respond, and my eyes had closed. They had taken me from the recovery room to a regular room. They were trying to put me in bed. The bed they were putting me in was broken. The head of the bed could not be raised. There I would lie flat on my back until I slid into a coma.

Silently I lay, unable to move—for how long, I do not know. I had no strength. I found it impossible to find the power to move any part of my body.

There were times when I had realization; I became conscious, but no one knew when I was conscious. I know people say, "Don't talk around a person in a coma. They can hear you." That was not always the case with me. I could only hear when I was in a state of consciousness. I was in and out of consciousness. At times, I realize I was just lying still. I would try with all my might to move some part of my body, but I could not. I understood I needed to be communicating. When someone came to my bedside and I happen to be in a conscious state, try as I may, I could not speak nor move. I could hear them talking and understood what they were saying. I even tried wiggling my little finger and found I could not. Every time I became conscious, I was afraid of being taken to the hospital morgue. I did not like the thought of being put into the freezer and frozen to death. The thought consumed me.

At times, when conscious, I would try desperately to lift my legs. I remember trying so hard again and again to move one leg. I could not. I wanted somehow to show those around me I was still alive. It seemed my legs had been placed into iron braces; they were so heavy. I could not raise one of them an inch to let people know I was alive—death had not claimed me—but I could not vibrate a whisper. I could send no signals that I was entrapped in my body. However, I did not give up trying to show signs of life. I felt my life was in a cage, trapped, and could not get out of its entrapment.

At times someone would be working on me. I listen to what they were saying. There were times people were standing near my bed. I felt as if they were looking at me, thinking, *She is dying*. I could not see them with my physical eyes. I had the power to form a mental picture of them looking at me. I knew no one had any knowledge of my fears of being put into the freezer and being frozen to death. My fears had built, and there was nothing I could do about it.

One day, my doctor and his nurse were doing something to me. I felt the doctor had a sharp instrument and stuck me in the foot with it.

I heard the nurse cry out, "Oh no."

"She didn't feel that," the doctor replied.

I knew he had done something that should have hurt. I feel he wanted to get a reaction out of me. I had not felt anything. Still I wanted to tell him, "Don't do that to me again." I felt helpless. I lack power to speak, to move, to reveal life.

My struggle with the will to live was overwhelming, and the forces that held me prisoner was very powerful. My situation was beyond my power to show life was still in my body. How can I relay this to someone? My desire was to show I was very much alive—there is life in this motionless being. How to convey this I did not know since I had no power to move any part of my body. Time after time, I gave way to unconsciousness.

The coma had intruded into my life with vengeance. It held on. The renewed fears in every conscious moment were tormenting. Fear was consuming my ability to feel safe. My awareness day after day was a frightening experience as I lay silent, motionless. How many days would pass before I would hear sound again? I do not know the length of time between the intervals of consciousness and unconsciousness. When would I have the ability to try and move again? I lay there in the essence of time, in complete darkness, and sometimes I am conscious enough to wonder, *What's going on? Am I dying?*

As soon as I could hear a noise, the need to let someone know I am still alive was uppermost in my mind. In my heart, I would cry out, "I'm not dead," frightened, afraid, certain they would put me in the hospital freezer, where I would meet my doom. I was determined to show some signs of life—I tried, but I only lay in stillness, without movement or sound. I could show no evidence that suggested life was present other than my heart beat; I was dead. I would cry out, but they were cries of silence. I was calling into the silence of my dark world. My lips did not move. No one knew that I was crying out to them, wanting to tell them I still exist. *You ought not think I am dead because I cannot move.*

I was thirty-three years of age. My doctor thought I would surely die. He was waiting for that moment to come. I thought my life would end in a hospital freezer. Alive in a motionless body, devoid of the strength to communicate is a horrifying place to be. If I could move my little finger, if only I could say something, they'd know "she is alive." *I have my same body, my same mind. My brain is commanding my body to move. What is the disconnection?*

What's standing between my will to move and my body's ability to cooperate with my mind? They have been working together for thir-

ty-three years. I did not understand why I was living in this twilight zone. The mystery of my state of being was incomprehensible. The powerful hold of a coma could keep me prisoner in suspended automation for days, even years. It was utterly beyond my comprehension. This intangible impairment, the silence, the darkness always before my face—I was like unto death, in a coma. I was at a loss. What was happening? I was praying and trying to understand what was to become of me. How did I get to this point of lifelessness and still be alive, entombed in a body I once knew and could direct? The mysterious feeling of hopelessness, thoughts would come over me as I lay fearful of death, without an audible voice. I cried into the silence again and again, "Help me," but there was no one that could hear my silent cries, no one to help drive away my fears, to tell me everything was going to be all right.

I learned later, while still in the hospital, I had been overmedicated during the preparation for surgery. They made an incision across my stomach, cutting through the muscular wall. I would have to learn to use the muscles all over again after they healed and strengthened.

There was a time while in a conscious state my mother came to visit. I remember overhearing her, asking the doctor about something concerning my lips. I remember the doctor answered, "Oh, that's nothing. That happens to some people." Now I was wondering what's wrong with my lips.

In bits and pieces, I am recalling a coma I once experienced. Sometimes I was conscious; sometimes I was unconscious. However, I was alive in a body that could not respond as if it had life in it.

The day arrived when I happened to be in a conscious moment. Out of nowhere came a voice that got my attention. Still lying flat on my back, I heard this voice, saying, "I'm tired of watching this woman die."

"No!" I cried out in silence. "I'm not dying."

The nurse came to my bedside, yelled in my ear, "Get up! I am going to walk you. You've got to help me. I can't carry you and the I V stand. I've got to walk you to another bed." She pulled my legs over the side of the bed. She put my arm over her shoulder and put her arm under my arm. She pulled me until my feet touched the floor. In that moment, realization came. I could not only hear; I could also obey orders. A new window had opened to me, and I was glad, happy to walk through this opened window.

The exercise of being moved out of that bed and walking brought me out of the coma. My eyes opened. I was in a ward that had four beds. All four beds were occupied, and the eyes of the occupants were looking at me as if I just came back from the dead. I did not have the power of verbal communication, but I felt like I had just been born. The nurse took me to a bed, where she could roll the head of the bed in an upward position. I remember approaching the other bed. There was a patient still in the bed. I heard the nurse say to that patient, "There is nothing wrong with you. You are in and out of this hospital every weekend to sober up. You are not sick." The nurse said to me, "Get in the bed. You have got to have your head raised, or you will go back into a coma. They should have never laid you flat on your back."

There was a seriousness about her voice. She had a small frame. As I recall, it looked like she weighed about a hundred pounds. The Lord had put me on that nurse's heart, causing her to be concerned about my welfare to the point of her yelling in my ear, "Get up. I want to help you. I am tired of watching you die." With the help of Almighty God, he gave that nurse the strength to lift me and walk me to another bed that I might live to tell the story of how God works for our good through other people.

God was watching over me while I was disconnected from the realities of life, lying flat on my back in a coma. God has extended my days into old age and has given me his peace. May the grace of God be with you and extend your days now and for evermore. May you live with him. I have passed the ripe old age of ninety-two years. All the praise and the credit for my being alive today and in good health, clothed, in my right mind—the glory of all this goes to God the Father and his Son Jesus Christ and to the Holy Spirit of God, who lives within us. Thank you, my Lord, for your presence in my life.

God is due all praise—give him glory. His will is being done on earth as it is in heaven. The kingdom of God lives within each and every one of his children. Glory be to God in the highest, and may there be peace on earth and goodwill to all men this day and forevermore. May freedom ring in the hearts of man.

22

Encyclopedia of My Mind

Let the obedient mind, the submissive mind of Christ Jesus be in you, as his mind was unto the Father God of Heaven.

—1 Corinthians 2:16

Literally the Bible tells us we are to put on the mind of Jesus.

> For who hath known the mind of the Lord, that he may instruct Him? But we have the mind of Christ. (Romans 12:2)

> And be not conformed to this world: but be ye transformed by the renewing of your mind, that ye may prove what is that good, and acceptable, and perfect, will of God. (Philippians 2:5)

Let this mind be in you, which was in Christ Jesus. We who possess God's divine nature through the Holy Spirit should maintain an attitude that displays Christlike behavior. The righteousness of God is manifested through the passionate love of Jesus Christ. The Beatitudes show the Lord is touched by man's infirmity. The difficulties we face in life are always before the eyes of God. He is touched by the way we treat one another.

Jesus is the same yesterday, today, and forever. He said, "I will never leave thee nor forsake thee." We have been rescued from darkness and brought into his marvelous light of redemption. The believer is secure in Christ, and Christ is secure in God. Jesus said, "I am in my Father and ye are in me and I in you." This is an inescapable truth; this is a powerful statement. Saints, the angels of God are astir, engaging on earth as God's invisible agents carrying out their assignments. We are God's visible agents on earth with an assignment to be carried out; will we be intense in our obedience to God as God's invisible agents? My answer is no.

If his light is burning in our hearts, don't hide it under a bushel. Keep his light on the table of your life for all to see. Know that God has authorized his power to work through his children. All that we do should be lifting God higher. All that we do, we do through kingdom authority that is flowing down to us from the throne room of God. Our work on earth should always be to the glory of God because His spirit is the one doing the work. It's never by human might. We work for God; it's him displaying his power through us. We are not here on earth to glorify self. God is due all the glory in heaven above and on the earth below. All glory belongs to Almighty God. We are to give him thanks for all things coming into our lives. God moves mountains, casting them into the depth of the sea through his redeemed. Let us continually offer the sacrifice of praise unto the Lord God. May the fruit of our lips never cease glorifying the Almighty. Worship the Lord God always in Jesus's name.

According to his divine nature that dwells within, we who love him and are his inspired vessels, his spiritual power is channeling through us for his glorification. We who are washed in his precious shed blood are the children of fulfillment. We stand in awe in the midst of the mysteries of God, possessing the hope of eternal life. Having put on the mind of Christ Jesus, we stand.

Heavenly Father, the desire of your servant's heart is to be obedient to you on earth as we will be in heaven. Jesus said, "I speak not of myself but the Father that dwelleth in me. He doeth the work through me, you see me doing." The power that worked through Jesus is present today, working through the children of promise.

God's spirit beings are standing by, waiting to be called forth to assist God's workers. To know Jesus and the power that raised him from the dead is present in us. We too are raised from the dead. Stir up the spirit within through faith and prayer. Let the divine spirit within rise to its fullest potential, rousing itself about in God's will. Get excited. Let the sparks of God's love fly with passion. Let's not freeze our divine powers. Make some noise with songs and praise. Take the good news of salvation to the world. Go give the message of hope to all with an ear to hear.

God has never changed. He has never lost his power. He is the same God he was before Jesus walked the earth. God can never lose his strength. He's almighty. Many of us are taking the credit for the work God is doing through us. It's never us; it is always the Holy Spirit working through us for the glory of God. Make no mistake—it's the Lord that performs the miracles that we witness. Not one of us can produce a miracle. Stop trying to take God's glory. God said, "I will not share my glory with another. No flesh shall glory before Me." He is the power and the glory. All glory belongs to him. We are to keep our hands off God's glory. He alone is the almighty healer. We will never rise to our full potential when we try to steal from God.

Many have their eyes on the preacher. We lift them up instead of lifting up God for the joy we feel during services. The Lord has no substitute miracle workers. He is the one and only, and he is the fulltime miracle worker, ceasing not to show his mercy and his grace. When we express the joy that is coming from the preaching of the Word, express that joy unto the Lord God, giving him the praise, not the preacher. Know from where our blessings are coming; they cometh from the Lord God Almighty. Give him all praise. The preacher is a servant, a vessel infused, with the working power of the Holy Spirit ministering to the people. The preacher is a container performing duties for his master's pleasure through the supernatural power of the Holy Spirit. We should never claim to be miracle workers. We are not the cause, God is. The power of the Holy Spirit is working through man for God's glory. When the presence of the Holy Spirit shows up, he may show out, falling on everyone in sight.

Never feel removed from God's omnipresent power of love. As long as we are in the world, keep looking up. Don't let go of faith; God's love is in us. We can never escape God's omnipresence. His presence, his power to love reigns within the very soul of man. Living in today's society, with all its changes of what is right and what is wrong has no effect on God's plan of restoration. We will be restored. Our spiritual being is renewed every day. The desire of Jesus's heart is the continuous building of his Father's kingdom and the restoring of his people. The gifts of the spirit are available to be used today as they were yesterday. Repent with a hold heart, and enjoy the fullness of God's blessings. He has invested the blood of his Son in our salvation and will receive back assertively—all indifferences are under his power. He has given his angels charge over his saved army of believers.

Every dreadful moment of life is a moment without trusting in the love and protection of our heavenly Father through Christ Jesus, his anointed Son. We are living in a battlefield called earth's life struggles. We stand in the need of redemption. Let the redeemed identify themselves as the workmen of God, fighting against the rulers of the principality. Satan's evil spirits know no shame. They are playing the game of deceit. Deceiving all mankind is their assigned task. The demon spirits are determined to do their master's bidding at all costs, even to waging war against heaven.

There is a battle being fought in the atmosphere. It's all around us. Satan has been trying for ages to take heaven by force. He knows he is fighting a losing battle, yet he fights on. We know the spirit and the flesh are at war in the mind of man. We are to ask the Father to deliver us from those deceptive spirits, using their seductive effects, their smoothing superficial reasoning being whispered into the soul of man for their kingdom's gain. They want to steal God's children's souls.

Learn to recognize the misleading voices, the swindlers that are tempting the flesh of man. Disobedience comes wrapped in exciting packaging, pleasing to the eyes, promising pleasurable gratification to man's senses. Our love for Almighty God ought to be enough to make us be determined to push back from evil doing. Know that

God takes no pleasure in seeing his beloved participating in the devil's workshop. Reliance in the time of trouble, define our trust in our heavenly Father, knowing he is strengthening our faith. Pray to God to help our unbelief. Believe our prayers are being answered as we speak them out. Wait on God, wait in faith, and watch him work wonders. He will build our faith, our confidence. He will keep us moving on the path that brings glory to his name. Pray for godly judgment and spiritual insight as we travel through life's many passageways. The natural man does not have the ability to sift out the injurious, mischievous spiritual workings that want to destroy the kingdom of God within our being. We must fight the spirit by the spirit, thus sayest the Lord.

We who love Jesus have put on the mind of Christ and are prudent, knowing it is wise to keep his way of thinking in the forefront of our minds. We are the righteousness of God through the shed blood of our savior. We who have embraced his cross know it's not about us anymore; we now represent Jesus. Our lives' journey is all about our redeemer, and there is no looking back. Whose army are we fighting in? To whom do we owe our allegiance? To our Father God through Jesus Christ—that is where we are to position our allegiance.

Sin is often camouflaged to look appealing, tantalizing our senses. We cannot always tell the difference between the obscurity of right and wrong; the shades of gray are always blending. It becomes hard to distinguish between the shoulds and the should-nots; they have intercepted our view. Temptation tickles, excites, stirs up that old flesh appetite. The attractiveness of sin can seem so right in a fleeting moment. We think, *Why not try it? It's something different. I owe it to myself to have a little fun.* The prizes life can offer us may be inviting. At times it's hard to make the sacrifice of walking away from the spice of sin. We think, *Why not? Take the chance,* Adam and Eve did in their garden of Eden. The enticing shadows of sin, giving strong desire, intercepting our feelings of sound reasoning—these strong physical feelings may abide until we yield to temptation. We are not a Godforsaken people because we falter, we stumble, we fall—we are a tempted people. Jesus was tempted; we are no better than him. We are tempted daily in thought and in deed. Our faith includes not only praying in faith; it includes waiting on God's timing. God will deliver us from temptation in his time. The pain of waiting on God's timing is worth the wait. It breeds patience, and patience is a God-given virtue. Virtues are an order of angels—did you know that? Virtue is conformity to a standard of right standing with God, an excellence mainly showing a strength of courage—valor, chastity, a patriot of Almighty God's army.

First Peter 2:9 tells us we belong to the priesthood of God. It is the birthright of every Christian. We are priests in the sight of God. Christ's mind is manifested in us for God's glory through true believers, letting the love of God work through them. We have the blessed privilege of accessing the Lord at all times for any reason. David said, "If I made my bed in hell, he will be there." God will never leave nor forsake his own.

We are to call on Jesus when we come to a fork in the road of life. He is our guidance, showing us the way home. There are times the mind is bewildered, divided. Life may seem to have thrown a curve ball that is bending our mental stability out of shape; we can't think straight. We are perplexed, not knowing how to reach out for help, or maybe we don't want anyone to know the shape we are in. We cannot make head nor tail of what is going on in our lives. There is a fork in the road of reasoning. We cannot see ahead to the road's endings. We are losing sight of reality, yet we are determined to keep moving, wondering what direction we should take.

Never take counseling from the fearful. Never let go of hope. God is on our side of the equations of life. He wants nothing but the best for his children.

Look out in the backyard. Once again, we see a new day dawning. The sun soon will be shining in our backyard again. Don't miss the rising sun; the magnificence of it all is awesome. Once more the winters of life have passed, spring has sprung, a new day is dawning. Look on the wonders of God's seasons and rejoice. Change is inevitable. Hang in there—the best is still to come.

23

He Sings Over Us

There is a song in my heart, and I am going to let it out.

When we are singing unto the Lord, it produces a welcoming divine atmosphere, an environment that says, "Come, Yeshua, come. You are welcome in this place."

If need be, if we find we have to sing unto the Lord in a loud voice in order not to yield to the surrendering imaginations that are bombarding our minds, trying to take the heavenly peace we are obtaining, sometimes the mind goes on a journey. When we are engaged in worshipping, singing, and especially in silent prayer, the mind drifts. Speak unto the Lord in an audible voice. We are to use our voice to drown out spiritual interference that is there to sabotage our intimacy with God.

When Yeshua Hamashiach, our Anointed Salvation, receives our singing, he may sing over the worshippers. Once in a prayer group, we were praising our Anointed Savior. We were singing with all our might until a prophesy came forth from Jesus: "I received your singing, and I sang over you." Jesus's words filled our hearts with a joy we can never forget.

We are to let our mouths become a vehicle of joyful sounds unto the living God Almighty.

> Speaking to yourselves in psalms and hymns, spiritual songs. Singing and making melody in your heart to the Lord. (Ephesians 5:19)

It is of supreme importance to the soul that the inner man feeds steadfastly on words of the Lord. Let us be crystal clear about our need to have the deepest intimacy possible with our Lord and Savior Jesus Christ. The sad truth is that few of us have come to learn how to sit and reflect at the feet of Yeshua our Messiah. There at his feet, we will deepen our relationship, being enlightened to the oneness with him. A hush may come and still the soul when finding ones true self sitting quietly, soaking immersed in his presence. We may find ourselves weeping tears of unexplainable joy.

Singing is a form of prayer without asking God for something. While in silent prayer, we may realize our minds have wandered. However, making melody, singing out in an audible voice will help break spiritual interference during prayer. Our worship sounds penetrate the surrounding spiritual atmosphere that is influencing our airways. Spirits are always out there, waiting for an invitation, an opportunity to invade the mind of every living thing. The joyful noise of worship will break through any unauthorized spiritual interference coming near us. We can cause the enemy to back away with songs of love and worship to the Almighty.

Keep your mind on Jesus. Christians can live in a joyful state before the Lord God; we can dance like David danced and sing like David sang unto the Lord. Can we trust in the Hebrew God of Israel like David did? David is recorded in world history because of his love and devotion to God. The way David dedicated his life to loving and pleasing and approaching the Lord God of Israel—with his whole being, he gave of himself with pure delight in the presence of the Almighty. There was an intimacy between David and his God, the Jehovah God of Israel. Read how David relied on his God—twenty-third Psalm.

Our God yearns for—longs persistently for—his children's display of affection for him. David had no problem expressing the beauty of his emotion through poetry and hymns, dancing in pure delight before the Lord. Some of us have a problem with the simplicity of showing love outwardly to the living God. David is called a man after God's own heart. My friend, it can't get any better than that—being called a man after God's own heart. What is God saying about our show of worship to him?

Throughout the ages, we have clung to Psalm 23. It expresses very clearly that God is our protector; he is all that we need. God is our provider. Read aloud the twenty-third Psalm. Do we hold sacred these words? Declare the twenty-third Psalm to be our foundation in life. Our war chest will stand fighting against the words of the unbeliever; they who do not know that God is able to defend to the very end. His name is the name that is above every name. Know the battle of life is not ours alone. We are to put our faith in God's promises. They will withstand the powers of time. Believe the twenty-third Psalm has our name written all through its pages. Our faith will attack the enemy's stronghold, giving us the breakthrough we have been praying for. Our defining moment is our trust in Jesus's name.

Heaven has always been filled with music. When God said, "Let there be," the harmonious sounds of creation went to work, bringing into being the greatest symphony of colors, lights, and sounds creating life. Their performance will never stop creating. God's symphony orchestra will never die. Our God and his heavenly host love music; there is unending music in the whole of heaven. Let us fill the earth with singing, making a joyful noise unto the Lord. As we travel through life's many troublesome highways and byways, let there be songs of praise on our lips unto the Almighty.

Our job on earth is to defuse the devil's power through faithful praying and worship to God. We will find many bombshells littering our pathways when serving the Lord God, and they will be unmovable in our own strength. Accept we, through faith and prayer, are standing on God's Word. In all that we do, let it be in communion with the Father through singing and humming melodies of love unto the Lover of our souls. Show God some love through our faithfulness and obedience.

Learn the mystery of the double portion. Trust and obey—there is no other way to God's heart. Jesus said, "If you love me, obey me." Faith is a gift. Once we unlock the door to faith, our trust in God's Word grows. Our breakthrough has come. Keep on trusting in the Lord. His faithfulness will never depart from our lives if we trust and obey.

We are to prepare our hearts to enter into that perfect plan of purpose God has set before us. Father, in the name of Jesus, I ask you to cleanse my heart with the precious blood of Jesus. Lord, I am serious. I want to glorify thee with a pure heart that is always open to you.

I am standing in agreement with you, my Lord, when you say, "Let the dead bury the dead." Jesus is the light, the giver of life. Outside of him, we journey among the walking dead. Jesus called Lazarus from the tomb of the dead. I too am entombed with transgressors. I stretch forth my soul to thee—strengthen my faith, O Lord. I am believing, leaning on thee; I trust in the power of thy faithfulness. There are times when I feel I am one of earth's many walking dead. Let my feelings be a liar. I am made whole in Jesus's name.

Jesus said, "Seek and you shall find" (Matthew 7:7–8). Stand on the promises of God. Stand with expectation of new life. Jesus ushered in the dispensation of grace. Grace is an amazing free gift. It is an anointing, saving gift; it's an astonishment, a wonderment giving the way to salvation. Accept that if not for the grace of God, we go into the pits of hell. The miracle of unconditional love is the grace of God, preparing us for eternity in his kingdom. Are we reverencing, worshipping, and glorifying God in Jesus's name? Jesus sings over his true worshippers.

24

Love Makes a Healthy Soul

Turning the pages of our minds, we will read love is the necessity to a healthy soul. Love is unique. It is the spirit that gives and feeds life. Love is hidden from some and revealed to others. Only God knows why some receive the spirit of love and some do not. Love is a glorious treasure and will last throughout eternity. Discover how the world can be changed through the divine love that is living in us. Having the knowledge of love and the ability to give and receive love is a mystery that is misunderstood by many. Love thy neighbor, and love thy enemy as we love ourselves. The spirit of love vigorously lives and thrives in the presence of God because it is one with Him.

Like burning incense rising, our souls go back from which they came, soaring their way up to the God that gave them. God is the spirit of love. His love is flowing and creating new life as he breathes divine rebirth. Are you born again? Salvation makes you a new creation through the shed blood of Jesus Christ.

There is a river of radiance flowing through God's children; they are to share this river with others. The secret of it all leads to God's promises of an abundant life.

When we can stand serene and secure when unsettling circumstances have found us, in these times of uncertainty, it is a blessing to know we can draw from our inner calmness, an ever-renewing reservoir, a well of flowing love that lives within the heart. Only in his presence will our souls find rest and peace through the circumstances of life as they come before us, and we deal with them in love. Focus on the serenity of the Father's love. Listen to his voice. Know the voice of the master as it calls unto his own, teaching us his ways. Know the peace found in true silence as it nourishes the soul while sitting at the feet of Jesus.

The bonds of love transcend generations. Love is a divine gift that keeps on giving. The capacity to love finds no fault; it strengthens and affirms. Unconditional love is found in lessons taught from above. There is wisdom found in having the gift of patience—try it. Experience life through the wealth of knowledge, but above all you're getting, it strengthens while it enlightens your decisions.

Listen in those priceless golden moments when God is whispering his love through grace inspiring us; through those many times you feel life is letting us down, his grace will abound. God's fragrant nuggets carry the odors of life's fragile passing time. Make the most of life. Understand life is a gift from above. Years may pass by, but when we find God's wonder-working plan for our lives, share that discovery with others. Help them on their way through the droplets of life.

Unconditional love—it's a glimpse into God's faithfulness forever. God said, "I will never leave you nor forsake you." Love is inspirational; it creates a joy that weaves a rare durable textured fabric of human insight that will cause us to be caring in a loving way to others, showing our spiritual growth. When God speaks to our hearts, it is soul stirring; his words are soul reshaping, bringing unspeakable joy. When God talks to the heart, unexpected, unexplained memories that exist in the subconscious may surface, causing us to realize our old hurts.

God has given us many gifts—think on them. He has presented us with a world of gifts. We have let many pass by unaware; we were uninfluenced by the world's opportunities. God offered mankind many favorable circumstances during life's journey. They were spiritually provided to us for our good, but we did not recognize from whence they come. Some think they have never experienced an answered prayer. They prayed unbelieving. Though they prayed, they were not expecting God to answer.

God receives pleasure from those who recognize his voice and stand on his faithfulness. We are sharing in God's will when we use the great gift of obedience. When we obey, we show our love for him and few there are that possess the miracle gift of obedience.

Recognizing the beauty of God's presence, knowing that we are being surrounded by his loving touch is an unforgettable experience. Realizing we are in the presence of God is an overpowering moment—a spiritual sense of being spiritually united and becoming one spiritually in Christ. Have we ever been immersed in a tender moment of spiritual bliss and wanted that experience, that moment of bliss to stand still become an everlasting moment in our being?

God's children abide in *faith* and in *hope* and are rooted in *love*; the greatest of these three gifts is love. God is love. In all we do, do it in love, pleasing God, not self. The Lord gave us free will. We are to use our free will, not Satan. Don't let Satan use our free will for us. The Holy Spirit lives in us to gently nudge and urge us to obey the voice of God. Know the world cannot change until we change.

Do you fret? Are we wearing away over yesterday's mistakes? If the answer is yes, why? Yesterday has passed, never to return. In Jesus's name, we are to pray, asking God to forgive our yesterdays. Don't look back; keep walking into today's activities—they are waiting on you. Do not be concerned for tomorrow. In due time, the tomorrows will take care of themselves.

Learn to listen to the rustling winds in the trees. They are singing a song of love to God. One day, having refreshments outside a small café in Florida, I found the warm gentle breeze pleasing. When looking at the trees, their leaves waving and dancing about, it seemed as if they were looking and bowing to me. I said, "O my, little trees, why do you stand there bowing and waving to me? Is there a spiritual message in the sound of your rustling leaves that is meant for only me?" O, listening to nature, the environment, is whispering its mysteries of God, telling his stories of love.

> And it repented the Lord that he had made man on the earth, and it grieved him at his heart. (Genesis 6:6)

Jesus, open my spiritual eyes that I might see thee and desire a deeper relationship with thee. Only through you, my Lord, can I become spiritually alive in thy ways. I want to live under the power of your love throughout my remaining earth days and through eternity.

There are the new tomorrows awaiting their turn to be brought into existence. The future tomorrows are given an allotted time to play out their participation of purpose. To be an observer in our journey to greater life would be a blessing. We will make our departure from earth's journey; this existence must come to an end, for there is greater life waiting to be explored.

O, what a difference a little love makes to those on their journey home. Again and again, I tell you God is love, and those who worship him must worship him in truth and in love. Jesus will come to you in many ways. Ask him to open the eyes of your heart.

> And their eyes were opened, and they knew him; and he vanished out of their sight. (Luke 24:31)

> And they said one to another, "Did not our heart burn within us, while he talked with us by the way, and while he opened to us the scriptures?" (Luke 24:32)

All the days left to me on this earth, Father, I pledge them to thee. When in intimacy with thee, I transcend the rational human mind. My entry into your presence is sublime. I am humbled as a child, seeking the love of her Father, knowing his arms are stretched out in love. I await the tenderness of his touch, so I run to him.

25

Indwelling of the Holy Spirit

Many people think the Holy Spirit is the most neglected person in the union of the Godhead.

We worship not the Holy Spirit nor do we praise him. We were never told to kneel and pray or praise the Holy Spirit. We were told to ask God for our needs in the name of Jesus. We are to thank God for the Holy Spirit. The Holy Spirit is our promised comforter. Jesus prayed to the Father, asking him to send another comforter to his people. God sent the Holy Spirit to live in the believer—after Jesus ascended into heaven.

The Holy Spirit is the third Person of the holy Trinity—Father, Son, and Holy Spirit are one. The Holy Spirit is a divine Person; he is fully God, coequal and coeternal.

In the old days, the Holy Spirit was referred to as the Holy Ghost. The Holy Spirit was not sent to earth to speak of himself; he hears and obeys the Father. He is the source of our personal testimony. He guides us in decisions and protects us from physical and spiritual danger. He is our comforter, the one who calms our fears. The Holy Spirit is the power of God in action on earth through us. The Holy Spirit intercedes for us with groanings which cannot be uttered by man. The Holy Spirit knows the mind of God.

The Holy Spirit proceeds from God and is one with the Father and the Son. The Holy Spirit brings conviction, regeneration, and transformation to the hearts of sinners. He can do this because he is one with the Father. He applies the saving works of the Son to the hearts and the lives of God's elect. The Holy Spirit unites the believer to Christ's imparting working benefits to and through the believer. He is working through the believer for the glory of God. Praise God for the Holy Spirit, who is living in the called of God.

There is only one true God—he is triune in nature. God subsists in three distinct inseparable persons. The members of the Godhead fully indwell one another, being the same in essence, performing in their distinguishable divine offices, glorifying Almighty God.

> The angel Gabriel announced to the young woman, a virgin named Mary, that she would bring forth a child. The Holy Ghost shall come upon thee, and the power of the Highest shall over shadow thee: Holy Ghost is working with the Lord God, and through Jesus Christ, they are one. The Holy Spirit is our divine inner spiritual guide, he lives in us. (Luke 1:35)

Jesus said, "I will pray the Father, and he shall send you another comforter that will abide with you forever" (John 14:15–26). The Holy Spirit is the promise of Jesus.

Jesus breathed on his disciples and said, "Receive ye the Holy Ghost" (John 20:22) We know that Jesus has the Holy Spirit within him and has the power to impart the Holy Spirit to whom he pleases.

Ephesians 4:30 tells us, "Grieve not the Holy Spirit of God, whereby ye are sealed unto the day of redemption."

Resentment and wrath are to give way to kindness and forgiveness. Since God has forgiven us, ought not we be about the business of forgiving others?

It is expedient to learn to recognize the voice of the Holy Spirit. He speaks to the hearts of God's children. A guardian angel is appointed to us from birth by God; Satan also assigns an angel to be on our case. God's appointed angel is our protector and defender. Satan has also assigned an angel from the pits of hell to steal our souls. Our appointed angel is one of God's skilled warriors, being in touch with God at all times.

> Casting all your care upon him; for he careth for you. (1 Peter 5:7)

We are to crucify our old man—our flesh. Satan is always tempting, whispering, appealing to man's sinful appetite that is buried deep within the human flesh. Man is inherently immoral, craving, desiring the forbidden fruits that temp the flesh of man; read Genesis 3:2–19—the garden east of Eden is still alive and well today.

> And the Lord said, Simon, Simon, behold; Satan hath desired to have you, that he may sift you as wheat. (Luke 22:31)

The Holy Spirit knows all things. He proceeded out from God our Father unto us through Jesus. Jesus prayed, asking the Father to send another comforter after he physically leaves the earth. God sent the Holy Spirit to mankind in answer to Jesus's prayers, asking the Father to send another comforter that would live in his people.

Whenever thoughts enter your mind, question the thoughts, asking God, "Did you send these thoughts? If I obey them, how will they bring you glory?"

The blood of Jesus washes away even the stain of sin.

> Behold, I stand at the door, and knock: if any man hears my voice, and open the door, I will come in to him, and will sup with him, and he with me. (Revelation 3:20)

The Holy Spirit searches all things, even the deep things of God. Every tiny morsel of our spiritual and physical being is searched. The Holy Spirit seeks the hidden obscure evil spiritual entities trying to hide out in our being; he destroys the evil one's corrupt influence that lie in wait, lurking, waiting for an opportunity to strike at the soul of man. The Holy Spirit stays busy cleansing our being through and through; with the precious shed blood of Jesus Christ, he scrubs our very essence. Jesus's shed blood has sealed us, and his seal cannot be broken. The Holy Spirit is our watchman on the wall of life, keeping watch over the saved of Christ.

God is the one working his gifts, the fruits of the Spirit through his servants by the power of the Holy Spirit. The Holy Spirit is the one that executes divine power, performing the miracles of God, answering our requests for God's favors in life.

> Let this mind be in you, which is in Christ Jesus. (Philippians 2:5)

The Bible tells us to put on the mind of Christ Jesus. "The Holy Spirit speaks not of himself" (Acts 2:39). He speaks that which he hears from Jesus.

The Holy Spirit nurtures and nourishes the soul of man, preparing him for the work the Lord has purposed for his life. Surrender to God. Let the Holy Spirit have dominance over our lives, guiding us through the mosaic pathway God has set us on. We serve a faithful, compassionate God. Stand back. Move away from self. See him direct our lives. God has given us a life he wants us to walk through with the guidance of the Holy Spirit. We are to surrender our control button to the Holy Spirit for the glory of God.

26

Launching Spirit Light

I expect to pass through this world but once. Any good, therefore, that I can do or any kindness that I can show to my fellow creatures, let me not defer nor neglect for I shall not pass this way again.

—Author Unknown

> Blessed is the man that walketh not in the counsel of the ungodly, nor standeth in the way of sinners, nor sitteth in the seat of the scornful. But his delight is in the law of the Lord; and his law doth he meditates day and night. (Psalm 1:2–3)

The key word in this psalm is the word *blessed*. It serves here as a pronouncement upon a man but a certain kind of man—a *peacemaker*.

A TV preacher once said, "I asked God, 'What are we doing today that displease you most?' God answered, 'The dogmatic determination to correct one another.'"

> Blessed are the peacemakers: for they shall be called the children of God. (Matthew 5:9–12)

> Thy kingdom come, thy will be done in
> earth, as it is in heaven. And forgive us our debts,
> as we forgive our debtors. (Matthew 6:10)

Jesus ushered in the dispensation of grace. The age of grace came in with our Lord Jesus Christ. Was Jesus a Christian? How did the name *Christian* derive? The Greek word *Christos* for the Hebrew *messiah* ("anointed one"). Christian "followers of the Christ" became the name of a group who followed the teachings of Jesus of Nazareth in first-century Israel and proclaimed him the predicted messiah of the prophets (taken from the *Christianity-World History Encyclopedia*).

Through Christianity, we profess belief in and follow the teachings of Jesus Christ. No longer are we under the law of Moses. We are under grace through the finished work of Jesus, who has fulfilled the old law. Jesus was the only one who could keep the law. It was impossible for man to keep the law, for Jews kept adding to the ancient existing laws. We were incapable of keeping the hundreds of laws. Man kept adding. God gave Moses ten laws. Man added over six hundred laws. The Jews had to keep all the laws. Jesus was the only one who could fulfill these laws.

Jesus, God's perfect sacrificial Lamb, gave us victory over sin and death through his finished work on the cross. His blood has expunged, obliterated, eliminated God's strong anger against our sin. Our sin had a strong offensive odor; it had come up before the nostrils of God. After the finished work on the cross, our Father casted our sin into the sea of forgiveness to be remembered no more, showing the grace of God unto man.

Salvation came to us through the finished work of Jesus, the shedding of his blood on the cross. On the cross hung our savior. "It is finished," Jesus said, and the Father said, "Well done, my Son. Come home."

God's kingdom came to earth through Jesus Christ. From the kingdom of God, Jesus came to us. He came to earth to share the good news of salvation through the grace of God by his finished work on the cross.

How do we forgive our debtors—those who have offended us deeply? Should we love them with the love of Jesus that lives within us? We too are debtors standing in the need of forgiveness. We have afflicted pain on others and held unkind thoughts and have acted on those thoughts in words and in deeds.

Reflecting on life, there are toxic amounts of pain and suffering in this world. Have we played a part in any of that suffering during a careless moment?

> "Let the wicked forsake his way and the unrighteous man his thoughts: Let him return unto the Lord, and he will have mercy upon him; and to our God, for he will abundantly pardon. For your thoughts are not my thoughts, neither are your ways my ways," saith the Lord. (Isaiah 55:7–8)

When we are singing and praising the Lord, we produce an atmosphere that reaches beyond the rim of earth. Our worship enters into heaven, and all heaven joins in our rejoicing, singing with us, praising and glorifying God.

Our deep worshipping affects the spiritual environment, signaling to the battling injured angels of God who come and lay before the altar of worship. The holy atmosphere created by powerful worshipping gives God's spiritual injured warriors a place in which to come and be healed. They lay surrounded by the holy atmosphere created by the sounds of worship that is influencing the area with waves of holiness. The warriors' wounds are healed from the heavy spiritual weight of God's ministering spirits joining in the worship. The warring angels of God minister to us by fighting against hell's opposing angels that are trying to fight their way into the church services to hold back our worship to God.

The opposing angels come out of the dark pits of hell. They are evil spirit beings from the underground caves of Hades, where they abode, bringing with them their deceiving spiritual interference that they marinated and soaked in their hellish vessels, making a special recipe that is prepared for the corruption of the world.

Satan would like to consume, swallow God's children—swallow them up and spit them out into the dungeons of hell. His combating entities are trying to overthrow God's authority in the heavens and in the earth. Satan's influencing behavior is everywhere, affecting the mind of man. His opposing demons come unto our ears with a smooth silvery tongue, trying to make us think they are God's chosen saints sent by him to instruct his children. The spirits of darkness are trying to preoccupy the mind of man, planting seeds of doubt, wanting to bring disbelieve in God's Word. These beings are from the chambers of darkness; they come to create disbelief in the hearts of men. They bring doubt and discouragement to the hearts of God's children. They want to create a wall of separation between us and our Father. These entities try to hinder our prayers. They want to stop our prayers from reaching the throne room of God.

> From the first day that thou set thine heart to understand and to chasten thyself before God, thy words were heard, and I am come for thy words. But the prince of the kingdom of Persia withstood me one and twenty days. (Daniel 10:12–13)

Thoughts are words not audible to the human ear; they are unspoken substance sent spiritually into the universe through the power of our minds. Spoken communication is audible, showing intent. Know both spiritual physical worlds are operating in the earth, expressing and presenting their influence to the mind of man. The opposing demon spirits observe our prayer life; they do not want our prayers to reach the ears of God. They interfere with the travel of prayers. Demons were interfering in Daniel's prayer route to God; they tried stopping his prayers from reaching their destination. They hindered them for twenty and one days, resulting in spiritual battling. Michael, the archangel of God, one of God's chief princes, and the angel Gabriel, the messenger angel of God, had to fight the prince of Persia, the demon who ruled the air over Persia didn't want Daniel's prayers going through his airwaves. The prince of Persia's job was to prevent prayers on their way to God's kingdom from getting through any air space under his rule.

God's army is always standing ready; they are nearby, awaiting the command to go into battle on our behalf. The mighty angels of God cannot be defeated. Victory is written in their breastplate. God's Word will not come back to him void. As he so wills, it shall be done.

My children, delight yourself in your God. Read my Word. Know that I am in my Word—my Word is true.

Know that we are living in a world functioning with unseen spiritual activity; we live in two coexisting environments that are communicating with the human soul. The seen and unseen worlds are animating in our midst. They are partially concealed but not remote.

Ask that our little faith be open to broader avenues of deeper faith—the kind of faith that moves mountains and cast them into the sea.

Are we yearning to go behind the divine veil of spiritual intimacy? Do we want the Lord's presence perfecting our peace? Will we tuck his perfection in our hearts? Are we feeling unworthy to enter into his sacred tranquility because of our weakened faith? Are we training our minds to connect with his stillness? A silent connection with God's stillness brings harmony to the quietness of the soul. Let our minds be concentrated on the visitation of God through communion in prayer. Expect the sereneness, the hush, the calmness of his presence that is giving us controlling power over our minds while in prayer.

Dominating, intruding, influencing thoughts will come, trying to penetrate our concentration when we are praying. The enemy wants to take away the tranquility of our souls when we are reflecting on God's Word.

Ask God not to let our restraining efforts be short lived when the enemy tries to engage our minds with runaway thoughts. If we must, speak out loud when spiritual interference come; speak in Jesus's name. Sing unto the Lord. Give him praise, glorifying his name, then go into meditation. The enemy may try to aggravate our minds again, but keep engaging the Lord, lifting up Jesus in song and praise.

Speaking aloud to God will help keep our minds focused on prayer, giving our inner ear the capability to listen for his voice. I know people say we have to be quiet to hear God speaking—that's not necessarily the case at all times. Once I was defending myself, and the voice of the Lord said to me, "You have said enough." I stopped talking. The unseen Spirit of God took over; I watched that person's demeanor change from hostile to apologetic.

"Minister Smith," she said. "I didn't mean to give you a hard time." I stood there in astonishment. How quickly, how peacefully God fought that battle in my presence. We can try and fight the enemy with our whole being, allowing us to spiritually and emotionally getting our spiritual balance off tack. We are no match for the enemy. We will struggle furiously when engaging the enemy. As a warrior of God, on the battlefield of our Lord, learn to wait on God's timing. We enter into serious spiritual warfare with the devil when God is using us to deprive Satan of his precious souls. What a privilege granted to be counted among God's physical warriors. Discernment is a fruit of the Spirit; it is an absolute necessity. This gift is inescapable, it gives man the capability to see beyond the physical rim. Discernment lifts the spiritual veil. We need this gift to escape the inevitable pitfalls of Satan's craftiness.

We may experience the wandering mind syndrome especially in the silence of meditative prayers. The enemy loves engaging his ability in feeding his thoughts into our minds. This thief with great determination; is after our souls' salvation. He has the ability to fool mankind. He is amusing himself, making us think we are thinking when in actuality, we are listening to the voice of ungodly persuasion. The enemy is competitive when playing the mind game. He is always nearby to bombard our minds with his thoughts. We need not entertain ungodly thoughts; the Holy Spirit will quicken us to the point that we will not feel right when acting on thoughts coming from the trickster.

With enticing words straight from the pits of hell comes misery and fear when we forget that the presence of the Lord God is always with us.

Let our mouth become a vehicle of offerings—offering joyful sounds of precious praise unto the Lord. We will never regret our decision to love the Master of all creation, believing his Word is true. Trust him, being God's vehicle of joyful sounds, letting Jesus know he is our beloved savior. Today Jesus is awaiting our praises. Praise him. Do not keep the bridegroom waiting, for tomorrow is not promised.

> Speaking to yourselves in psalms, and spiritual songs, singing, and making melody in your heart unto the Lord. (Ephesians 5:19)

Saints, what a precious assignment—making melody in our hearts to Jesus. Our Lord God is always desirous to commune with his inheritance. We are his inheritance. He made his request known in the garden east of Eden; this very moment, that request is still standing. He is still wanting communication with mankind. He made Adam. They walked and talked in the cool of evening. The angels of heaven are communicating continuously with song and praise unto Almighty God our Father. There is no end in their worship to the Almighty. Let us be a part of that heavenly celebration. We have a mouth—we can use it. Heaven will hear our singing. May our hearts be delighted. May all the earth sing with the heavenly choir unto the Lord God Almighty—being one in spirit.

> And I heard as it was the voice of a great multitude, and as the voice of many waters, and as the voice of mighty thundering, saying, "Alleluia: for the Lord God omnipotent reigneth." (Revelation 19:6)

The health of our souls is of supreme importance. The inner man should be fed divinely each day.

Let it be crystal clear—man was born with a divine appointment. Our destiny, our future was destined. God gave us a spirit of free will. We are to prayerfully use it. We need a deep desire for intimacy with our Lord and Savior Jesus Christ. Few have come to know how the inner man evolves vigorously, thriving when fed on a diet of God's Word. The sad truth is that many have not learned it is possible to come and sit at the feet of Jesus, reflecting on his truth as he speaks to our hearts, receiving forgiveness, being expunged from vile sin. There at his feet, we deepen our relationship. We come into spiritual oneness in his divine presence.

Be still, O my soul. Experience this holy hush. The absence of all sound has come upon me; only divine whisperings are flowing through my being. The state of heavenly serenity has engulfed my inner self. The enrichment of my soul is unfolding, thriving in peace. Sitting at the feet of Jesus are precious moments to a traveling soul. The intimacy is feeding my inner man. My soul is unfolding, vibrant, tranquil, spiritually alive in Christ Jesus. O my soul, be thou stilled in the presence of our Lord. Know the calm, the rest we are experiencing while sitting in quiet bliss, peacefully soaking in his holiness. In this minute, the space of a moment, comes an apprehension. When we are perceiving bad vibes from the enemy of our souls, who is trying secretly to steal our peace while we are yet sitting at his feet, receiving wisdom from on high, we are receiving an experience in the recognition of spiritual war games being played out in our psyche.

What will we do with this experience? Jesus is present. Call on his powerful name. We have caught a glimpse into the great and glorious peace of God, and that made the devil mad. He does not want us experiencing that peace which surpasses, exceeds all human comprehension. While sitting at the feet of Jesus, we are lost in time, for there is no concern with time in eternity with an eternal Jesus. By force, the devil will try and rob us, deprive us of our divine experience. He will try to make us forget we ever had a divine experience with Jesus. We have had a glimpse into the window of eternity—infinite time opened before our spiritual eyes, our inner man. In a split moment in time, we came into the presence of our Master and became one in spirit.

Through silence, we are experiencing our spirit man's feeding, and we share in heavenly hymns unto the Father, the Son, and the Holy Spirit, seeing ourselves sitting at the foot of God's throne, singing unto him with his angelic beings. What peace there is seeing the inner man beholding the face of the Creator.

Thanks, Father—thy kingdom has come unto men through Jesus Christ and his obedience to thee. Thy will is being done on earth as it is in heaven through the dispensation of grace. We are standing on the promises of God. The provision of salvation has come through the shed blood of Jesus. The will of God has been accomplished through His Son. Lord, you have showed yourself many times; you are visible to whom you want to be visible to. It is written some are infidel from the womb; they are the nonbelievers.

Some have eyes that cannot see, ears that cannot hear to know that God's Word is life. Many cannot accept the Word of God nor are able to receive his offering of eternal life. We were created for God's pleasure, and for his pleasure were we created. God the Father, God the Son, and God the Holy Spirit are one Being; they make the blessed holy Trinity. God is the union of three divine persons in one Godhead, unto whom is it given the full knowledge and mysteries of God. I cherish the mysteries of God; though I understand them not, I stand on the promises of God. All life was created through the divine mystery of God's spoken words. God's mysteries have engulfed his eternal selected chosen family. We who are his chosen—we are tried—and sometimes we may ask, "God, where are you? Do you see how hard things have become for me?" Experiencing suffering for the glory of God is not a hiccup; it is our roadmap to eternal life.

The inner man is a not our spirit; the inner man is our soul, our true selves, the true persons of who we are. The kingdom of God lives within his chosen. Salvation has awakened us to see who we really are in the eyes of God. If our faith is in the shed blood of Jesus. God has brought us a mighty long ways from the gates of hell through our faith in Jesus. Our relationship with God is intangible and beyond explanation. God gave his only Son for our souls to be returned unto him. A repenting soul that loves God will live in his presence throughout eternity in an unending enthronement of his love. Are we longing for a relationship with Jesus? There is a oneness with the Father through his Son. Our worship to God will never cease. Repent, and be obedient; there is no other way to have a relationship with the Almighty.

Worship can clear the air, driving away hovering ungodly influences. They control and linger in the midst, wanting to occupy our minds to possess our psyche. Lifting up Jesus is always seasonal—no precise timing, no ritual—his love is an open-season affair. He wants to help us overcome our adversaries. Whenever a breakthrough is needed, lift the circumstances up to Jesus. In Jesus's name, circumstances are not inevitable or inescapable. Plead the precious blood of Jesus over all situations, and watch them become minor. We are to be tested—it's a part of living. God only sends trials to test us, allowing us to have an experience that will show spiritual growth. All God's children must have a testimony: "And they overcame him (the devil), by the blood of the Lamb, and by the word of their testimony," were they saved (Revelation 12:11). We do not have to put up with unauthorized spiritual interference that is constantly causing difficulty in our lives, taking away our ability to think clearly, making it difficult, taking our ability to concentrate on the affairs at hand. Don't surrender to that slue-footed pretender; he is a liar from the pits of hell. In faith we are to keep our chins up. Jesus is on the job.

An unoccupied mind is enticement for evil spirits. They are wandering around, looking for a home. These evil spirits go up and down in the earth, looking for someone to devour.

Children of God, our unspoken as well as our spoken words go before the Father. Our old adversary, the devil, would like to come between us and our God. The devil puts as much interference in our lives as he's permitted, wanting to hinder our concentration on Jesus, speaking to our minds while we are praying. The emitting consuming fire coming from the fury of the holy angels of God is protecting us; they are shining and emanating sweet scents on the prayers of God's saints. An air of serenity, happiness comes from God's protection and his amazing grace that gave us immunity—purchased through the blood of Jesus Christ. Constantly alert and battling without any fear, the angels of God are protecting God's children.

> Daniel had to wait twenty and one days to
> get an answer to his prayers. (Daniel 10:13)

With faithful prayers, fight back the enemy. Learn to wait on God's timing. Let our souls be filled with heavenly songs as we offer musical praising and worship unto you, Lord God Almighty. Keep our souls free, my Lord. We who love and serve thee are free indeed. Whenever we feel the desire to sing and talk aloud to our Redeemer, it is a good time. He loves hearing from his children. Magnify the Lord. Know we can do all things through Christ who strengthens us. Though I am weak, I am strong when I am walking in thy Word, O Lord.

In the book of Psalms, David sang praises to God, remembering all the goodness God had put in his life. I cannot emphasize enough worship sounds are alive; they never die. They have God's DNA in them. They live on. They have everlasting life. They are spirit. They have healing power as they are being spoken. Worship penetrates through spiritual interference, so worship with all your being. Give God praise.

The unseen spiritual world is a part of our daily life. We are to keep praise in our hearts at all times. In this world, there are two different kinds of existence that walk among us. The spirit world dissimulates, hiding under false appearances when they want to. God's children are sheltered from spiritual activity to a degree. God passionately put a spanning separation between the worlds. God put a deep chasm of protection between the two worlds, giving us the sense of being submersed in the capacity of his love, and we are. We stand, washed in the warm penetrating power of Jesus's saving blood. The piercing secret to life is faith, trusting God's pervading Word to become diffused throughout every part of our being. The shield of love is defensive armor, protecting our eternal life. We are submerged in the obscure clouds of God's broad ever-increasing love. God covered his children, giving them a resting place in him. When Jesus comes back for his people, we will look up from the earth, seeing the presentation of war appearing in the clouds, riding on a white horse—not a donkey this time.

My testimony of seeing a vision when I needed the hand of God to appear to me is drawn from my memory bank to a time of worship past in a little church I was attending. I want to share this dramatic episode with you because it shows our worship never dies. A time when my life was hanging in the balance of man's hands, God send a long-gone-by Sunday worship service to aid me through a time I needed to know he was with me. This experience is true and is one of many wonders I have witnessed God do. I poured my soul out to God many times in praise and worship, and they are all stored in heaven. Our prayers are God's treasures, stored in God's divine vault until they are needed.

I was living in Florida; it was a hot day, ninety-five degrees. I felt the heat of the sun, but I was out working for the church. I kept on working. I did not feel overheated. The sun was shining, and I was having a lovely day.

Late that night, I was awakened; my heart was leaping like a fish out of water. I woke my husband. I told him I'm having a heart attack. I got out of bed and tried to put my clothes on, but I could not. I lay on the floor. I said to God, "If you let me live until tomorrow morning, I'll go to the doctor at 8:00 a.m. I don't know why I said that. The doctor's office did not open until 9:00 a.m., and as a rule, the doctor did not get into his office until 10:00 a.m. However, I was there at 8:00 a.m. without having a doctor's appointment. I said to the woman at the check-in window, "I don't have an appointment, but if I don't see the doctor, I will die." As I was speaking, I saw the doctor peeking from a distance. He motioned to the receptionist to let me come back to the examining room.

After the short examination, he told me, "Your blood tests have been showing you are an anemic—you have no blood. Your body has between four and five pints of blood." The doctor asked me, "Do you have health insurance?"

"Yes, I do." I answered.

"I'm contacting the hospital to see if they have a bed available. Yes, there is an available bed. They have assigned you to a room, bed A. Get into your car and get there as quickly as you can." My husband drove to Ocala, to the hospital. After doing all the paperwork, they put me on a cot and pushed me into a very busy hallway, where I lay for hours before they put me in a small waiting room facing the nurse's station. Soon a doctor and a nurse came to my bedside.

They asked me, "Have you had any seizures?"

"No," I said.

They didn't believe me. They looked at one another. They asked, "Have you had a loss of consciousness?"

"No," I replied. Again they did not believe me. I could see they were not believing a word I was saying; as far as they were concerned, I was a liar. They made up their mind—they would not try to save my life.

I asked, "Haven't you ever had a patient with four or five pints of blood?"

"Yes," they answered.

"Well, you see, I'm not the only one," I replied.

The nurse said to me, "They are dead."

She and the doctor stood looking down on me as if they called into question my ability to tell the truth. I looked at them and then I looked away. In that moment, I was seeing an event taking place in the spirit world. God let me know he knew where I was and what was going on in my life. God let me see into the supernatural. I saw a congregation in worship—a body of believers gathered together. The event I was witnessing, I believed, that service had taken place sometime ago. God was letting me see a rerun of events, showing me that our prayers and our worship never die; they are contained in heaven until we have need of them. The whole church was singing and praising God.

I looked around and saw my pastor's wife. She was in the pew behind me, singing and smiling at me as if she was pleased to see me. I looked over, crossed the aisle to see a young man who thought he could not speak in tongues. He wanted the holy utterance, and he was speaking it. The vision episode that came to me was on a screen, like a TV screen. It showed the whole church worship scene. I felt God sent me a scene from the past, letting me know his presence was with me. I was dying from the lack of blood; I needed that miracle of seeing my past. God showed up in his own way, showing me a scene—a vision from my past—as I was worshiping. I looked up at both the doctor and the nurse and said, "The church is praying for me." They looked at each other, and they turned, walked away. As they were leaving, the doctor said, "I'll order you one unit of blood. If it doesn't work, we have no more blood for you."

At 3:00 p.m., my private doctor came to visit me. He could see me from where he stood at the nurse's station. He stood, looking at me and the blood hanging from the floor stand.

"What is that you are giving her?" That blood is pink. She needs red blood, the reddest blood you've got. I've been up to Mrs. Smith's room. A man was in her bed. Her insurance is paying for him. I want her in her room by 4:00 p.m., and I want her in the operating room by 5:00 p.m.

The nurse said, "I just got in touch with her surgeon. He's going to a party tonight. He said he would do her surgery tomorrow."

"This is an emergency. Tomorrow she won't be here. He can go to the party after her surgery."

I was receiving divine intervention although I felt like I was in limbo—was I dying? I had asked myself this question some sixty years ago when I was in and out of a coma.

> What is man, that thou art mindful of him? And the son of man, that thou visitest him?
> (Psalm 8:4)

Christians, we can live on earth with its surrounding environmental contamination of polluted air and water. With a great peace in our hearts, learn to approach God like David did—with a joyful heart, singing and dancing unto the holy God of Israel. You can plainly see the intimacy between David and Jehovah God, the God of Abraham, Isaac, and Jacob. The twenty-third Psalm shows David's life was all about his love and trust in God; his dependence on God's faithfulness was evident. David lived all his life loving God although sometimes his lifestyle got him into big trouble. David was a warring man, but through it all, he relied on God's sufficiency and forgiveness. Many times, God gave David victory over his enemies.

David was a young boy. He knew God was with him when he challenged and killed the great giant Goliath, the Philistine's strong man (1 Samuel 17). David was not embarrassed to show God affection before the people. You can feel his love for God through the readings of his writings, in the hymns he sang to the Lord God of Israel. David's singing and dancing were offerings only unto God. It was his great pleasure to play musical instruments to God. His sounds of praise, his worshipping and his dancing were anointed by God. It pleased God to see David not ashamed to display exceedingly rich worship, bathed in the warmth of his love for God, showing off his strong heartfelt passion, honoring the Lord God Almighty openly. God created us for his pleasure; for his pleasure did he create all things.

David was set apart. God said, "David is *a man after my own heart*." My friend, it can't get any better than that—being called a man after God's own heart. David demonstrated his faith and was committed to following after the Lord. Acts 13:22 says, "After removing Saul, God made David the king of Israel." David was the only person in the Bible described as "a man after God's own heart." God testified concerning him: "I have found David, son of Jesse, a man after my own heart." David was God's choice, imperfect but faithful. He loved God with all his heart. A psalm written by David after Nathan the prophet came unto him after he had gone into Bathsheba: "Create in me a clean heart, O God, and renew a right spirit within me."

European church belief is not rooted nor founded in its motherland of worship. The church as we know it, its characteristics is steeped in European culture. European thinking does not allow worshipping like David worshipped; they think it's heathen, barbaric, self-indulgent, and very unnecessary to serve God in that manner. Europeans feel their concept is the way to please God. They have conceived in their mind that they—and they only—demonstrate fervent respect in God's presence. They think, Show no emotions. Genuflect. Bend the knee before the altar. Go sit down, be quiet, be polite, be still before God is the European traditional thinking. To them, anything else is religiously and politically incorrect, not protocol. Be still. Serve in strict adherence. Be correct, and show proper behavior before God. Christmas is the time we celebrate the birth of Jesus Christ. We have been instructed not to say "Merry Christmas" but to say "Happy Holidays" so we do not offend non-Christians. Giving God our hearts in love like David did is pleasing to God. Dancing and singing before the Lord God Almighty in the spirit makes the statement of God's presence.

When they tell us God is not deaf, be quiet. Acting crazy, dancing during church service is primitive and not of God. I have felt the Holy Spirit moving between my toes, tickling, engaging from toe to toe. I could not keep still. The Holy Spirit was having his way, tickling my toes. I started moving; I was doing the holy dance. The holy dance is an outward praise unto the power of God's presence in the body of worship. I danced before the Lord with all my might. The Holy Spirit was amusing himself with my toes. He too was dancing before the Lord on my toes.

There are preachers that say to God's workers, "You said God told you to do what—he's got to tell it to me first. Don't you put your hands on my people." The Holy Spirt is doing his work through those God has anointed for a pacific ministry. When people are being slain in the Spirit, dropping to the floor under the power of the Holy Spirit, some preachers will say, "You are telling me God has anointed your hands in this service and wants you to use them? Don't you lay your hands on my people in my church—I don't care what God is telling you."

Satanic interference can come into play through jealous preachers. Worshipping under man's restricted religious precepts has removed the miraculous miracle power of God out of many churches because some preachers do not have a relationship with God; it only seems they do. When you quench the Holy Spirit, you interrupt and hinder the displaying of God's holy fire at work. When you take it upon yourself to quench God's divine action, you become the one in command, not the Holy Spirit. Many preachers are egotists; they are not walking with God. They are walking with the mighty dollar and "self first." Let God be God. The Holy Spirit is the breath, the power of God—a burning flame, a fire sent to earth to work through God's people for his glory (Acts 2:3–4).

When God is working through his servants, some preachers do not know it is God working through his called-out ones. Don't try and put God in the box you have compartmentalized on his behalf; he is bigger than any box man can dream of building to tuck him away. Man is assertive in his limits and confined in his conception of the presence of God at work in the churches. Man's religious precepts of what God's work looks like is one thing, and how God works his work is another thing. God reveals himself to whom he wants to reveal himself to and in the way he wants to reveal himself. Many of us have tried over and over again to put God in our small box—shame on us. We will never be mentally nor will we be physically capable of adjusting God to fit our imagination of him. God works in mysterious ways. His wonders are to be performed, not man's wonders.

Throughout the church age, most Christians cling to the words of the twenty-third Psalm; we are drawn to this psalm because it shows God-Jehovah the Lord will provide all our needs, El Shaddai, the All-Sufficient One. The twenty third Psalm is clearly expressing that Adonai is the protector of those who love him, serve him, and believe in his Word. Many churches today prohibits their members from demonstrating David's kind of love when glorifying God. Let the religious leaders know they cannot stop the people from singing like David sang nor dancing like David danced before his God. God will open up doors where the Holy Spirit is free to express God's power; why not let it be in our churches? We are saved souls, signed, sealed and delivered unto God, cleansed and made anew through the shed blood of Jesus; think about what I just said because it is mind boggling, knowing we are all sealed in God's heart without stain or blemish. Make a joyful noise unto the Lord, all ye earth—he awaits our fellowship.

Satan is still working out of his same old dirty trick bag that he has used on every generation. This very day, he is using that old trick bag on world governments. Our political leaders are falling for his evil trickery all across this rotating globe we call home. He has fed false information to the hearts of all nations. The people have given their acceptance, and they are running violently with his evilness.

Our trials are not ours to fight alone. Through faith, we are in partnership with Jesus Christ. Our battles are already won; they were defeated on the cross. Jesus is working for us and through us. We are to keep our chins up—do not worry; worry is not a part of free living. Worry will decrease faith, bring confusion; its interference hinders us from attaining our God-given potential. Turn the worry into faith. Our opponent, the devil, is an illegal spirit being from the pits of hell. Put on the whole armor of God and keep standing for the Lord in faith. The Holy Spirit sees our brokenness. The Holy Spirit sees our unborn future, events that are yet to come into our lives. God is holding them in his hands, so don't worry—just give God praise for the life to come. The Holy Spirit is on the job, attacking the enemy's strongholds. Before we know to pray against the unknown troubles that are traveling through the spirit world with our name on them, God has already taken initiative. There should never be a time to doubt the existence of our God's power and faithfulness to act on our behalf.

Words have everlasting life. They are eternal, so let them be words of kindness and worship that glorify and edify God and the world; throughout eternity, let our voices ring. Let our words be edifying, illuminating all of heaven and inspiring the human race. Both good and bad words are living substance. They will live forever. They go racing through dark spaces into the unending eons of time. They are alive and on the move, inflicting as they go. When we select and choose to send words from our warehouse of consciousness, be aware that our words might pass our way again. What effect will they have on our lives when they return to their sender? Our tomorrow is just around the corner. It has been said when we cast our bread upon the waters, after many days, it will return. What we put into the waters of life may eventually show up, and there will be no hiding place from who you are. Can we run from our shadow?

Life is pendulous without visible support. If there is no faith, life is suspended, swinging in the air, blowing from unknown to unknown because of doubt and unbelief.

> But let him ask in faith, nothing wavering.
> For he that wavereth is like a wave of the sea
> driven with the wind and tossed. (James 1:6)

Faith is a gift—let it guide us into the safety of God's eternal arms. The children of God have an advocate with the Father, Jesus Christ the righteous (1 John 2:1). Jesus Christ the Son of Almighty God is our advocate; in his body, he bore our breakthrough. Jesus, our peace offering of salvation. Before creation, God placed our sin in Jesus's blood, for life for life is in the blood. God sent Jesus to set the captive free from the firm grip of sin by the shedding of blood.

Life is in the blood. Jesus poured forth his life-giving blood that we might have life and have it more abundantly (John 10:10). Once the power of his shed blood was released, instantly the receiver, the sinner was made clean, set free from death unto everlasting life.

Everyone hoping for eternal life in the kingdom of God must be washed in the blood of Jesus Christ. It is the only way to have a renewed mind, making us a new person in him. Our inner man has become a new creation by the washing of the blood. Our sins are forgiven by grace through the shed blood of God's holy sacrificed Lamb, Jesus. Jesus took our sins to the cross with him, for they were in him; they too were nailed to the cross. The forgiveness of sin, even the stain of sin, was washed away. The born-again believer was saved, set free from the damnation of hell by the shed blood of Jesus.

God is the same yesterday (*past*), today (*present*), and the *future* tomorrows. Today we can apply the blood of Jesus Christ in our everyday life by asking him into our hearts. Take our daily activities to the cross. Lay them at the feet of Jesus. Ask for forgiveness. We should plead the blood of Jesus over our lives as we go about our daily routine. Jesus is still in the soul-saving business, and every soul is special in his sight. We are unique, cherished, and distinguishable in our God-given purpose.

It is a defining moment when we realize the Holy Spirit is continuously at work in us, working on our behalf, keeping us in purpose while we are sojourning. The Holy Spirit was sent to us by God through Jesus—he is a gift through impartation by the Son of God.

The Holy Spirit is on assignment, living in us to guide our every thought. Quench not the Spirit of God that has been imparted in the believer. Let him do his work. He is being directed by Jesus and is one with our Lord. The Holy Spirit is in obedience to the will of God, doing only the work he was designated to do (Thessalonians 5:19).

> For the spirit (Holy Spirit) searcheth all things, yea, the deep things of God. (1 Corinthians 2:10)

I would like to share this story with you. One morning, at the break of dawn, a voice came to me. This messenger spoke into my ear these words: "There is a room prepared for you in the kingdom."

"Of who?" the Holy Spirit inside me asked.

The voice of the spirit answered, "Of God."

At that time, I was working for the Lord as a street minister and very much in love with Jesus and wanting to please him. I just knew the messenger of God was telling me that God had a room prepared for me in his kingdom. I didn't think I needed any verification of the meaning of his message; the message seemed clear to me. I never questioned the messenger about whose kingdom was he speaking of. I was so very happy with the message. I had listened with my hold heart to the messenger. While I listened, the Lord let me see inside my inner self. I could see three spirits: Jesus's spirit, the Holy Spirit, and another spirit—I could not perceive its identity; it may have been my spirit. I was so still, listening for more that might come from the messenger.

When the Holy Spirit said to the messenger, "Kingdom of who?" the messenger answered, "Of God." I was so excited about having a room prepared for me in God's kingdom. I had to go tell someone my good news. I told a Christian friend about the message I had received that morning. I remember her saying, "You got a room. I've got a mansion prepared for me when I get to heaven. I don't believe you got a messenger from God." She said, "Why would the Holy Spirit have to ask whose kingdom the messenger was referring to? The Holy Spirit ought to have known whose kingdom the messenger was talking about."

Her rejection of my spiritual visitation annoyed me. I gave what she had to say much thought, concerned for a day or two about her disbelief of what had happened. Finally, I said, "Lord, help me to understand why the Holy Spirit asked whose kingdom the messenger was telling me about."

The Holy Spirit answered me, "Had I not asked in whose kingdom was your room prepared? In time, Satan would have said, 'I've got a kingdom too.' Was the messenger referring to my kingdom? You would have been prevented from answering Satan because the designated kingdom had not been revealed to you. Satan would have taken your lack of knowledge and used it against you. He would have sent a spirit of fear to cast a shadow of doubt on the message. I deprived him of the privilege of placing fear in your heart by not knowing the chosen kingdom of your eternal abode. The spirit of fear would have taken ownership of your heart for a season."

By the Holy Spirit asking the question, "Of who," gave the messenger an opportunity to answer, "Of God." God, I thank you for the Holy Spirit. The Holy Spirit's job is to search all things—even the things of God. There are two kingdoms vying, striving for the superiority concerning man's soul and wanting the rule over man's soul throughout eternity.

Obedience is fulfillment to the soul and joy to God's heart. It gives God great pleasure creating working vessels of representation of his likeness, the image of him in the earth. Know our bodies are living temples where the breath of God lives.

Have we been trying to fight our battles alone? Do we think we can fight the battle of life all by ourselves? No. Living through life's battles in our own power and terms was never our assignment. The Lord said, "Cast your cares upon me, for I care for thee."

Jesus Christ ushered in the dispensation of grace. Grace is for whosoever: "Let him come unto me," Jesus said. "And receive the free gift of eternal life." Heaven is promised to those who have accepted Jesus Christ as their Lord and Savior. If we have received Jesus as Lord of our lives, he becomes our redeemer. We've been redeemed, freed from Satan's secure hold on our souls, and rescued from hell's lake of fire. We have been saved from our souls' eternal damnation.

Heaven is filled with melodious music. The angels of heaven fill the kingdom of God with sounds of songs of praise. Let the whole earth make a joyful sound unto the Lord. There are those with an ear to hear these celestial bodies in song as it travels throughout heaven's atmosphere.

It is appointed unto man to encounter many uphill battles; through prayers in faith, we are never walking alone. The highways of life are troublesome, but the trouble is limited. Better to travel this troublesome journey than walk eternity's everlasting troubled roads in hell.

> Man that is born of a woman is of few days, and full of trouble. He cometh forth like a flower, and is cut down: he fleeth also as a shadow, and continueth not. (Job 14:1–2)

Man's constant longing for freedom and peace of mind can be a reality, a dream come true while on our earthly journey; through a relationship with Jesus Christ, all things are possible, for the joy of the Lord is our strength. There are many ways to defuse the power of Satan by practicing faith in Christ while traveling life's highway of many trials and tribulations; Jesus is the answer. Let us not fail to use prayer and worship as our defense, our protection against the works of the enemy. Our Lord Jesus is the faithful King of kings and Lord of lords, having dimension over our souls and is the answer to our every need. There will always be bombshells littering the pathway to heaven. We will experience oppression, sufferings resulting from evil persecutions sent straight from the pits of hell to our address. We are the promised-land children, walking hand and hand with Jesus toward the New Jerusalem.

Understand that earth time is allotted time given to mankind to fight the good fight of faith. Our faith will be tried. We are to use our earth time wisely to find our purpose and get in it. Our time and peace on earth, being that it was preordained, we are to use it with determination to obey Almighty God. Intentionally strive, aim at purpose; our lives' goal should be living deliberately in the measure of faith that God has given us.

When we want to live our lives on our own terms, expressing life any way we choose and being referred to as the ever-loving goodtime daddy of the night, know life can come back at us like a haunting dream that keeps returning and making no sense. Our lives were not given to us for selfish indulgence. Life is not all about us and our wants; it's about God and his will to be done on earth as it is in heaven through his chosen.

It is natural to feel we are missing out on some things in life. What is it we can't wrap our minds around but we keep thinking we need it? Give up the belief we can rule all the flavors of our destiny. Did I hear someone say, "I don't want the intangible, the abstract beings ruling my life"? Do we pray? Are we relying on an invisible God to hear and answer our petitions, wanting him to show favor concerning our requests? If God is not ruling our lives, who is? When God is absent as ruler of our lives, there is a spiritual void; Satan certainly will rush in to fill any emptiness we are carrying in the enter bosom of our hearts. He would like to own the chambers of our minds, having them become his hiding place and his playground throughout eternity. The mind directs all our bodily functions. If our minds are not listening to the Holy Spirit, our eternal rest is at stake. Don't trade away the one and only soul we will ever have.

There is a new life, a godly life through Jesus, waiting for us to open our hearts and invite him in. If we are not in obedience to God's will, then whose will are we in obedience to? Think about the choices we make. Are they of God's will or of Satan's will? Who are we obeying—that is the question we should be asking ourselves every day. The choices we make today determine where we will spend our eternal life.

> Verily, verily, I say unto thee, "Except a man be born again, he cannot see the Kingdom of God." (John 3:3)

Only God's blood-washed children will enjoy God's kingdom. What we believe in life can happen for us, so keep the faith. Ask Jesus to take over our lives. The right moment is now—now is the time to ask him in. Jesus is as near to us as the breath we breathe. Why not ask him in?

> Behold, I stand at the door, and knock: if any man, hear my voice, and open the door, I will come into him, and will sup with him and he with me. (Revelation 3:20)

The Bible gives us biblical truth. No man is able to save himself, neither is a man an island unto himself. We live in a mosaic society. In our own power, we can do nothing to defuse the enemy's power that is coming after our lives; without the blood of Jesus working through us, we are defeated.

> My people are destroyed for lack of knowledge: because thou hast rejected knowledge, I will also reject thee. (Hosea 4:6)

My people, because they will not ask me to feed them, perish from their lack of knowledge concerning my will. The enemy will rush in like an flood overflowing coming against the ignorance of my people.

When we fail to call on the power of the blood, we suffer needlessly. We are to plead the blood of Jesus over our lives each day. Satan's power is irremovable when we confront him with human knowledge and strength only; the enemy will play us like children playing with their yoyos.

There is spiritual warfare in operation all around us; we are to fight the spirit with the spirit. Our strength alone is a toy in the hands of the enemy. He is laughing in the face of the whole human race. We think we can duke it out with Satan without the help God has provided—think again. The devil sees man trying to figure out, "What in the world is happening to my life?" Having a peaceful, happy life is insignificant to the enemy, meaningless to the devil, who is robbing and stealing, stripping away the peace of the world. He has taken our joy. He wants us to stay under his influence. He is playing mankind like a violin with war after war. He hates man; he wants to destroy us. We are inconsequential in his quest for power over the world. He is violence, a threat to who we are in Christ. No one will ever find their true selves until they embrace Jesus as Lord of their lives. Jesus is Lord. Cherish that old rugged cross. Our sins were nailed to it, and they died there in Jesus's finished work.

When we see a fellow human being, that sin has laid flagellant, beaten to the ground. If they ask to be helped, they want to do penance, to lay bare their soul. Kneel. Pray with them in Jesus's name. Don't use dogmatic determination to correct a broken spirit. Our lives are often interrupted by our transgressions. Think on that before casting the first stone.

Be aware. Know that we too live on a street called infringement. We too stand in need of correction. Compassion is what Jesus gives to the souls of the brokenhearted. All have failed and came short of the glory of God. I had an uncle Jack; I dearly loved him. He was an alcoholic. He lived alone, and he talked to himself all the time.

When I was a young child, I would ask him, "Uncle Jack, are you going to heaven when you die?"

He would answer, "I live in hope if I die in despair."

I don't know if my uncle knew the meaning of the word *despair*. I'm sure he did. Anyway, I loved hearing him say that. Though my uncle was an alcoholic, he was one man that never disrespected or tried to violate my youth. I felt safe around him. I did not want any harm to ever come near him. He did not cuss nor swear. I never saw him mistreat anyone. He was not a vulgar man in any way, shape, nor form. He was not the hoity-toity type. Uncle Jack looked like a thin old White man. He had a lady friend. Her skin had a deep chocolate hue. "The blacker the berry, the sweeter the juice," he would always say when talking about his lady love's deep ebony complexion. He loved her deep complexion, and I so loved her clothes; they looked like they were from the 1920s, when people were dancing the Charleston.

The Holy Spirit helps us grow in grace, strengthening us and deepening our faith. The Holy Spirit gives us the ability to withstand hardships, increasing our endurance. Patience is learned through endurance. Can we picture depicting a world without patience? God has long patience, waiting for his people—we are the precious fruit of the earth. Obedience to God is a precious jewel, and it's greatly cherished in the kingdom of heaven. Patience is a virtue; it is a spiritual principle embodied in mankind, and patience shows the love of God in our souls (Luke 21:19). In your patience, possess ye your souls.

Do not ask anything from God with a doubtful heart. We are to believe we receive as we speak. Show faith. We are to harbor in our hearts an attitude of praise. Keep pure thoughts—they are unspoken words. We should have our spiritual ears perked up, for spiritual communications are always taking place. God hears our thoughts. The enemy of our souls is always engaging our psyche, trying to influence our minds with unholy thoughts. Stay in continuous communication with the Lord through songs and deeds; there is always an exchange of thoughts taking place between the spiritual and the physical world. We are always interacting with these spirits, their presence sending thoughts, causing behaviors, either good or bad.

Our perception receives the message, and what should we do with them? Outward worship is one thing; divine inward spiritual contact is intimacy, and that is what God wants. Intimacy with the divine spirit is most important to our spiritual insight. We are to close the door of our mouth sometimes, worship the Lord God in the privacy of our hearts; it is our inner closet. Outward religious signs, the application of oil, and the washing of feet—we are to keep manifesting these outward religious signs. They show man's institutionalized religion system at work. God wants intimacy. He wants the heart of man. Inward dedication speaks volumes to the Lord God.

Mary Magdalene anointed the feet of Jesus. Weeping, she washed his feet with her tears and wiped the tears away with her hair. She did not stop kissing the Lord's feet, showing her great love.

Can you picture Mary, from the town of Magdalene, showing such deep tender love for Jesus as she anointed his head and cleaned his feet with her tears, and with her hair she dried our Lord's feet? What was going on in Mary's heart as she displayed tender affection to our Lord? (Luke 7:37–50)

> And whatsoever ye shall ask in my name, that will I do, that the Father may be glorified in the Son. If you ask anything in my name, I will do it. (John 14:13–14)

Learn the mystery of the double portion. Trust and obey Jesus. Have faith in the Word of God. There is no other way to receive a double portion. Jesus is our anointed savior sent by God for the salvation of mankind. "Whomsoever will let him come unto me, and I will make him fisher of men." Obedience is the key ingredient to life everlasting. Jesus said, "If you love me, obey me." Unlock the doors that lead to life; open the door that reads grace. Grace is God's free gift to humanity; it opens the door of favor. In all our doings, keep faith in God's Word; God and his Word are one. As we walk through the many doors of life, we are to keep faith in the forefront of our minds. We are to hold our faith high above our head; it is a precious commodity, a jewel above all else.

Faith is a gift everyone will not inherit in the same portion. Demonstrate, utilize the faith God has given us. Put faith into action. Let the world see God at work through his faithful believers. If we faithfully use the faith God has given us, we will watch our faith take wings. Faith the size of a mustard seed will move any hideous mountain that will occur in our lives. Our faith is confronted daily, put to test—that's called experiencing life in faith. Our lives were preordained. We must live out our predetermined purpose to the glory of God. We were born for a purpose. Once we find our purpose, we are to quickly get into it and do what is required of us.

> Likewise the Spirit also helpth our infirmities: for we know not what we should pray for

> as we ought: but the Spirit itself maketh intercession for us with groanings which cannot be uttered. (Romans 8:26)

> For it is written, "As I live," saith the Lord, "every knee shall bow to Me, and every tongue shall confess to God." (Romans 14:11)

Jesus never said life would be easy; life certainly was not easy for him. Think of his suffering the days and hours before he went to the cross—the pain of the nails being thrust through his flesh, through his bones, and the sudden plunge of the blade the spear penetrating, piercing through to his heart, drawing out his life's blood to hurry his death because the Sabbath day was at hand. We call the day of his crucifixion Good Friday, and so it is. Hold on—Sunday is coming. Grasp the resurrected life that is ours. For the sinner, Good Friday is their gift from God that set the sinner free. Jesus had to be sacrificed. God's precious Son was sacrificed for whosoever could believe on him. A blood sacrifice was required for the forgiveness of man's sin; it was an ancient ritual. Before the death of Jesus, every year the blood offering of a goat was required for the people's sins. Jesus shed his blood once for whosoever would come to the cross of salvation. He said, "Let him come." The blood of Jesus reached back to the beginning of time until this present moment in time and to the future times yet to come. There is living power, wonder-working power in the shed blood of Jesus. May our souls be immersed in the blood of the Lord. O Lord God, may we continuously with joy be absorbed in the precious shed blood of Jesus. Fridays must come into our lives, but the power of God gave us Resurrection Sunday, our key to eternal life.

Never in our wildest dreams can we imagine what God wants to reveal to us in this life. Let him who has an ear hear—hear what the spirit of God is saying. The soul that is absent of love—it's absent of the concept of God's nature. Love is a gift and is the most needed ingredient in life. To the glory of God, love activates the spiritual blocks that build divine working power. Not having love is being disobedient to God. We cheat ourselves. We deceive ourselves. We defraud ourselves out of God's kingdom by not loving one another. God will not work his power where there is no love. Let us go to the altar of our hearts, tearing there as the Father ministers to our souls. Put God first in life no matter the cost. Answering God's calling without wavering will bring us into a partnership with the Almighty.

With loving participation, when undertaking our divine assignment, we do well to do it with purpose. Our eternal life is at risk. With a loving heart for God's authority involving our relationship, as we cooperate with his divine presence, having a living experience with him brings benefits, resembling a loving kinship that is beyond man's understanding. Uniting in prayer with God is divine.

Whose mind is stayed on the Lord has created a very good habit. If we are participating in a prayer group that is led by the Holy Spirit, we have something to be thankful for. A union of believers in prayer is as powerful as an atomic bomb. Are our minds always present, stayed on Jesus when we are praying? May our minds be steadfast, fixed on God when talking to him. Don't let our minds be like Swiss cheese filled with holes. Are our minds absent from our conversation drifting here and there? Are we just in a prayer position uttering words into thin air, or are our minds steadfast on God in Jesus's name?

Cleanse me moment by moment, my precious savior. I want to walk before you, my savior, as a light to the glory of God. Where impurities abide, replace them with pure compassion. Jesus, your mercy is renewed every second of every day. I receive the great promises in your Word. I am serious when I say, "Use me, Lord, for your glory helps me to live for you. Sweet Jesus, I want to worship thee with a pure heart. Put in me the heart of an overcomer. My everlasting desire is to live in faithful submission to your will now and throughout the totality of time. I once was dead, but now I am alive because Jesus came into my life; my life was once like unto the valley of dry bones. I was one of the world's walking dead, roaming here and there without purpose. I did not know you" (Ezekiel 37:3–10). That which was dead in the valley of dry bones, you spoke life over them, and they lived. In your sight, am I less then those dry bones? Speak to my dried-up bones that they may live again.

Your ways, my Lord, are far above my ways. I understand not thy ways, my God, yet I am in full agreement with all you do. When I get to heaven, I will receive divine knowledge. My eyes will be opened to understanding (John 11:39–44). You called Lazarus to life when he had been entombed for four days, and Jesus, you have called many from among the walking dead of the earth and renewed their lives. Thank you, Lord God Almighty, for the free gift of salvation through the shed blood of Jesus. Our souls were bankrupt, broken, and spiritually penniless, unable to pay our sin debt. Jesus, you are the Lord and Savior of all who will come to you asking forgiveness.

Do we believe Jesus is who he says he is and can do all he promised to do? Jesus is the truth and the light of the world—believe in him. There are times when Jesus may seem far away. We feel we have not heard his voice in a very long time. Jesus said, "I will never leave you nor forsake you." Stand on the binding promises of God. At times we may feel like unforgiven children. In our weakest moments, faith is still there, waiting to be called forth from our innermost beings. We are to plead the blood of Jesus over all our fears and doubts and lean not on our own understanding. We are to cast the weight of our desires on the solid rock of foundation—Jesus. Remember, the spirit of our anointed Savior forever lives within the soul of his children. Let's have a little talk with Jesus. Tell him all about our quality times and our troubling times. We have freely received from Jesus. Thank him for loving us so richly. We are immersed in him in spite of the fact we are not always in obedience. We are to become a new creation, buried in the blood of our redeemer. See that we ask Jesus into our hearts as we speak. We give you the glory, the honor, and the praise for washing and cleansing us in the water of your Word. You have freed us from all unrighteousness by the power of your holy Word. God and his Word are one, and Jesus is the Word of God. Follow his lead.

We have been freed from the unmerciful wicked one who offers enticement that leads to hell. Know that we have been given citizenship in God's kingdom. Fear not, my little ones. Your cries have come up before me as sweet fragrance. I have gathered your tears into vessels of grace. As a mother hen gathers her little chicks under her wings, I will gather you too, my little ones, unto myself, keeping you under my protection.

The concept of a suffering Messiah has always been a stumbling block for many to comprehend. Some ask, Why would a God suffer? God's ways are not our ways; his ways are high above human understanding. Jesus's sufferings on the cross is a powerful integral part of God's redemptive plan to gather his children unto himself. In fact, Jesus was completed through his suffering of the cross. His death and resurrection signifies our death and resurrection in him. Not that his deity lacked imperfection; his entry into humanity was without fault. Jesus had no defect. He was perfect in every way. The Father's requirements were that he become sin to redeem man from Satan's firm grip on the soul of man. As man, Jesus was enabled through suffering and the shedding of blood to become the captain of man's salvation. Suffering was allowed to come upon him. He participated and empathized with us. Death was the means of his destroying Satan's hold on man's soul and securing our redemption to everlasting life in God's kingdom.

> For whom the Lord loveth he chasteneth, every son whom he receiveth. If ye endure chastening, God dealeth with you as with sons; for what son is he whom the father chasteningth not? But if ye without chastisement, whereof all are partakers, then are ye bastard, and not sons. (Hebrews 12:6–8)

When God asks you to do something, don't say, "I don't want to." I made that mistake even though later I obeyed. What a miserable wretch; what a disappointment I am. I've grieved the Holy Spirit through strong feelings of anger, not being able to forgive in the moment, self-pity, fear of what others would think about me. I ran the full gamut of human sin and emotions.

I know we are to make allowance for those who have insulted us, forgive their errors and weakness—even to the point we may cry when we think about the pain and hurts they brought into our lives. The highway to heaven is designed with billions of deeply engraved pavers. Inscribed are the names of the forgiven. If we ask God to forgive us in Jesus's name, our names too are engraved on one of those pavers that are flowing up the King's highway leading to heaven.

Since the creation of time, Jesus is the best gift ever given to man. We were born sinners, but by the grace of God, we are a part of God's holy family. I get all excited thinking about my new life that is yet to come.

Still, on this journey, let us give thanks to God by sending prayers of love to our Lord while standing in expectation of our unending peace awaiting our arrival. Every day feed freely on the things of God. Spend time with the Father and his Son; it is spiritual nourishment to the soul.

I am alive in God because Jesus is alive in me. The realization of God's truth is of importance to our spiritual insight and growth, his grace a unique gift through the Holy Spirit of promise. Jesus is the promised Word of God made flesh. He was sent to earth to bleed and die for our sin. O death, where is thy sting? The sting of death has been removed because of what happened on the cross of Jesus. The miracle power of forgiveness lives in the Savior. Our worst sin has been forgiven through the precious shed blood of Christ Jesus. Forgiveness is a must. God's love is wrapped in his forgiveness. Where would humanity be without God's forgiving power? He sent his Son into the world to die that we might be forgiven and brought into new life. Forgive, my friend, forgive. Our eternity is wrapped in forgiveness.

Hear ye all the earth. Listen to the voice of almighty God, and give him glory.

Glorify God with praise—he is due all praise. Let our songs be songs of praise.

When we are washing dishes, sweeping floors, do all that we do—do it unto God.

27

He Was There All the Time

That day I did not have to go to work, and I did not feel like going to the mall. I decided to sleep in. I was fast asleep. It seemed abruptly I awoken. I realized I was looking across the foot of my bed toward a small window above the dressing table. The corner near the window had a grayness, an appearance I was not used to seeing. The area looked shadowy—why? I saw a figure standing in the shadows. A man was standing in the denseness; I could not see him clearly. My awareness heightened, my brain signaling danger. Fear was upon me. I thought while I was asleep, someone has gotten into the house; now they are standing concealed in the shadows. I sat upright, straining my eyes to see who on earth could that be. The figure began walking effortlessly, it seemed, without bending a knee, more like a glide, yet the figure kept moving toward me. I crawled to the foot of the bed, my eyes glued on the approaching figure.

He drew near—I remember thinking, *That looks like Jesus to me.* If there be a Jesus, I'm grabbing a hold of him. When he got close enough, I reached out, trying to grab his garment. With all my strength, I tried to get my hands on his loose flowing gown. My intention was to never let go of him. I thought to myself, *I want to go where he goes and be where he be.* While I was reaching out to grab his clothing, he turned and walked so smoothly through the wall like the wall was just a puff of air. With all my efforts, I was unable to touch his clothing. He moved so swiftly. I felt he didn't want me to touch him. I wanted him to take me wherever he was going.

Two years passed before the remembrance of his visitation came back to my memory. Jesus temporarily removed my power to retain his visitation—why I do not know.

I had an enthusiastic friend who was a recent born-again Christian, just overflowing with joy. She was always telling me, "Maxi, you need Jesus." She was a very good friend; otherwise, I would have told her, "Keep your religion to yourself." We had formed a friendship when taking some adult classes together. After our classes ended, we stayed in touch. We both loved Jesus in our way. I was a nonpracticing Catholic; she was a Protestant Evangelist. We could sit for hours, talking about the Lord Jesus, and drinking a little Martini & Rossi Asti as we fellowshipped.

One day, I was in deep depression, very unhappy. I felt less than human. It was like I was having a vision; I could see myself gloomy, looking into a ghostly place. I was dressed in dirty rags, sitting on muddy ground at what appeared to be the gate outside the grounds of the grim reaper. I was peering through a rod-iron fence into a heavy fog. It was grim and obscured. A smoky mist covered the large swamplike yard. It was a damning looking place.

I felt so lonely and alone. My spirit man was at its lowest. I was in extreme distress, downright miserable, feeling wretchedly inadequate and unloved. I felt like an outcast without a foreseeable future of any worth. I could not anticipate anything of value coming to me. I felt sorry for myself. I was in despair. I felt lost. I was alone, and I was so lonely. Sitting there on the ground in that awful place, peering through into a dark desolate place, I thought that must be hell. I could hear the phone ringing—who could that be? I don't feel like talking to anyone. I made myself answer the phone.

"Hello." Not really surprised when I heard my dear friend's voice.

"Maxi, how you doing?" she inquired.

"Not good. I'm so unhappy," I told her.

"Maxi, you need Jesus," she said. "Get on your knees. I want you to repeat after me the sinner's prayer." Then she asked, "Are you on your knees?"

Right away, the devil rushed to me and said, "You can tell her anything. She's over there. You're over here. You don't have to get on your knees. She won't know the difference."

The Holy Spirit was near me and spoke, saying, "Why tell a lie about a little thing like that?" he asked.

"That's right," I agreed with the Holy Spirit.

I dropped to my knees and began repeating the sinner's prayer; I saw through the dining room window what appeared to be a shooting star. It disappeared. I kept watching through the window (I thought, *A shooting star this time a' day*). Again, I saw the streak of light; it was a shooting star. I kept repeating the sinner's prayer, still watching to see if I would see the shooting star again; all at once, there it was. An image of a man was sitting in the dining room window. It was Jesus dressed in radiant white. He was gloriously beaming brilliant light that flowed from his person. His engulfing presence was lights unspeakable, magnificently possessing splendor, overflowing, gleaming across the room. The appearance of unimaginable glorious brightness came through his holy being. His holy presence glowing unspeakable, in flaming radiance, purity, and holiness was blazing from his presence.

Jesus moved close to where I was kneeling. Without words, he summoned my soul to him. Jesus looked through my spirit, to my soul. He was interested in ministering to my soul. He separated my soul from my spirit. He had first separated my spirit from its body of flesh. Spiritually, I was standing before my Lord. He looked through my spirit and ministered to my soul. I looked over at my body, still kneeling on the floor, repeating the sinner's prayer. My spirit being was standing quietly as Jesus ministered to my soul. Jesus imparted the Holy Spirit into my soul. The Holy Spirit shot through my soul like a bolt of high-powered electricity, an electrifying surge of energy that will never die. The flash of holy empowerment went through me, an experience that I will only receive once. I believe this Spirit will go with me from life to life. My soul will not go through this experience again; the Holy Spirit will never leave me. The holy electrifying power went through the phone, to my friend, touching her so powerfully until she hollered, "Maxi, I believe you've got the Holy

Ghost." The phone was so full of electricity I had to let it fly out of my hand; it fell and rested in its cradle. Jesus turned from my spirit. He walked down the hall, off the dining room. I ran, looking to see where Jesus went. He disappeared in the darkness of a cloud that was standing in the room.

My friend called me right back to tell me, "You go tell somebody what Jesus did for you. The devil will come and try to steal the memory of your experience. You just received the impartation of the Holy Spirit."

"I don't know who to tell," I asked her. "Can I tell you what just happened to me?"

"Yes, you have to tell somebody. The devil is a thief. He wants to take the moment of your rebirth away from you," she answered.

The Holy Spirit had been there all the time. He knew that day Jesus was coming to me and imparted his holy presence into my soul. The Holy Spirit was there, observing that lying devil at work, trying to steal my salvation. The deceiver was trying to get me to lie to my friend, to tell her I was on my knees while I was still standing. I did not lie to my friend, but I have to give all the credit to the Holy Spirit, who was near me, saying, "Why tell a lie about a little thing like that?"

Satan wanted me in his power with a lying spirit influencing my tongue during my born-again experience; God's will will always be done. The Holy Spirit did not let me lie and say I was on my knees when I wasn't. God is able to keep all that is his. The devil wanted my soul for his hellish pleasure. Tormenting my soul forever was his aim. He is the one making unhappy souls, wanting to rob our souls of eternal rest. No one nor nothing can rob God.

Jesus said in John 18:9, "Of them which thou gavest me have I lost none."

The Holy Spirit is always on the job. He is everywhere at the same time, knowing all things, searching the depths of the deep things of God. Nothing gets past the Holy Spirit; he is everywhere present. He is the very breath of God, one with the Father, all-knowing, all-seeing, and all-powerful. God tells us in his word to try the spirit by the spirit. We are to question the thoughts coming into our minds. Thoughts are coming to us all the time—from whom did they come?

After I received the impartation of the Holy Spirit, God gave me a three-tiered ministry. Number one, I was called into the ministry of praise and worship, expressing love to God with praise, song, and dance. The Holy Spirit can get down between your toes, and your feet just can't stay still. I would glorify God with holy dancing. Number two—called into intercession. I was an intercessor, interceding in prayer for others, entreaty—petitioning God's mercy on behalf of their request. Number three, I was to be a prayer warrior. Warfare brings engagement and struggle with the demonic powers. Being a prayer warrior, I came against many powers of darkness sent to me by Satan to torment me. These evil spirits tried to defeat my efforts to obey God. They brought fear into my face by showing themselves to me, trying to stop me from working out my divine assignments.

Satan's work sometimes can resemble divine purity, having the appearance of holiness, but their deceit comes from superhuman powers, putting spiritual intermediates between you and God. There were times I came to the point while working for God, I felt I was a failure. I would say, "God, how can you use me? I'm such a crybaby." Destruction was coming from every side of my life. My marriage was falling apart, yet I carried on. People who appeared to be serving God—some were actually Satanists. They would not teach from the New Testament; they taught only from the Old Testament. I felt they did not want to use the name of Jesus. They wanted me to feel I didn't have the ability to serve the Almighty, yet I carried on and cried constantly. At times I felt I had no strength in me. I felt beaten down; however, I lost not the ability to serve my Lord. I accomplished the task assigned me. I watched my Lord at work, performing miracles.

God is with his children. The battlefields of obedience is never easy. Read the Bible stories of God's workmen, and you will understand what I am talking about.

We are God's soldiers, and we will engage in spiritual warfare. The day we invited Jesus into our lives, we enlisted in his army. Jesus will make us skilled warriors by teaching us the drudgery of pushing onward while in the thick of opposition. Winning through learning how to fight the battles of warfare, we don't give up, we keep on, keeping on knowing Jesus is with us. The cross was not easy for Jesus. All the filthy sin of the world covered him while he hung on the cross. Think how painful all that sin must have been, but he had to bear it for our salvation.

Even God, his Father, looked away from the filthy sin that covered and dishonored his Son. Sin was destroying, taking away mankind's eternal rest. Our sin had to be placed on Jesus. No other being was worthy to carry out God's divine will of redemption. God so loved mankind he gave his only Son to redeem us from hell's burning flames. God is calling us to do a work for him. Obey. Answer his call. We have been removed from the poisonous stains of the painful sting of death.

Our God has dispatched ministering spirits that surround his workers. They are working among us, defending God's workers from the dangers of defeat at the hands of the enemy. Victory belongs to God through his children of obedience. The devil's power has been destroyed because of Jesus's finished work while he was on the cross of redemption. Also, he is being defeated daily by God's triumphant faithful prayer warriors. Satan tried tempting Jesus—the Son of Almighty God. He failed miserable in his attempts. Jesus is our only prevention against Satan's powers. Satan is trying to succeed in his ongoing quest to conquer God's kingdom and make it his habitation once again.

Lucifer is a nullified spirit. He has been overthrown by God's mighty and holy angelic army and by the prayers of God's faithful. The human foe has been defeated, arrested, and is awaiting trial. Our hostile spiritual opponent will live in his dungeon of intense blazing fire. These utter dark dungeons were created for him and his faithful followers. Our Father Jehovah God Almighty already has convicted Satan, found him guilty of treason. His great illegal crime was attempting to overthrow heaven. He will receive his full penalty during the white throne judgment. He will be tried and cast into utter darkness. His power will be inflicted unto him, restricted limited to ruling only his kingdom of darkness. The punishment of being sentenced to everlasting darkness is a serious defeat for Satan in his efforts to gain a foothold in the glory of heaven. He wants power over the souls resting in the kingdom of God. He used to play the symphonic instruments in heaven and had a melodious voice. He was the leader of heaven's choir. After living in the divine light that proceeds from God's holy being, he tried to overthrow God and was kicked from heaven to earth, where he is running rampant. To a certain extent, Satan has unrestrained power over the earth for a time and a season. Knowing he shall reap the harvest of his evil deeds in endless darkness, he is running in high gear. His time of sabotaging the earth is short lived. God's everlasting punishment is ever before his face. Knowing he can never escape the punishment that is coming to him at the hands of God, he is trying to bring as much harm upon the earth as quickly as he can. He keeps eating away at man's heart, crippling man's soul, making us unable to love and forgive one another.

Forever throughout Satan's kingdom comes startling loud screams. The violent cursing, enragement with uncontrollable anger and fighting without end, tearing one another to pieces, causing great pain continuously in the underworld of darkness, and he is requesting your presence to the kingdom of uncontrolled hatred.

When Jesus comes back, the new heaven and the new earth will be revealed, and these new worlds will never come under satanic attack. Whose kingdom are you momentarily serving—do you know?

28

Sin Was Nailed to the Cross

Some people feel it is not necessary to expose every wrinkle in their soul to public view, and they are right. We are to give place to the soul's agony. Allow life's built-up steam to escape its confinement. Put your concerns out there and breathe in then exhale. We need an escape hatch from some of the pressures of life, from days long gone by, allowing new life to thrive and flourish, experience a newfound freedom, the joy of releasement from pent-up emotions; holding onto some things far too long can be dangerous to our mental and physical health. Get rid of old guilt by emptying the soul to a confessor of sort because our true confessor is God Almighty. Remember, the devil lives in the details of the past; we have given our closemouthed knowledge permission without limits to access the happiness of our lives. Beware of whom it is we are confessing the innermost secrets of life. Make sure God is telling you to take this person as confessor and confidant. The devil is on a lease when it comes to interfering in the lives of God's believers; his liberty in harming us is under contract. He has to get permission to approach and inflict harm on the children of God. Read Job 1:6–12.

Satan has to get permission to whisper his deceit into God's servant's sense of perception. Satan likes exercising control where he can, in places where he has no permission. He tries to infuse his principles. This master of deceit has to get permission from God to invade the lives of God's called-out ones. The enemy wants to thumb his nose at God by conquering the will of God's chosen few. God sends angels to fight our spiritual battles, Lift up Jesus in worship. Joshua marched around the walls of Jericho; we too are marching in the battle of our Jericho. Keep faith, and watch the opposing walls of the enemy come tumbling down. We have to be very careful to whom we confess, giving our innermost possessions; if it's the wrong person, we can count on this—the evilness of that person will laugh in our face while slandering our name. Know to whom we are laying open our souls. We don't want our face washed in our past day after day. Most people are tattlers, and they can't help it. A tattler wears many faces. They say, "Let us pray about this matter." Eventually, they say to someone, "Did you know what so and so told me—that they did such and such a thing. Can you believe that? I didn't know they had that in them."

After we have exposed our sins, every time we look at the person we confess to, they see only our sin. Every time God looks at the sinner, he sees the finished work of his Son's blood and what it has accomplished. He knows we have been washed, made clean, and given new life through the blood of Jesus Christ. Blood is life giving, supplying life to man. Blood is the life of all living beings. Without blood, there is no life.

It does not matter where God has brought us from; what matters is where he has taken us to. Our sin has been blotted out for his glory and are seen no more. The finished work on the cross has done it all. We are beaming, shining bright lights in God's sight. We have been saved from the destruction of death. We have been made brand new through the shed blood of his Son Jesus Christ, our Lord and Savior.

When we pray, believe the request has gone up before God. May our prayers be tied to his Word. His Word is his will. Know that God and his Word are one. Many pray, "If it be thy will, let thy will be done." We know that God and his Word are one. His Word is his will. Let our prayers be fastened to the love of God and his faithfulness. Let us come to God as a little child, come in love, expressing what is on our hearts. For all that we do, let it be done to the glory of God.

God has let his will be known. He gave ten commandments to Moses; Jesus gave two powerful commandments to us—love the Lord thy God with all thy strength and all thy might; love thy neighbor as thyself. We are to join our neighbors, feeling their pain and their joy. We are one with our neighbor through Christ Jesus, so let's celebrate our neighbor.

We are to look to God for our completion. Only God has the power to bring completion to the human soul.

Jesus said, "Holiness is what I want. Be holy as I am holy," said the Lord.

29

Fear

Fear is the expectation of a bad outcome. We cannot afford to live fearfully. The way you live is the way you die. What is fear? Fear is triggered by the perception that danger is near. Fear is a strong emotion; it is paralyzing, can make us powerless to think in our best interest. Fear is one of the basic emotions affecting both man and beast. Our fear instinct tells us danger is near; it seems something is not quite right. The sense of danger brings a feeling of insecurity. When fear engulfs us, be cautious. Call on God, and listen to our gut instinct. Be submissive to God's spiritual guidance and panic not. Wait on God.

Fear is not of God. Stand on his word and faint not. We do not have to sink under every heavy load that life brings when we have the ability to put our faith in God's ability. We do not have to leave ourselves wide open to the devil's centuries-old tricks. He goes around like a roaring lion, seeking whom he may devour. God has smitten Satan upon the jaw and broken off all his teeth. He can't chew us up; he can only nibble on us. Jesus disarmed him thousands of years ago. He is powerless and toothless. We don't have to lie down and roll over for Satan, letting him try to gum us to death. Why should we live in the fear Satan has provided us with? Jesus bruised the head of Satan and put him under his feet a long time ago on the cross of redemption. Fear is not a spirit sent to us by God.

Look up and despair not. Trade in fear for God's faithfulness. Walk in faith. Get in line with God's Word, and live a life of peace in our hearts.

> For ye have not received the spirit of bondage again to fear, we are to keep our eyes on Jesus. (Romans 8:15)

We are not to put our eyes on the problem, keeping them there. We are to keep our eyes on Jesus. David's Psalm 23:4:

> Yea though I walk through the valley of the shadow of death, I will fear no evil.

We are not to let Satan go undetected in our lives. When we realize the spirits of fear and doubt has come upon us, in Jesus's name and in praise, resist these feelings until they flee. Peter, showing his love and trust in Jesus, jumped out of the boat into the water to meet Jesus. Through the howling winds, Satan was whispering into Peter's heart, and his faith began to sink. Fear had entered into Jesus's beloved disciple. "Peter," Satan whispered. "Are you walking on water? You know men can't walk on water." At that moment, fear entered Peter, and he began to sink. Under the influence of Satan's voice, Peter's confidence and strength failed. He cried out, "Lord, save me." Jesus knew Satan had sifted Peter's confidence to continue the walk. Jesus immediately stretched his hand out and caught Peter, saying, "O thou of little faith, wherefore did you doubt?"

Fear is one of Satan's properties; he owns that spirit. When we get on Satan's property, he has the legal right to come after the invited intruder. Beware. So easily we become intruders. Stay off his property that we might inherit eternal life. Our lives are all about making decisions. We are to make our decisions prayerfully.

Job said, "The thing I feared most has come upon me. That which I was afraid of is come unto me and has smitten my soul." The spirits of fear are all around us, living in the air we breathe. Fear is in our homes, where we feel safe. These spirits of fear know what we are thinking, and they act on our thinking. We are to confess what we want to come to pass.

Satan hates us. Why? We are made in the image and likeness of God, whom he hates. We reflect the light of God and are capable of giving love. Satan is jealous of our persona. The image we reflect is the beauty of divine rule. Satan has the mark of the beast, and that is the image he will always reflect throughout the infinite immeasurable ages. He looks like a hairy no-tailed monkey. His spirit is grotesque. He is incapable of loving. Satan made his choice long ago, and his choice got him kicked out of heaven. Now he is tempting us to make a choice. Choose obedience to the will of God. The enemy wants us to doubt the Word of God. He will not live in heaven again. He does not want you to make heaven your home.

Perfect love cast out fear. Fear had torment in it, and fear is not of God.

Abraham believed God; it was counted unto him for righteousness (Romans 4:3).

> God who quickeneth the dead, and calleth those things which be not, as thou they were, and they are. (Romans 4:17)

In life, our faith will be tried, put to the test. We are to stand in faith and be able to give the testimony that was set before us before we were born into this world. All God's children will have a testimony. Tell the world of the peace God has allowed to come into our lives. "By the blood of the Lamb and the words of our testimony are ye saved," says the Lord.

Satan is greedily awaiting human souls. He is drooling ravenously. He is hungering for a morsel of humanity. He looks forward to devouring the souls of those who cannot resist his powers. He preys on both the weak and the strong of the earth. He likes a good fight. He feels he can always win over the will of man. He does not have the power to create life to fill his chambers of horror. He is envious that he cannot breathe out new life. He can only try trickery on the lives that are in existence. God only has the breath of life. Life is created out of God's love. Satan is void of love. He is filled with hate, and hate is all he will ever know—his hate he presents to all the world.

30

Listen

There is a need to listen to others with an inward ear. Learning to listen does a world of good for the many that need to be heard. We all have a story that should be told. There is a great need for listeners—will you be one? Many are so involved with self; they cannot hear the cries of the world. Listening is a neglected practice; it's a skill that I am still trying to learn the art of. Learning to listen has unique requirements. Patience is one of the techniques, paying attention, showing concern. Do not let your mind wander—that is all important to the one telling their story. They want to know you hear and you care about their feelings. They want to feel they have been understood with a nonjudgmental mind. Being able to hear their cries and feeling their pain is a necessity when giving a heartfelt response. Many are hesitant to say what is on their minds. Learning to read between the lines is discerning; it is a spiritual skill. We are to keep our opinions and judgments to ourselves unless asked. Get over the natural urge to speak out when others are talking. Listen. That is why they are talking to you. Life is all about communication. Having an interchange of thoughts and opinions is a good thing if we can do it with insight. The Bible tells us above all learning, get understanding. Get wisdom, but above all, get understanding. Understanding directs the senses to act on the right side of wisdom's knowledge.

Having companionship with one another is absolutely a necessity. We need fellowship for our human existence. We are social beings. Knowing someone is there for us does something for the psyche. We need someone to hear us. We have a need to get our feelings out into the open. Some people want us to keep our needs, our cries in bondage. Shush—be silent. Don't talk about that. We all have our troubles. No one wants to hear that kind of stuff. Keep it to yourself. They will say, "We all are going through something. Keep your troubles to yourself. I don't want to hear that negativity. You are talking negative." A dying man wanted to say something to those standing at his bedside. They reacted by telling him he was talking negative, and they walked away from him. The man lost his ability to utter a sound. He died wanting to tell his story.

Some people are reluctant to speak the secrets of their hearts, feeling unsafe to do so. They need encouragement rather than criticism. Many are disposed to secrecy, not wanting to bear the blame of their unhappiness, feeling they will come under serious scrutiny. Some may feel if they let the cat out of the bag, they will lose control over their lives because of others judging them, saying, "It's all your fault."

The listener has to make the person feel it's all right to unlock their emotions. They are free to air their feelings. They are there for them.

The recipient wants to feel a sense of having your permission to tell it like they see it. Your undivided attention is priceless. They will be looking at you to see if they have your attention and approval as they speak from the quiet places of their hearts, exposing their soul, revealing the unpleasantness of their pain that has for years caused them to have a disease called fear that has chewed away their peace of mind, causing anxiety untold.

It is important for everyone to be heard. Make an observation of the person's body language as they are going through the moments of disclosure. Be there for them. As they talk, they are becoming your patient. They have put themselves in your hands as you receive their never-before-told stories. They pour their soul out to you, and you are sitting there, listening. They have determined that your sincerity is with them, and they are making a decision whether or not to trust the listener. Depending on the response and body language of their listener, the patient now feels free to open the vault to their inner sanctum and bear their pain and faults. They wanted to come out of their sacred place—a place where they were free from others' intrusion and judgments being cast upon them, a secret place where they felt safe with their terrifying remembrance, being free from the blame of the world.

Recalling the past is not always pleasant. It's not exciting to relive old grief. Most of us need help in order to let go of dreadful hurts. Let the patient know it is okay; you are there for them; you do not mind hearing their fears and their anger. Be mindful of your treatment toward the confessor. Find no fault in what they are telling you. Be gentle. Let them know through kind gesture they have your approval to be themselves in your presence. Give people space to be who they actually are. Don't make them feel like they have to be people pleasers.

Showing our ignorance by being indifferent to human pain has no place and no excuse. We are to have a heart for others. The Bible tells us we are our brother's keepers. A spirit of service should be living deep within every caregiver. When we are friends, we play a very important role in someone's life. Keep in mind we do not know what tomorrow will bring. It may be our turn to be at the receiving end. Hopefully, someone's merciful heart will be there for us.

31

Jesus Appeared Five Times to Me

The first time I remember seeing the spirit of Jesus, I was suddenly awakened. When I opened my eyes, I saw in the far corner of the room a cloudlike denseness. There stood a figure simulating a man. The figure started to move effortlessly, gliding, moving toward my bed. His loose flowing gown was to his feet. He drew near. *That looks like Jesus*, I thought. *If there be a Jesus, I'm going to grab a hold of him.* I had crawled to the end of my bed, reaching desperately, trying to get my hands on his clothing. I had in mind, *Once I get a hold of his garment, I'm not letting go.* Near the foot of my bed, he turned from me and walked through the wall. I wanted to go with him. I felt he did not want me to touch him and touching his garments would be the same as touching him. I would be connecting and would be receiving power from on high through his garments.

The Bible tells us there is power in the garments of Jesus. People touched his clothing and healing flowed from him to them and healed all matters of diseases and they were restored both spiritually and physically. They had faith to believe if only they could touch the hem, the borders of his garments, they would be healed.

The second time I saw Jesus, I was on my knees, saying the sinner's prayer over the telephone. The Holy Spirit was there in the room with me. How do I know that? He spoke to me. The devil had spoken to me first. My friend who was at the other end of the phone line asked me to get on my knees and to repeat the sinner's prayer after her, and I was so ready to do that. The devil spoke, saying, "You can tell her anything. She is over there. You're here. Tell her anything. You don't have to get on your knees." The Holy Spirit said, "Why tell a lie about a little thing like that?"

That's right, I thought. *Why tell a lie about a little thing like that?* I dropped to my knees and started repeating the sinner's prayer. Ordinarily I closed my eyes when praying, but not this time, I don't know why. I was repeating the sinner's prayer while looking to my left through a small lead glass window. There on my knees, I saw what looked like a shooting star. It disappeared. I kept watching through the window. I was amazed, surprised seeing a falling star at this time of day. I kept looking to see if I would see the falling star once more, still repeating the sinner's prayer and watching through the small window. All at once, there was the star sitting in the small dining room window, his back resting against the window frame. It was Jesus, appearing in garments, radiant, dazzling, with brilliant white light flowing from him. Purity and holiness were blazing through him. Jesus—a flaming tower beaming gloriously.

Jesus moved close to where I was kneeling. Without words, he summoned my spirit out of my body. My spirit stood before Jesus. Jesus looked through my spirit and ministered to my soul. He was interested in my soul. I looked over at myself. I was still kneeling on the floor, repeating the sinner's prayer. When Jesus imparted the Holy Spirit into my soul. A bolt of high-powered electrifying energy surged through me. An unforgettable experience had taken place. The power of the Holy Spirit went through me and through the Phone over to my friend she hollered, "Maxi, I believe you've got the Holy Ghost."

The third time I saw Jesus, it was early morning. He appeared to me partially from the shoulders up. I was immersed in a tub of bath water. His appearance lingered above the water. He allowed me to study his face. He knew I was going to tell all my friends I saw Jesus while taking a bath this morning. They will not believe me. That's okay; I'll tell them anyway. He did not look at me. His eyes looked past me, looking with intensity into the vastness far beyond human range. His eyes were hazel. His hair resting on his shoulders was light auburn, his garment light brown, with a square neckline. His skin looked as if he had a light suntan. His face showed no emotion; an expression of purity and peace is the only way I can explain his appearance.

The fourth time I saw Jesus, I was sitting on the couch in the living room. I had the Bible in my lap, but I was looking out the window, I seen a slender young woman walking a little white dog. The young woman was wearing white shorts. She had long blond hair. She looked as though she didn't have a care in the world. I thought to myself, *It looks like she has lived a good life. Don't even know what hard times are. I've suffered all my life. Well, do I know what hard times are.* As I thought, I looked toward the open staircase. I saw, to some degree, a man standing. He was far enough up the staircase that the wall was hiding his upper body. Only his lower left side was visible. He was wearing a white vesture. Around the waist was a thick cord belt having fringes at the end. The white vesture was trimmed in about eighteen inches of fine white lace, partly covering a pair of black trousers. This was a priestly garment worn when the priest is preparing to give Holy Communion. How do I know that? For years, I served as an altar person. It was Jesus; he wanted to communicate a message to me concerning the thoughts I had about the woman who was walking the little white dog. Judge not—judgment belongs to me. That scripture came to mind.

I fell back against the couch with the Bible pressing against my chest. I thought, *I've sinned. I had no right to judge that woman. His judgment is the only judgment that sets the sinner free.* In that moment, Jesus let me know, if he wanted that woman saved, he could burn out any evil spirits there may be in her with the spirit that comes fourth from his eyes.

The fifth time I saw Jesus, I and my husband were in bed. I was watching evening TV. My husband was asleep. Jesus entered the bedroom. He walked across the room. He looked straight ahead. He walked through the wall, never looking once my way. He was wearing a garment made from a finely woven fabric; it was emerald green trimmed with a wide gold trimming that went around the neck and down both sides on the front of the garment. It was a pencil-straight garment. There were many little buttons down the front of his cloak. His hair was blondish, long, and straight. It was combed down, resting on his back. Jesus is a priest. He had on clothes the priest used to wear years ago.

There had to be a reason for Jesus to appear. As I said, my husband was sleeping, but there was something Jesus wanted me to know. I was not aware an evil spirit was sleeping in the bed with me. As soon as Jesus disappeared through the wall, the spirit raised my husband's body. He grabbed my wrist, wanting to become sexual. "In Jesus's name," I said. "Take your hands off me." His body fell from me. I believe my husband was still asleep and did not know he was being used by an evil spirit. That demon spirit glared at me. It was a frightening experience.

This demon spirit was influencing my husband's behavior. Jesus's presence revealed the hidden.

32

Elohim the Creator Knows Our Address

To live and work in the darkness of ungodliness is to exist functioning at an inferior level of life. In this world, we live in active spiritual surroundings. We are living in communication with spiritual forces, many having no knowledge that they are being influenced or are being troubled by spirit beings. The underworld is very much alive and thriving, bringing its temptation to everyone. From the kingdom of Satan continuously, temptation comes. It is a transitory experience we must live with daily. In the midst of our storms, remember to praise Elohim the Creator; in that way, we are fighting the spirit with the spirit. Press into Elohim's presence. Don't turn and run from him. Refuse to doubt our creator Elohim; otherwise, if we doubt, we send vibes that transmit a weakness in our faith. There are times life seems touch and go, bringing weariness. Endurance and patience may become exhausting, but they will win in the long run. Remember, Elohim has long patience awaiting the precious fruit of the earth. He is awaiting our return to him.

Elohim knows our address. Learn to listen to creation. It is all around, thriving in its purpose. When we listen to the winds that blow and howl, the roar of the ocean's surge as it tossed its waves and billows across the sandy shores, we are listening to the voice of Elohim, the creator of all things. His pleasure is giving serenity and peace lovingly to those of his. Elohim has sent angels to help us stand up under the pressures of life, for pressure must come for rebirth to take place.

Today there is a great need for the pool of Bethesda to be placed in our backyards and stirred continuously for the healing of the soul and the body of man.

It is incredible yet saddening—man has a way of broadcasting his hate and his lust to the world. Man's corruption, his bad behavior continuously goes out before the ears and eyes of the young and the foolish. Sinful suggestions are ever before us—thanks to the Internet. What can be done about the unhealthy ideals being offered to the human psyche? That is the question. Many have become vulgar. There is no more shame in the games they play. It is easy for some to be lulled into a sense of false security by the great pretenders of the world.

The Lord has given us an exciting world, but we have ruined it with our greed—me, me, me—our selfishness, our excessive desire for more and more of everything, even things that belong to someone else.

We have impoverished our souls as much as we have impoverished our land and the waters within, making a disaster out of the world that we have to live in. We have made an economic and social wreck of things, destruction on every side of life. Wages cannot keep up with the rising cost of living. We have two classes—the haves and the have-nots—the middleclass status is disappearing. Are we oppressed and filled with fear over our behavior and want to correct the tragedy we have caused? I hope so. Were we called into this world to make it a better place. Think about it.

In spite of our imperfections, whatever the state of our imperfect beings, we find life is a stern taskmaster. Still we are on a wonderful journey if only we would just work together in love and respect. We are not estranged from God. We are not a hopeless people. We are teachable. We can die in our worries, or we can live worshipping God for his amazing saving grace through his gift of renewed life. The Holy Spirit's unseen hands are always at work, knitting our lives back together. We know we are not to have a faultless journey home. There are blemishes. We understand life has its struggles, but we are to proceed, for the joy of knowing God is our strength. We must stand strong in faith.

33

Healing Is the Children's Bread

Father, I come to you in the name of your Son Jesus, asking that the children's bread be given to us in this place this day. May the giving of your bread bring glorification to you now and forevermore. I stand in faith, knowing you always receive my prayers and answer my many requests. You love hearing the voices of your children praising you for their needs, Instead of begging, "Please, please give me," your Father wants his children to come to him with thanks. Place your prayers before him joyfully. He knows our needs because he lives within our souls. Thank God the Father, for having intercessors on earth. When God's children intercede, they are to intercede in Jesus's name, knowing the Father receives glory through His Son.

There are people who do not have enough faith to believe for their healing or any of their prayer request; they need someone to stand in the gap for their lack of faith. Many are praying, deficient in faith. We are not to try and hide our inabilities from God. He knows all about the condition of our faith. Ask Jesus to receive our weak faith. Say, "Take this little bitty faith, Lord, the same as you received the widow's might. She gave all she had. We too lay before you all we have in faith. Help our unbelief."

The servants of Almighty God are prayer warriors. Their prayers are covering the world for those who are weak in faith, having no confidence. God will answer the prayers of those with no faith. Let them reach out, saying, "If there be a God, I am talking to you. I am calling on the one who created all things. If you can hear me, please let me know." God wants us to put all the hurting and unbelievers under prayer.

Did you know that someone is praying for you? Wherever you are, no matter how big a hole we've dug for ourselves, he will help us out of our predicament. Ask him then wait and see. God has the power to heal all our sickness and disease through the prayers of others. You know we are to pray for one another. God has prayer warriors praying twenty-four-seven. God has appointed many to intercede in prayer for world peace. Listen—can you hear angels crying for the weak in faith? Jesus stands before the face of God, interceding for us. Remember the shortest verse in the Bible says, "Jesus wept." He is still weeping for us even after shedding his precious blood on the cross for our sins. God's deep sorrow is being expressed in heaven for Prayers for the backslidden. The backslidden conversion to God from their lack of self-control; after they have tasted the goodness of God.

We are to pray for world peace, for souls to be saved. Stay in obedience. Keep prayer in our hearts. In the name of Jesus, ask God's mercy and grace to be shed on all living things. God releases power through prayer. Healings and blessings flow when we can step back and let God have his way when he is using you in prayer, for he is still in the soul-saving business. God's presence is in the midst of his people. He is always at work in our hearts. God is releasing ministering spirits to help during the times we are battling back the enemy on the battle fields of life, battling for spiritual, mental, and physical healings.

When we are slain by the spirit, we have the appearance of being asleep. We are being spiritually ministered to as we rest in the Lord. The healing spirits of God rebuke sickness, and we receive our healing. Hold on to what God has done for you. Don't doubt, wondering if you are really healed—that kind of wonderment gives permission to Satan to deal with your mind concerning your healing. Satan will try and steal our healing, by putting doubt in our minds. The Word of God tells us Satan is a thief. Satan does not want us to be spiritual, mentally, financially healthy, nor free from doubting

God. He is crafty, subtle, and cunning; he can take our healing when we doubt; he will cause us to feel pain even though we are healed. He will give a parching to the soul, and we will deal with that false dry sensation. He is good at what he does. He wants to do a job on the whole human race, and he is busy doing just that.

For the asking, you can draw everlasting life from the wells of salvation. Only the strong in spirit will survive the journey of life.

> If we confess our sins, he is faithful and just to forgive us our sins, and to cleanse us from all unrighteousness. (1 John 1:9–10)

> Verily I say unto you, whatsoever ye bind on earth shall be bound in heaven: and whatsoever ye loose on earth shall be loosed in heaven. (Matthew 18:18)

> Jesus holds the keys of hell and death in his hands. (Revelation 1:18)

Jesus has defeated Satan. Satan is the true enemy of man's spiritual and physical health. He comes against our faith; our peace of mind is in our faith. Without faith, there is no true peace. Satan has nothing good to offer the human race. Satan is doomed, accursed by God forever.

Jesus is our only savior. He is calling to us—will we answer his call? Commune with Jesus. Ask him to show the purpose of our lives. During our daily activities, seek Jesus's presence and find that he is near.

34

The Holy Spirit Was in the Cloud

I was serving as a volunteer chaplain in the original Detroit General Hospital. One day, Sister Adelaide, the head chaplain, came to me, asked if I would go to the third floor and minister to a gentleman who had just lost most of his family in a bad car accident. It was during the Christmas holidays. He and his family had been visiting relatives in the state of Kentucky. They were driving back to Michigan. "Without any remembrance of what had happened or how it happened, lost in thought, how is it I'm sitting in a ditch, looking up at a crushed car." At first glance, he thought, *That can't be my car. Oh, God, don't let it be. What about the injured?* All these thoughts were running through his mind. *Is anyone alive? Is anyone trapped?* Wondering, he ran to the vehicle. He forced himself to go and investigate the wreckage. *Am I the only one left?* He was hoping that was not true. *I am sensible behind the wheel. I am a good driver, vigilant in every way. I take precautions. I watch to avoid the expected and unexpected danger. I am a good driver and a careful driver. How bad are the injuries?* he was thinking to himself. How did this happen? Is there anyone alive? Why did I survive? He had many questions—where were the answers?

Weakened by grief and a sense of growing guilt, he peered through the wreckage. It looked as if everyone was dead—no movement, no sound, blood everywhere. He pressed his face against the wrecked car and cried, "Oh, God, help me."

A passerby had seen and reported the accident and came back to help. There were no cell phones in the 1970s. There were four passengers—his three children that looked lifeless and his wife, who showed no indication of life. Confusion was mixed with his disbelief at what he was seeing. Rejecting the sight, the car filled with his loved ones' lifeless bodies, he could only sink into himself, suffering in quiet grief, his head bowed in prayer.

When I stepped inside his wife's hospital room, the atmosphere was thick, heavy with the presence of the Holy Spirit. Without words, I was touched by his grief, and the throbbing pain showed in his face. He sat in silence. His suffering showed. The sadness had surface from deep within and was lingering on his face. I introduced myself. I said, "Your wife will live. The healing power of the Holy Spirit is present."

"I know," he replied.

"I have been asked by Sister Adelaide, who is the head of the chaplain's department, to visit with you and pray for your wife. May I?"

"Yes," he answered.

I said to the Lord, "God, I know I'm not needed here. Father, I thank you for allowing me to witness the presence of the Holy Spirit at work. Lord, I was asked to come and pray for this patient, and I will have to give an answer to Sister Adelaide when she asks, 'Did you pray for the patient?'"

While I was praying for the patient, the Lord did not prevent me from seeing the huge expansive dark cloud that was breathing and pulsating the sounds of many beehives, buzzing and engaging in active sounds like aggressive live wires at work, sending out their electrifying powers with their humming. They contain inconceivable voltage, a force that could kill you or heal you. This electrifying energy I was witnessing was spiritual, intelligence, flowing to and through the patient that lay helpless on her bed—a spiritual entity at work transmitting healing power from its cloud to the woman. God allowed me to witness this wonder of his work. I can attest God the Father is everywhere present, displaying his mercy and his grace.

God is high above any invention man can dream of. The cell phone is a wonder. Talking to someone, seeing them when they are thousands of miles away is a wonder. I am anxious to see man's next contribution to society. God is above all that man can think of or produce. Inventions will come, and the wonders of manufacturing man's inventions will always be with us. God said, "Man will grow wiser and weaker." God said his Word will not come back to him void. I am anxious to witness man's inventions yet to come.

35

Predestined to Be Redeemed

"What is this unrest lying deep within my being—is this feeling allegoric?" I ask. Why am I still looking for something, living in hunger, living a mystery that satisfies not?

Why is my lifestyle not enough to gratify the feelings that seem to put me at a loss? Am I experiencing a loss of the unknown?

I know there are many who are unable to make peace with themselves nor the world that is spinning around like a drunken madman. How do we keep a relationship in full bloom while living in this mad, mad world of who is who and what is what?

Sometimes I am overwhelmed with the raw shocking unconscionable unjust garbage, spiritual temptations that have found their way into my nonphysical perception and wrestling with my peace of mind.

One day, my conscious mind said to my unconsciousness, "What is going on in that world within your soul?" The unconscious replied, "That's a wonderful question. I'll think about it, and we will talk later."

What might be found in the chambers of one's heart of hearts? I gathered what few threads of stillness and sanity I possessed, and I thought about it. I found that place in my heart, where I have hidden most of my secret possessions, and I carefully consider them all. I like keeping control over that which I hold dearly. If I deprive my sanctity of its privacy, making it unprotected and unsheltered, the hidden would not be hidden anymore. Do you want me to come naked before you, laying bare my soul—nothing hidden? I have found a certain pleasure in the quietness surrounding the untold. A voice came to my inner ear with a softness, emerged in loving sounds; it seemed as though it awoken my soul from a place of deep absence in the thickness of darkness where I had been spiritually sleeping much too long. I offered no resistance to this awaking. I was aroused by its glowing light. I listened. A peaceful inner rest overcame me—a rest I have never known came unto my being. Again, I listened to the light. Renewed in spirit, I found myself crying. In a different world, I found myself where my inner man could cry without apology, a feeling of being understood far beyond my wisdom my scope of understanding. Words cannot make known what I felt in the deepness of my soul. That day, I knew a spiritual stimulus was taking place. I welcome the intensity of peace that kept expanding. A divine exception came from within, and I did not fight it. Spiritual communication was taking place, and I could only stand by, witnessing the impartation, for flesh must stand back, for the spiritual is the only true life.

The unseen was touching the unseen, bringing with it peace inexpressible. I cannot explain the sensation of pure undeluded love shadowing my being. A sense of excitement came to the stillness within. Unspeakable was the joy.

God has opened my spiritual eyes to see and understand the inner chambers of my heart. What a mystery was opened unto me.

Once I tasted the peace and the rest of God, I hungered for more intimacy with the Prince of Peace that lives within my soul.

Our lives were predestined by divine will, a decree established in advance of creation's influence to sway the chosen toward an action or an opinion, a tendency, a proneness to a particular kind of man's perception.

Predestined—an act of God who has preordained all things. The relegation to exile souls, to be assigned to an appropriate place or situation on the basis of classification by man, whose appraisal to submit to someone or something for an appropriate belief, an action that transfers to a lower-ranking division, either a kind of salvation or damnation.

For those whom God foreknew, he predestined to be conformed to the image of his Son that they might be firstborn in his family.

An example of the principle of justification by faith. (Romans 4:3–8)

For what saith the scripture? Abraham believed God, and his faith was counted unto him for righteousness. Now to him that worketh is the reward not reckoned of grace but of debt. But to him that worketh not but believeth that justifieth the ungodly, his faith is counted for righteousness.

Even as David also describeth the blessedness of the man, unto God has imputeth righteousness without works, saying, "Blessed are they whose iniquities (wickedness) are forgiven and whose sins are covered."

Blessed is the man to whom the Lord will not impute sins.

Faith is not a work performed to earn righteousness. Rather, it is the means through which God can impute the righteousness of Jesus Christ to the sinner. He is then "accounted" righteous, not "made" righteous. David's sin counted not against him because of his faith and love of God. Through faith, Abraham staggered not at the promise of God through unbelief but was strong in faith, giving glory to God.

With Abraham, as with others, justification was the result of saving faith. Anyone who comes to God and trusts Christ for salvation will be justified. A sinner is not rendered guiltless but pardoned. Christ has taken our sin on himself and has imputed his righteousness to the sinner.

Jesus ushered in, ordered in, revealed the promises of God through the dispensation of grace. Grace unmerited divine assistance, grace the mercy given to the human race for their regeneration, or sanctification, a virtue coming from God, a state of sanctification enjoyed through the shed blood of Jesus's divine assistance.

Abraham, father of a multitude, has an everlasting covenant with God.

Abraham was justified before the Law was given. The Law does not annul the Abraham covenant; it was merely added alongside it until Christ came to fulfill the Law; for us also, to whom it shall be imputed, if we believe in him that raised up Jesus our Lord from the dead. Christ died a substitute for sin that we be redeemed and become professed followers of Jesus Christ, paid the debt we owed and were unable to pay. Jesus the substitutionary death. God imputes the righteousness of Jesus to the account of a believer. The imputed righteousness of Jesus is the only remedy for imputed sin.

Jesus's death broke sin's control over us, so walk in the newness of life, free from sin's control, knowing the old man is dead. Our old self has had a burial. Our resurrection has given us new life in Christ Jesus. We are a new creation, divinely reinstated through the favor of God's amazing grace, the wonder of being redeemed back by the blood of Jesus and placed in the position we once held before the foundation of the earth was laid.

36

Above All, Get Understanding

The transforming power of the shed blood of Jesus Christ on the cross gave us access to the holy of holies. We can approach, draw near to God, knowing we will be received into his presence to make our request unto him. The Holy Spirit searches the deep things of God. By grace do we give evidence of the deep divine nature of our Father at work in man. What joy divine when trusting in the blood of Jesus Christ. Do we want to be divinely inspired? Cozy up with the Bible, and pray for wisdom; but above all, ask for understanding.

By grace, through the shed blood of Jesus, we received salvation and are buried with him through faith. God adds justification and has declared righteousness unto the believer. We are now citizens inhabiting the kingdom of God, entitled to all the rights and privileges of our heavenly abode. O what glory divine when resting in the everlasting arms of Almighty God.

37

Confront Your Truth

As a professed Christian, I had to confront the horrifying truth. I have been somewhat of a bigot. I am shocked, appalled at what has gone on in the unconscious chambers of my mind. Looking back, I realized I did not keep my tongue from speaking judgment or telling what is called little white lies. When opinions came to my mind, they came out of my mouth. I utter them—sometimes without thinking. Silence is not always golden; neither is it always the best mode of operation. Some things ought to be put on the table for discussion. We learn from others' experiences. We need to analyze things, weighing in on the power that comes from each other's insight. Our participation in events without any knowledge of what we are getting into is called learning the hard way. Good advice is recommended regarding decisions on many things we are to make in life. Investing in certain markets, when is it the best time for buying or selling our investments? The many choices to be made in life can be staggering. We need each other's advice, coming out of their bank of lifelong learning. Be careful not to be offensive when someone asks us for advice. Feel an obligation to guide others when asked. Agree with the decisions of others and not be guided only by our own judgment. Hear what others have to say.

Comparing and considering the popularity of some, their advice may play a bigger part in estimating how much favorable consideration we give to their input. Being a team player and a peacemaker will cost us something.

When it comes to a person's race, or their skin color, I notice some people are intolerant of those who look different from them. Hold on, my beloved, God is not finished with any of us yet. We are not to always be angry. We are not incorrigible. We are saints of God. We may have been depraved people but no longer do we feel cast down. We are Christians, teachable, and willing to accept the opinions of others on the rights and wrongs of life. My opinions may be right for me but not right for others—I understand that. We all have the right to live in peace and to regard the rights of all people. To have freedom from hate and fear is a human right. Let's learn to love, to live, and to let live.

38

Racism in an Unsympathetic World

It is critical for our well-being to survive the allegations and the lies while forgiving the defrauders and the gossipers. There are many whose recipe for living is pointing out what is wrong with someone else's life, causing others to be despairing and unhappy.

The trustworthy—where are they? Has trustworthiness gone out of style? What has happened to the character, the reliance of friendships? Am I gullible, looking for a needle in the haystack? Either there is a right and wrong hanging in the gallows of decision. Are we blindsided to human needs?

Our accusers, our haters, are definitely jealous. They want what keeps you ticking. They would like to have your personality and your prosperity. They see you thriving, being successful. Your train is connected, going in the right direction; it just keeps on rolling—they hate that. Racism and envy want to throw a monkey wrench across the tracks your train is running on; they want to bring your train to a standstill. Your progress sets their souls on fire.

The jealous accusers don't know curiosity killed the cat. How bizarre the haters—they are definitely spewing out their hate and unhappiness in the world.

We are to condemn racism every chance we get. Racism is seriously in the face of non-Europeans. Being in a country that is trying to ignore racism like it does not exist and refusing to notice or act on the well-known underground movements of White supremacy is an insult to humanity. In this country, racism stands before us, constantly reoccurring like a bad dream that keeps returning.

Thinking back, when I was seventeen years old, I saw a notice in the window of a Jewish hair salon. The sign read KINKY HAIR STRAIGHTENED HERE. I went in and asked one of the stylists for an appointment. Looking me in the eyes, she informed me, "We don't do Negro hair."

I replied, "The sign in the window said kinky hair straightened here."

Still looking me in the eye, she told me, "Some Jews have kinky hair."

I knew that. As a child, I saw these old Jewish kinky-haired men. Picking up junk for some it was a good living. These junk men were picking up old rags, pieces of iron, bottles, and cans for extra income. I am remembering a time before the second world war, the days of the pushcarts. The children would hunt for old pieces of iron to sell to the junk men. They would give us ten to fifteen cents for our findings.

What happened to those kinky-haired Jews? Their intermarriage with the Europeans is the answer. Today we have the Russian Jew, the German Jew, and so forth into European society did they blend.

Many European descendants living in this country feel entitled to all the rights and privileges that justice and liberty will afford them. Many non-Europeans do not enjoy the same binding rights of the country's pledge of allegiance to flag and country. There is not yet equal justice for all in this country. We are pledging an allegiance to promises still unfulfilled; liberty and justice for all has not been reached in this country for all its people. However, it has been provided to those of European roots. Their White skin and straight hair gets them the rights to the American dream. Europeans coming into this country understand America's past history, and they play on it to their advantage. The conditions put upon those of non-European roots are ungodly and is an insult in the face of God. Europeans feel they should be privileged because of the lack of pigment in their skin. They come from the old country feeling superior to all of the other races that are living on the face of this earth. Apparently, some Whites do not want to see equality for all American citizens. Their jealousy burns within them against non-Europeans. Some of America's old-standing laws are influencing White power groups. Many members in these groups serve on our police force, killing Black men with the protection of their badge, and they have no shame in the actions they take against the Blacks.

There is controversy—opposing views on how the laws in this country are handled: fair to Whites, not so fair to Black Americans and other races who go to war for the freedom of this country. On the backs of Africans through slave labor, this country has been built to its present glorious state.

I overheard a young White man say, "My ancestors died fighting for this land. It is my land."

I said to him, "What about the indigenous people? The Indians were here before the ship named *The Mayflower* arrived on the east coast from a distant shore, bringing Europeans to a new frontier."

He answered, "Those Indians didn't know what to do with the land. We built this country—nobody is going to take it from us."

This is my country. The Europeans say, "We found it—it's our land." This country was never lost; it was occupied by people that only had bows and arrows to defend themselves from danger. The Europeans had guns, muskets, muzzle-loading; their guns got them land that belonged to another race of people. The Europeans named these human beings Indians because they thought they were in India. The European feel they paid the cost to be the boss of this land and the lands all over the world. The Whites laugh among themselves; they claim non-Whites are inferior, less of an importance in human value than White skin, which lacks in melanin. Non-Europeans have less brain power and are less intelligent than them; they feel their skin coloring speaks to superior brain power. Some White Americans feel all non-Whites are ignored to their customary beliefs, to White culture, so they are dismissive and should not claim America as their home. People of non-European roots have no rights to equal rights, as far as the concept of the ruling powers are concerned. Anyone who does not think like the Europeans are heathen and uncivilized.

The European descendants say, "We came, we saw, and we conquered. In time, we will possess and economically rule the world." Not so fast. You want to rule the world—you never will. What you have, you took by force the same as any other dictator, any other land grabbers of old. North America and Africa were seized by starving homeless Europeans. The fleeing Europeans looking to escape from the Black plague found lands outside of their homeland. The Whites have taken credit for being the founder of Christianity. Ethiopian Orthodox Church (called Tewahdo in Ethiopia) is one of the oldest organized Christian bodies in the world introduced to Ethiopia in the fourth century. The Kingdom of Aksum in present-day Ethiopia and Eritrea was one the first Christian countries in the world. Enoch, father of Methuselah and the great-great-great-grandfather of Noah, who built the ark—these people can be traced to Haile Selassie, Emperor of Ethiopia, descendants of King Solomon and Queen of Sheba.

America, the land of the free and the home of the brave with liberty and justice for all is untrue. Is America where all can live a life of equality? Think again—that is not true. Inequality is practiced all over America as a customary way of life for the bigot. Take a moment and reflect on the numerous interactions. Fate under the White man has dealt the world a terrible blow because of their historical lies. Look at the countries they have destroyed and the governments they brought down with their greed and gunpowder—the ultimate meaning of suffering, for some is living in a country where there is not even playing field for all its citizens.

Racism in America is alive and well. The proud boys are saying, "We want our country back—all to ourselves." They have said, "We have devised a bombshell of a plan, so if you are not from Europe, get out of the country." Their plan will not actually arrive in time to destroy or get rid of nor wipe out any race. God has the last say in man's devices with his plotted ungodly Affaires in mind. Man's secrets, his hidden evil works are of no consequence to God; they are the workings of Satan, and God has Satan on a restricted lease. Can there be another January 6, 2021, when the capital building was under siege by groups of angry White Americans who were trying to sabotage the US government and take their land back?

There is a devastating quest for love to be shown to the world. Be kind to one another for the sake of obtaining world peace, keeping civilization as we now know it. Mental health is a must for all there are many with mental disorders functioning throughout our society. Please show a little kindness to one another. The world is devoid of so much love; it seems love has been left off the menu of today's must-haves. Where did the love go? She ran away. Will she come back another day?

When Jesus returns for the thousand-year millennium, when holiness will prevail, Christ will reign on earth. There will be a period of great happiness and love—will continue without interruption. Love will show her face again for one thousand years.

39

Even in the Darkest Night, There Is Light

Out for a walk in the dark of night, looking out into the endlessness of space. Billions upon billions of countless twinkling stars aligned the depths of the deep. Like flawless stunning diamonds flung into its deepness, scattering across the endless pool of black velvet, lighting the sky. The starry sky all arrayed, adorned with splendor, showing imposing lights that studded the blackness of the night—o the grander of the scene.

How hallowed it all seemed to me when in pursuit of my destiny. What is the intermittent secret that makes it seem so effortless as the universe in its Milky Way galaxy continuously and patiently keeps spending in endless space? What is that infinite secret, the universe echoing sound waves, for billions upon billions of eons—indefinite time, its distance immeasurable?

When circling through space and viewing the earth from our spaceship, an astronaut said, "The Earth is a beautiful, shining blue star. It's the most outstanding planet in the universe, having an intensely blue light that is glowing in the endless depths of darkness of space."

A shooting star is a burnout planet falling through space. Our Earth one day—will it become a burnout star, a meteor appearing and disappearing as a temporary streak of light across the sky? What if our fixed star is fixed no more and cannot any longer revolve around the blazing sun—what if?

What if our environmental changes take too long to take place and we don't fix the environment problem soon enough—what if? Our Earth revolves around the sun as it is spinning roughly one thousand miles per hour on its axis; the Earth is suspended, hanging in the midst, hung on nothingness, yet it stays fixed. The mysteries of the earth's stability to stay in place is its speed, and it is beyond human understanding. An airplane's speed keeps it in the sky, but it has to be powered by something else to stay in the sky. Gasoline products its staying power. Other aircraft such as the helicopter can stand still in space for a short length of time. Is our Earth becoming another burnout star? Earth's increased temperatures—are we in any way at fault for its climate change, yes, will we live to see and feel its birth pains, ending the human story?

About the Author

Out of the dust of times came the Great Depression of the 1920s and 1930s. I was born during those economic times that shook the world to its knees. This worldwide economic crisis shocked millions. My parents were a young couple with limited means; they were not equipped to raise their three little girls. They did what many other people felt they had to do. They sent their children to other family members. I was given to a great-aunt. After eleven years of intentional abuse at her hands, I ran away. My biological mother was told I was missing and was assumed dead. My friends told my mother where I was staying. She went there and took me with her. In the early seventies, the Holy Spirit moved across America, and he found me and filled me with his Spirit. The Lord directed me to go tell the world that God loved them. In Detroit, at that time, the Cass Corridor was a drug haven; there was where I began my ministry.

The streets became my pulpit. Prison ministry was my passion. I came against opposition during those early days of the seventies. Female ministers were not accepted by some men of the cloth. Through life, I learned not to give up on God. Hold on to faith. Faith is a muscle growing stronger as we stand steadfast in the truth of God. My message to the world, show kindness as you walk through life.

Sept 21st ANKND INTEEN 3RDTY